I SAMUEL

Dale Ralph Davis

1 SAMUEL

Looking on the Heart

'The best expository commentary I have read in years.'
Eric Alexander

Dale Ralph Davis

Dale Ralph Davis is pastor of Woodland Presbyterian Church, Hattiesburg, Mississippi. Previously he taught Old Testament at Reformed Theological Seminary, Jackson, Mississippi. He has also written commentaries on:

Joshua (ISBN 978-1-84550-137-2)
Judges (ISBN 978-1-84550-138-9)
2 Samuel (ISBN 978-1-84550-270-6)
1 Kings (ISBN 978-1-84550-251-5)
2 Kings (ISBN 978-1-84550-096-2).

Unless otherwise cited, Scripture citations are the author's own translations.

Copyright © Dale Ralph Davis

ISBN 978-1-85792-516-6

10 9 8 7 6 5 4 3 2 1

This edition published in 2000,
reprinted in 2003, 2005, 2007, 2008, 2009 and 2010
in the
Focus on the Bible Commentary Series
by
Christian Focus Publications Ltd.,
Geanies House, Fearn, Ross-shire,
IV20 1TW, Great Britain

www.christianfocus.com

Previously published in 1988 and 1996 by
Baker Book House, Grand Rapids, Michigan, 49516-6287.

Cover design by Alister MacInnes

Printed by Bell & Bain, Glasgow

Mixed Sources
Product group from well-managed
forests and other controlled sources
www.fsc.org Cert no. TT-COC-002769
© 1996 Forest Stewardship Council

Contents

Preface

Writing a commentary on the Books of Samuel, 1 Samuel in particular, is like facing Goliath: such a massive bulk of questions and dilemmas stand in one's way. For example, one can't help but be intimidated by the spate of recent studies, both articles and monographs. One can hardly read everything and write something. Then there are numerous textual difficulties and an ongoing discussion over the corruption of the traditional Hebrew text and whether the fragments of Cave 4 Qumran show a more excellent way. Or how is one to evaluate supposed sources and complexes (Shiloh traditions, the Ark Narrative, the Saul Cycle, the History of David's Rise)? How many tentacles does the Deuteronomistic octopus—that ubiquitous mascot of current Old Testament studies—have wrapped around the Samuel materials? And how ought one to evaluate historical issues like the rise of kingship in Israel and the seemingly conflicting attitudes toward it? Maybe Goliath has swiped David's stones and is pelting students with them!

However, I feel compelled to ignore direct and extended discussion of these matters. Not because I am ignorant of them or want to demean scholarship. (In fact, I used to become exasperated with students who refused to wrestle with such problems.) But I have my reasons: 1 Samuel is a long book and I do not want to bog down in such details; the reader can find discussion of critical issues in the introductions of many commentaries, in books on Old Testament introduction, or in articles in standard Bible encyclopedias—no need to repeat it all here; and since I have had to spend so much time in the past focusing on historical and critical questions, I have the right to have some fun. That is, this time I want to eat the cake, not look at the raw eggs. Hence *Looking on the Heart* concentrates on the literary quality of the narrative and, especially, on the theological witness of the text.

I might say that I regard the work as a theological (or, if you prefer, an expositional) commentary. It is not a devotional or a homiletical commentary. I have cast the exposition in homiletical form because I think it helps digestion and coherence. But these expositions are not sermons even though illustration, application, and exhortation appear. I believe the commentator, no less than the preacher, has the right and the duty to do something with the truth and life claims of the text. I will plead guilty to having preached many 1 Samuel passages, but that was often done in a different form than appears in this commentary. I am grateful for the encouraging response to my previous volumes on Joshua and Judges— I have discovered that the Lord's people from Idaho to New Zealand delight in his word!

I assume the reader will have Bible in hand as he or she uses this commentary. I have made use of a number of English versions; if no version is specified, the translation of the biblical text is my own.

This volume must be dedicated to our three sons, Luke, Seth, and Joel, with thanks for the entertainment and education they have given me and in prayer that they press on in the faith each has professed. You then, my sons, keep on being strong in the grace that is in Christ Jesus (2 Tim. 2:1).

Advent 1992

Abbreviations

BDB	Brown, Driver, and Briggs, *Hebrew and English Lexicon*
IDB	*Interpreter's Dictionary of the Bible*
IDB/S	*Interpreter's Dictionary of the Bible/ Supplementary Volume*
ISBE	*International Standard Bible Encyclopedia*
JB	Jerusalem Bible
JSOT	Journal for the Study of the Old Testament
KJV	King James Version
LXX	The Septuagint
MLB	Modern Language Bible (New Berkeley Version)
MT	Masoretic Text
NASB	New American Standard Bible
NEB	New English Bible
NIV	New International Version
NJB	New Jerusalem Bible
NJPS	Tanakh: A New Translation of the Holy Scriptures according to the Traditional Hebrew Text (1985)
NKJV	New King James Version
RSV	Revised Standard Version
TDOT	*Theological Dictionary of the Old Testament*
TEV	Today's English Version
TWOT	*Theological Wordbook of the Old Testament*
ZPEB	*Zondervan Pictorial Encyclopedia of the Bible*

Introduction

Where Shall We Cause Division?

It was a whole chicken; and it was in the early years of our marriage. My wife was an excellent cook and had frequently baked or fried chicken, but always chicken that had already been chopped into its respective pieces. She was perplexed. Was there an orthodox way, known to those in the know, by which a chicken ought to be dismembered? So Barbara left the Presbyterian manse to inquire of our Baptist neighbor next door. Mrs. Jenny was a delightful soul, a veteran of many seasons on the farm. Her tear ducts worked overtime, so that she seemed to be crying even when not sad. And she was not sad but highly amused that a neophyte cook would seriously inquire about the proper way to hack up a whole chicken.

But biblical materials matter more than chickens, and if a biblical writer (or editor) cuts his materials at particular points or joints, we should note and respect that. Although our focus is on 1 Samuel, we must, momentarily, look at the "whole chicken," 1–2 Samuel, since all this material was originally one book.

The author or editor of 1–2 Samuel has placed four summary sections throughout this massive amount of material. These summaries are his division markers, the indicators for the overall structure of 1–2 Samuel.[1]

---

1. I have not been able to trace the recognition of these summaries back beyond Thenius; see C. F. D. Erdmann, *The Books of Samuel*, Lange's Commentary on the Holy Scriptures, in vol. 3, *Samuel–Kings* (1877; reprint ed.; Grand Rapids: Zondervan, 1960), 18–20. Brevard S. Childs (*Introduction to the Old Testament as Scripture* [Philadelphia: Fortress, 1979], 267, 271–72) recognizes something of their structural importance, but H. M. Wolf ("Samuel, 1 and 2," *ZPEB*, 5:254–64) is the only one I have found who allows this structure to govern his use of the material. There are, incidentally, some nice correspondences in 1–2 Samuel as a whole; e.g., the house of God at Shiloh at the beginning (1 Sam. 1) matched by the future site of the house of God in Jerusalem at the end (2 Sam. 24; cf. 1 Chron. 21:1–22:1); and

Textual Block	Primary Focus	Summary Section
1 Samuel 1–7	Samuel	1 Sam. 7:15-17
1 Samuel 8–14	Saul	1 Sam. 14:47-52
1 Samuel 15–2 Samuel 8	David/I	2 Sam. 8:15-18
2 Samuel 9–20	David/II	2 Sam. 20:23-26
2 Samuel 21–24	Kingdom	

Hence, in the case of 1 Samuel, our major divisions come at the end of chapters 7 and 14. Following these divisions I propose a general outline for the book:

> I.   A Prophet from God's Grace, 1–7
> II.   A King in God's Place, 8–14
> III.   A Man after God's Heart, 15–31

Enough of chickens, summaries, and outlines. There's a woman weeping in Shiloh. We need to get there and find out what that's all about.[2]

---

a weighty kingdom passage near the beginning (1 Sam. 2:1-10) and near the end (2 Sam. 23:1-7).

2. We know neither the date nor author(s) of 1 and 2 Samuel. Some scholars hold to a very complex compositional history that places anything like the present form of the text into the Babylonian exile or beyond (see Georg Fohrer, *Introduction to the Old Testament* [Nashville: Abingdon, 1968], 217–26). Others would hold that, excepting minor alterations (like the note of 1 Sam. 27:6b?), "the books seem to date close to the end of David's reign" (William Sanford LaSor, David Allan Hubbard, and Frederic William Bush, *Old Testament Survey: The Message, Form, and Background of the Old Testament* [Grand Rapids: Eerdmans, 1982], 229). See also Wolf, "Samuel, 1 and 2," 261.

Part 1
A Prophet from God's Grace

1 Samuel 1–7

1

Cradle and Kingdom
(1 Samuel 1:1-2:10)

It was the last straw. True, it happened every year. But the time comes when the spirit snaps. The festive mood of the religious celebration only depressed her all the more. Suddenly, she was gone. We find her at the tabernacle entrance; we watch but don't intrude. Obviously Hannah wants to pray, which she might do if the great, heaving sobs subside.

In one sense Hannah had almost everything an 1100 B.C. Israelite woman could want. She had Elkanah, a husband of social standing (note how his roots are spelled out in 1:1), moderate wealth (else he could not have supported two wives, v. 2), genuine affection (vv. 5, 8), and faithful piety (v. 3a; the antics of the priests, Hophni and Phinehas [v. 3b], severely tested piety, but then all Israel had to put up with them). The problem was that though Hannah had Elkanah, she didn't have him. She shared him. With Peninnah, an overly fertile, mouthy, thorn in the flesh (vv. 2, 6-7). We may wonder whether this domestic conflict can have anything to do with the kingdom of God. We will simply have to dive in and see.

The Beginning of God's Work (1:1-8)
The problem in the home in Zuphite Ramah[1] was not entirely new. Hannah had no children (v. 2b); Yahweh had closed

---

1. The name is Ramathaim-zophim in the traditional Hebrew text (v. 1). "Rama-thaim" means "Double Heights"; many think that the difficult "zophim" should be

her womb (v. 5b). The fact was enough; the aggravation was worse, especially when she was worshiping at Shiloh.

Though it would not comfort Hannah, it helps us to remember that Hannah is not the first barren woman noted in Scripture. We remember Sarai/Sarah and how Genesis 11:30 ("Now Sarai continued barren; she had no child") hangs like a dark cloud over the next ten chapters of Genesis. The mathematics of Genesis 25 (vv. 20-21, 26b) show that Rebekah had no children for the first twenty years of marriage, and Genesis 29:31–30:24 details the soap-opera turmoil swirling around the barrenness of Rachel. Yahweh raised up mighty Samson from the fruitless womb of Manoah's wife (Judg. 13). And who would have guessed that old, childless Elizabeth would give birth to John the Baptist (Luke 1:5-25)?[2] Barren women seem to be God's instruments in raising up key figures in the history of redemption, whether the promised seed (Isaac), the father of Israel (Jacob), saviors or preservers of Israel (Joseph, Samson, Samuel), or the forerunner of the great King (John the Baptist).[3]

Hannah, therefore, shares in a fellowship of barrenness. And it is frequently in this fellowship that new chapters in Yahweh's history with his people begin—begin with nothing. God's tendency is to make our total inability his starting point. Our hopelessness and our helplessness are no barrier to his work. Indeed our utter incapacity is often the prop he delights to use for his next act. This matter goes beyond the particular situations of biblical barren women. We are facing one of the principles of Yahweh's *modus operandi*. When his people are without strength, without resources, without hope, without human gimmicks—then he loves to stretch forth his hand from heaven. Once we see where God often begins we will understand how we may be encouraged.

slightly altered to read Zuphite(s), which element would distinguish Elkanah's Ramah from that in Benjamin. Hence it is dubbed the Zuphite Ramah. Some would locate the site at Rentis, about nine miles northeast of Lydda in the western slopes of the hill country of Ephraim. See W. H. Morton, "Ramah," *IDB*, 4:8.

2. We might add the story of the Shunammite (2 Kings 4:8-37) to this tally.

3. The virgin conception and birth of Jesus should be added to this series. Though different in kind, it is similar in "difficulty." Gabriel urged the improbability of Elizabeth's pregnancy as an incentive for Mary's faith (Luke 1:36) and alluded to Sarah's case (Luke 1:37 reflects Gen. 18:14) for additional support. The virgin birth then is no mere dogma but also a sign that salvation is wholly God's impossible deed!

Yahweh's work, however, began not only in barrenness but also in distress (esp. vv. 6-7). Childlessness was stigma enough for Hannah, but having it rubbed in was intolerable. Peninnah apparently used special worship occasions (vv. 3-4) for getting Hannah's goat. Peninnah herself likely chafed under Elkanah's obvious affection for Hannah (v. 5).[4] We can imagine how it must have been...

"Now do all you children have your food? Dear me, there are so *many* of you, it's hard to keep track."

"Mommy, Miss Hannah doesn't have any children."

"What did you say, dear?"

"I said, Miss Hannah doesn't have any children."

"Miss Hannah? Oh, yes, that's right—she doesn't have any children."

"Doesn't she *want* children?"

"Oh, yes, she wants children very, very much! Wouldn't you say so, Hannah? [In a low aside] Don't you wish you had children too?"

"Doesn't Daddy want Miss Hannah to have kids?"

"Oh, certainly he does—but Miss Hannah keeps disappointing him; she just can't have kids."

"Why not?"

"Why, because God won't let her."

"Does God not like Miss Hannah?"

"Well, I don't know—what do you think? Oh, by the way, Hannah, did I tell you that I'm pregnant again?! You think you'll ever be pregnant, Hannah?"

Year after year it went on—baiting Hannah, irritating her, winding her up until the sobs broke out, goading her to complain against God.[5] In any case, it drove Hannah to God, drove her to the throne of grace, to the presence of Yahweh, to fervent

---

4. Verse 5 is difficult. We cannot be sure how to take *mānāh ʾaḥat ʾappāyim.* If it means "a double portion," the verse would be saying that Elkanah gave Hannah "a double portion because he loved Hannah." If one follows the Septuagint (LXX) the verse states that he would give Hannah "a single portion—yet he loved Hannah." See S. R. Driver, *Notes on the Hebrew Text and the Topography of the Books of Samuel,* 2d ed. (1913; reprint ed., Winona Lake, Ind.: Alpha, 1984), 7–8. More recent discussions have added no more certainty.

5. For this last, see C. F. D. Erdmann, *The Books of Samuel,* Lange's Commentary on the Holy Scriptures, in vol. 3, *Samuel-Kings* (1877; reprint ed.; Grand Rapids: Zondervan, 1960), 49.

supplication, from which, eventually, came Samuel. Let us not play down the heavy grief of Hannah's—or our own—bleak circumstances, but let us moderate our despair by realizing it may be but another prelude to a mighty work of God.

The Freedom of God's Presence (1:9-18)

The sacrificial meal (see Lev. 7:11-18; Deut. 12:5-14) was over; abruptly Hannah rushed away to the tabernacle entrance or court. She was oblivious to the peering, suspicious eyes of old Eli (v. 9b). Bitter in soul, she began to pray to Yahweh with many, many tears (v. 10). Sometimes tears themselves apparently constitute prayer, for the Lord hears "the sound of [our] weeping" (Ps. 6:8).

There was nowhere else to turn. She had to flee Peninnah's cruel mockery; she found no solace in Elkanah's well-meant but inadequate sympathy (v. 8); not even the clergy understood her. Old Eli, who had learned to indulge his wicked sons (2:22-25, 29-30), could yet get riled over an inebriated woman (vv. 12b-14). Hannah could only turn to "Yahweh of hosts" (v. 11), the God whose universal rule "encompasses every force or army, heavenly, cosmic and earthly,"[6] the God with the total resources of the universe at his command. This God, Hannah's God, is clearly no provincial, ethnic mascot, no deity emeritus of an Israelite ghetto. "Yahweh of hosts"—his very title calls our faith to stretch all its imagination to catch up to such omnipotence.

Hannah's petition is rather amazing (v. 11):

> Yahweh of hosts, if you will surely look upon the affliction of your maidservant and so remember me and not forget your maidservant, but give your maidservant a male seed, then I shall give him to Yahweh all the days of his life, and a razor will never touch his head.[7]

She addresses Yahweh of hosts, cosmic ruler, sovereign of every and all power, and assumes that the broken heart of

---

6. John E. Hartley, TWOT, 2:750. See also Walther Eichrodt, Theology of the Old Testament, Old Testament Library (Philadelphia: Westminster, 1961), 1:192–94.

7. "No razor"—is this child to be viewed as a new Samson? Compare Judges 13:3-5 and my discussion in Judges: Such a Great Salvation (rpt. Fearn: Christian Focus, 2000), 173n.

a relatively obscure woman in the hill country of Ephraim matters to him. (Believers use some of their best logic in prayer.)

It is also instructive to compare Hannah's petition here to Yahweh's statement in Exodus 3:7, when he assures Moses, "I have certainly seen [looked at] the affliction of my people who are in Egypt." Hannah assumes that the God who has "certainly seen the affliction" of a corporate people can as certainly be expected to see the distress of an individual servant. Nor does she ask that her son—should Yahweh grant him—be famous or prominent; all that matters is that he will belong to Yahweh.

But perhaps the most outstanding mark of Hannah's praying is the liberty she enjoys before Yahweh. Look at the scene again. Here is Hannah in such intense anguish. She is praying but "speaking in her heart" (v. 13); her lips were moving but there was no audible sound. So Eli mistook her earnestness for drunkenness. Another soused woman, half-crocked after the sacrificial meal! But his sharp rebuke was met by Hannah's sad confession: "No sir, I am a woman with a heavy spirit; I have not drunk wine or strong drink; rather, I have been pouring out my soul before Yahweh" (v. 15).

There is the freedom Hannah knows. She is a woman with a heavy spirit (many of God's people are) and she has been pouring out her soul before Yahweh. "I pour out my complaint before him, I tell my trouble before him" (Ps. 142:2). In her bitterness of soul, with many tears, out of grief and despair, she pours out her anguish. Yahweh is a God who allows her to do that.

Now there is a myth circulating around the church that often goes like this: "Believers in the Old Testament period didn't have the freedom and personal approach in prayer that we do. Their worship consisted of a very external, formal, cut-and-dried sacrificial procedure in which ritual killed off any spontaneity or intense spirituality." Hannah would say that is hogwash. True, Hannah is still in 1 Samuel 1 and not in Hebrews 4; but once you see Hannah in prayer, how can you doubt that she has found the same throne of grace and knows something of the same boldness with its Occupant?

Christians then should allow Hannah to be our schoolmistress to lead us to Christ, to instruct us in communion with God. Many Christians need to realize that Yahweh our God allows us to do this—to pour our griefs and sobs and perplexities at his feet. Our Lord can handle our tears; it won't make him nervous or ill at ease if you unload your distress at his feet.

The Dedication of God's Gift (1:21-28)

Eli's accusation turned to benediction (v. 17) when he finally understood Hannah; Hannah went away settled (v. 18), Yahweh remembered her (v. 19; cf. v. 11), and Samuel arrived (v. 20).

The primary concern of verses 21-28 centers on the fulfillment of Hannah's vow (see v. 11) to give her son to Yahweh, that is, for service at his sanctuary. Hannah wants to wait until she has weaned Samuel (v. 22), which in the Near East could easily take three years (cf. 2 Macc. 7:27). Elkanah cautiously consents (v. 23). The year arrives and so does Hannah—with Samuel, three bulls,[8] up to a bushel of flour, and a skin of wine (v. 24).

We should pay special attention to Hannah's words in verses 27-28 as she presents little Samuel to Eli. Four times she uses a form of the Hebrew root š'l (to ask), a fact which English translations obscure because it is difficult to anglicize fluently. If we tolerate a rougher rendering we could read it like this:

> For this child I prayed, and Yahweh gave me my asking which I asked from him; and I also have given back what was asked to Yahweh; all the days he lives he is one that is asked for Yahweh.[9]

---

8. Most English translations follow LXX and Syriac in verse 24, reading "a three-year-old bull," a reading that gathers indirect support from verse 25a, where only one bull is explicitly said to have been slaughtered. We can be a bit bullish for the "three bulls" of the traditional Hebrew text. R. Payne Smith pointed out that Hannah's ephah of flour was approximately three times what was required as a cereal offering for one bull, according to Numbers 15:9 (*I Samuel*, The Pulpit Commentary [London: Funk and Wagnalls, n.d.], 13; also G. J. Wenham, *The Book of Leviticus*, The New International Commentary on the Old Testament [Grand Rapids: Eerdmans, 1979], 79). Three bulls would constitute (almost) an extravagant offering—but not impossible considering Elkanah's wealth (he could support two wives) and Hannah's gratitude.

9. This is the rendering of Smith, *I Samuel*, 13, with slight modifications. Smith commented: "The conjugation translated 'to give back what was asked' literally means 'to make to ask,' and so to give or lend anything asked. The sense here requires the

Hannah's words pick up Eli's blessing in verse 17 ("May the God of Israel give you the asking [lit.] which you asked from him") as well as her own apparent wordplay when "she called his name Samuel, for 'From Yahweh I asked [šā'al] him'" (v. 20).[10] Hannah's worship then (back to vv. 27-28) gratefully rehearses Yahweh's gift and places that gift fully at Yahweh's disposal. "He is made over to Yahweh," as the New Jerusalem Bible renders the clause in verse 28.

There is a unique element in Samuel's position. He is destined to become Yahweh's prophet who guides Yahweh's people by Yahweh's word through a most critical epoch (3:19-20); he will be God's specially chosen instrument for a major task in redemptive history. So in one sense Samuel and Hannah and Elkanah do not stand on the same level as all believers do.

And yet we do share some common ground. Any parents who are living in covenant with the Lord should find themselves following Hannah in general principle even if not in precise practice. We should solemnly and passionately desire that each child be "made over to Yahweh." His gifts should be given back to him.

When I was a child there were times, though very few, when my father was away. That meant my mother would lead family worship in the evening. I always half-dreaded that because, after the Scripture was read and we were on our knees, Mom would pray for each of us five boys by name, specifically and in detail, beginning with the oldest down to the caboose (me). I say I half-dreaded this because it was difficult to hear the earnest desires of a mother's soul without tears coming to my eyes (and, after prayer, they were always fresh because I was the last prayed for). Naturally, it was not macho for an eight-, ten-, or twelve-year-old lad to shed tears. But it was tough to

---

restoration by Hannah of what she had prayed for (comp. Exod. xii.35, 36), but which she had asked not for herself, but that she might devote it to Jehovah's service."

10. "Samuel" probably means "name of God" or "his name is God." The point, however, of Hannah's statement in verse 20 does not rest on the Samuel-šā'al (to ask) wordplay, for the words *from Yahweh* are emphatic in the Hebrew and carry Hannah's primary point (see P. Kyle McCarter, Jr., *I Samuel*, The Anchor Bible [Garden City, N.Y.: Doubleday, 1980], 62, and Lyle M. Eslinger, *Kingship of God in Crisis: A Close Reading of I Samuel 1–12* [Sheffield: Almond, 1985], 83), namely, that her son is a gift from the God who had closed her womb (vv. 5, 6).

be tough. Here was a Christian mother, on the basis of what she knew—and didn't know—"making over" her sons to the Lord. They were hers, but it was more important that they be his—and for that she prayed.

The View of God's Kingdom (2:1-10)

Hannah prays again at Shiloh (2:1a). Here in 2:1-10 we have her response, her prayer of praise, for Yahweh's gift. I want us to walk our way through Hannah's song before explaining its significance.

Hannah's song may be divided into three sections: verses 1-3, verses 4-8, and verses 9-10. Verses 1-3 express Hannah's elation over Yahweh's particular salvation, over the relief he granted to Hannah in her distress:

> [1] My heart glories in Yahweh,
>   my horn is raised high in Yahweh,
>   my mouth opens wide against my enemies,
>   for I rejoice in your salvation.
> [2] There is none holy like Yahweh;
>   Indeed, there is no one except you;
>   and there is no rock like our God.
> [3] Don't go on talking so high and mighty;
>   don't let arrogant talk go out of your mouth,
>   for Yahweh is a God who really knows,
>   and actions are under his scrutiny.

The repeated personal pronouns in verse 1 ("my," "I") indicate that Hannah begins with her own experience. She breaks forth in a confession of faith in verse 2 and directs a word of admonition in verse 3. The counsel of verse 3 is not directed specifically at Peninnah, for the first two Hebrew verbs are plural, as is the "your." It is a general warning to all self-sufficient boasters. Hannah gives praise for Yahweh's salvation granted in her crisis. We might call this "micro-salvation."

In verses 4-8 Hannah expands on the matter; the way Yahweh delivered her is characteristic of the way Yahweh rules his world:

⁴ The bows of the mighty warriors lie shattered,
   but those ready to fall bind on strength.
⁵ The ones who are full hire themselves out to get bread,
   but the hungry have ceased famishing.
   Seven have been born to the barren
   but the one with many sons gets feeble.
⁶ Yahweh kills and gives life,
   brings down to Sheol, then he brings up.
⁷ Yahweh impoverishes and makes rich,
   brings low—also makes high.
⁸ He raises up the poor from the dust,
   he lifts up the needy from the ash heap
   to make them sit with princes,
   and he makes them inherit a seat of honor,
   for the supports of the earth are Yahweh's
   and he placed the world on them.

Hannah moves from the particular (vv. 1-3) to the general (vv. 4-8). What Yahweh has done for Hannah simply reflects the tendency of his ways. When John Calvin had suffered the death of his wife Idelette, he wrote his friend William Farel: "May the Lord Jesus ...support me. ..under this heavy affliction, which would certainly have overcome me, had not He, who raises up the prostrate, strengthens the weak, and refreshes the weary, stretched forth His hand from heaven to me."[11] Calvin was saying he would surely have been crushed but he knew a Lord who raises up the prostrate, strengthens the weak, and refreshes the weary—and that Lord had again acted in character in Calvin's grief. That is what Hannah is saying here. I was ready to fall and Yahweh gave me strength; I was barren and he made me fruitful; I was poor and he made me rich. But that is not really surprising, for that is just the way Yahweh is (vv. 4-8)!

Horizons broaden, the view expands in verses 9-10. We have come from Hannah's experience (vv. 1-3) to the way Yahweh rules (vv. 4-8) to how it will be when Yahweh fully, completely, and visibly rules (vv. 9-10). That is, we have come from micro-salvation and from Yahweh's characteristic ways to "macro-salvation."

---

11. Thea B. Van Halsema, *This Was John Calvin* (Grand Rapids: Baker, 1959), 155.

[9] He will keep the feet of his covenant one(s),
but the wicked will be silenced in darkness,
for it is not by strength that a man can conquer.
[10] Yahweh—those who fight with him will be shattered;
he will thunder against them in the heavens.
Yahweh will judge the ends of the earth—
may he give strength to his king;
and may he lift up the horn of his anointed one.[12]

Here is what will happen when Yahweh rules and acts as he is wont to do (vv. 4-8). Here is the final result, the grand finale—the deliverance of the covenant people, the shattering of Yahweh's opponents, the judging of the ends of the earth. Hannah expects Yahweh to accomplish this through his king, his anointed one.[13]

You must catch the logic of Hannah's prayer. It is easy to react superficially to these opening scenes in 1 Samuel: "What's the big deal? So Hannah has a son now—that's nice—and that rival wife Peninnah who has kids coming out her ears has had to eat crow; so now things have been calmed down a bit at Elkanah's flat in Ramathaim-zophim, wherever that is." No. This is no piddly little affair—this is a manifestation of

---

12. The last two lines are to be translated as a wish or a prayer. The verbs are imperfects with simple *waw*, almost a certain indication of the nonindicative mood (a point once made in a seminar by J. J. Owens). English versions uniformly render these lines as statements; however, both Ralph W. Klein (*1 Samuel*, Word Biblical Commentary [Waco: Word, 1983], 13) and McCarter (*1 Samuel*, 68) translate subjunctively.

13. Commentators almost uniformly deny this psalm to Hannah because of verse 10b—or, at the very least, they deny verse 10b to her, because Israel had no king in Hannah's time; hence she would not have spoken of Yahweh's "king" or "anointed one." The common view is that the compiler has placed a somewhat later psalm—somewhat appropriately, to be sure—into Hannah's mouth (e.g., Hans Wilhelm Hertzberg, *I & II Samuel*, The Old Testament Library [Philadelphia: Westminster, 1964], 29, 31). However, the assumption that one must have historical experience of kingship before alluding to it does not always hold water. In fact, it's a bit leaky. A. F. Kirkpatrick long ago pointed out that "king talk" was not impossible in Hannah's mouth: "The idea of a king was not altogether novel to the Israelite mind. The promise to Abraham spoke of kings among his posterity (Gen. xvii. 6): the Mosaic legislation prescribes the method of election and the duty of the king (Deut. xvii.14-20): Gideon had been invited to establish a hereditary monarchy (Jud. viii.22). Anointing too was recognized as the regular rite of admission to the office (Jud. ix.8). Amid the prevalent anarchy and growing disintegration of the nation, amid internal corruption and external attack, the desire for a king was probably taking definite shape in the popular mind" (*The First Book of Samuel*, The Cambridge Bible for Schools and Colleges [Cambridge: Cambridge University Press, 1896], 55–56). Robert P. Gordon

the way Yahweh rules and will bring his kingdom (vv. 5b, 8). Hannah's relief is a sample of the way Yahweh works (vv. 4-8) and of the way he will work when he brings his kingdom in its fullness (vv. 9-10). The saving help Yahweh gave Hannah is a foretaste, a scale-model demonstration of how Yahweh will do it when he does it in grand style.

Each one of Christ's flock should ingest this point into his or her thinking. Every time God lifts you out of the miry bog and sets your feet upon a rock is a sample of the coming of the kingdom of God, a down payment of the full deliverance, the macro-salvation that will be yours at last.

True, such tiny salvations are only samples or signs of the final salvation. A happily married woman may wear a diamond ring and/or a wedding band. And, if you asked her, she would likely admit that the ring is a token or a sign of the love her husband has for her; she would acknowledge that it is *only* a sign or a symbol and that the ring is certainly not the love itself but that the real thing is much greater than the sign or symbol of it. But she will not for that reason despise the ring; she won't reason that since it is only a symbol she might just as well sell it at her garage sale. No, because of the deeper reality it signifies she treasures it, though it is, admittedly, *relatively* insignificant.

Likewise, you should not despise or demean these little salvations Yahweh works in your behalf, these little clues he gives, these clear but small evidences he leaves that he is king and that he has this strange way of raising up the poor from the dust and lifting the needy from the ash heap to make them sit in the heavenly realms with Jesus Christ. Ponder every episode of Yahweh's saving help to you; it will help you believe Luke 12:32.

Young John Calvin, forced to leave his native France, was traveling eastward hoping to reach Strasbourg or even Basel.

(*I & II Samuel: A Commentary* [Grand Rapids: Zondervan, 1986], 23) would permit the psalm to Hannah but views the prayer of verse 10b as a later addendum, much like Psalm 51:18-19 might be to the bulk of Psalm 51. On the function of Hannah's song in the Books of Samuel, see Brevard S. Childs, *Introduction to the Old Testament as Scripture* (Philadelphia: Fortress, 1979), 272–73; Eslinger, *Kingship of God in Crisis*, 99–102, 110–12; and Willem A. VanGemeren, *The Progress of Redemption* (Grand Rapids: Zondervan, Academie Books, 1988), 206–7, 215–16.

His desire was for a haven in which to study and write and thereby support the new Protestant faith. A straight line to Strasbourg was impossible, for a war was in the way. It was 1536, and Francis I and Emperor Charles V were having their third war; cannon, carts, and equipment plugged the roads. Calvin must detour to the south, pass through Lyon. He hoped to reach Lausanne on a certain day but failed; he would have to spend the night in Geneva. There short, stocky, fiery William Farel got hold of the young scholar and threatened him with the judgment of God if he did not stay to carry on the reformation in Geneva.[14] Could we say that we owe Calvin's impact in the Reformation to Francis I and Charles V? After all, it was, humanly speaking, their war that forced Calvin to pass through Geneva.

I would not argue that case; but it is stimulating to raise such questions. Were Francis and Charles unwilling and unwitting benefactors of Geneva? By the same token (getting back to 1 Samuel), do we owe it all to Peninnah? I know that in one sense that is a perverse way to put the matter. Yet without Peninnah's goading, mockery, and malice would Hannah ever have been driven to the distraction that moved her to desperate prayer? As one looks back how crucial becomes the fact that Hannah was crushed with grief and moved to prayer. For Hannah this was grievous personal distress—yet in it Yahweh drove her to prayer through which he brought forth a lad who would shield his whole people. God moves our prayers and magnifies their effectiveness. The severe trial of Hannah proved to be the salvation of a whole people. Without Peninnah that may not have been the case. Do we owe it all to Peninnah? Certainly not. We owe it to the God who takes even the smirks and digs and venom of Peninnahs and uses them to fill a cradle with another kingdom servant. Can we not see the wonder of Israel's God? Can we not see the comfort of his people?

STUDY QUESTIONS

1. Bible stories of barren women given children by God encourage us in our 'impossible' situations. Consider the relevance of this to you at this stage in your life with God.

---

14. Van Halsema, *This Was John Calvin*, 59–60, 76–78.

2. Am I ever in danger of substituting 'human gimmicks' for dependence on 'the God of the impossible'?

3. 'Our despair ... may be another prelude to a mighty work of God.' Seek illustrations of this from Scripture and experience.

4. Consider the place of logic in prayer. What about 'Lord, you said ...... therefore, please do it!'?

5. Which is your greatest concern for your children, grandchildren, nieces, nephews – fame, prosperity or godliness?

2

Judgment Begins at the House of God
(1 Samuel 2:11-36)

Aspiritual resurgence looked out of the question for the American colonies in 1740, the year of the Great Awakening. Samuel Blair of the Middle Colonies wrote that "religion lay as it were a-dying and ready to expire its last breath of life in this part of the visible church."[1]

We expect opposition from society at large, but what can we do when the creeping death seeps inside the church, especially when her human leaders are indifferent in faith and unholy in life? It is a bleak hour indeed when the light of the world is part of the darkness. The regime of Hophni and Phinehas was such a time. Yet even then Yahweh did not abandon his people; he was there—in both judgment and grace—when judgment began at the house of God.

The Secret Manner of God's Work (2:11-26)
Yahweh is so quietly at work that we cannot hear him, but the mess at Shiloh is so visible we cannot miss it. Hence we will look at the mess first.

A surprise indeed! Hannah's prayer (2:1-10) has just alluded to the arrogant (v. 3), the mighty (v. 4), the wicked (v. 9), those who contend with Yahweh (v. 10). And here

---

1. Iain H. Murray, *Jonathan Edwards: A New Biography* (Edinburgh: Banner of Truth, 1987), 159.

they are! Not, as expected, Canaanites or Philistines, but the priests of Israel.[2] Worship is a farce at Shiloh. A worshiper is cooking his portion of a peace offering for the post-sacrificial meal he and his family will enjoy together. Here comes the ubiquitous priests' servant with his infamous three-pronged barbecue fork; he plunges it into the worshiper's pot or kettle, and whatever the fork brings up he carts away to the priests' quarters (vv. 13-14). The priest was already allotted the breast and the right leg (Lev. 7:28-36), but the Shiloh fork-man was sent to stab for more.[3] It was worse. Before the fat is burned in honor of Yahweh (see Lev. 3) the priests' lackey appears demanding fresh (uncooked) cuts from the worshiper (v. 15). Should the worshiper remind the priests' man that proper reverence should be shown Yahweh by first burning the fat on the altar, the young cleric would turn thug and threaten to take raw meat by force (v. 16). What sheer contempt Hophni and Phinehas had for Yahweh's offering (v. 17). Such was their liturgical offense.

Yet more was rotten in Shiloh. There was a moral offense (v. 22). Everyone in Israel knew about it: Hophni and Phinehas had sexual relations with the women who tended the worship center (cf. Exod. 38:8).

They were scoundrels all right (v. 12; Hebrew, "men of Belial"), and verse 12b uncovers the root of it all: "They cared nothing for Yahweh" (NJB; or, as RSV has it, "They had no regard for the LORD"). Literally, the Hebrew is, "They did not know Yahweh." How tragic that such words describe the spiritual leaders of God's people. Given that root, who wouldn't expect the fruit? In such a case boredom in public worship and immorality in personal life are not a surprise. Only a tragedy.

Yet in the middle of this liturgical and moral morass at Shiloh a careful reader can detect a hint of hope. There are

---

2. Karl Gutbrod, *Das Buch vom König*, Die Botschaft des Alten Testaments, 4th ed. (Stuttgart: Calwer, 1975), 24.

3. I think verses 13-14 are describing one of the priests' offenses. The Hebrew particle *gam* in verse 15a seems to imply as much (as if to say, "And if that wasn't raunchy enough, they even did this..."). Among translations, NEB takes verses 13-14 as describing a proper action with the offense committed in verse 15.

these short notes about little Samuel scattered through the text and standing in quiet contrast to the deeds of Hophni and Phinehas. They are silent witnesses of Yahweh's provision. We might highlight them like this:

Samuel serving, 2:11
   Liturgical sins, 2:12-17
Samuel serving, 2:18-21
   Moral sins, 2:22-25
Samuel growing, 2:26
   Prophecy of judgment, 2:27-36
Samuel serving, 3:1a

These brief Samuel-notes are noteworthy. They tell us that Yahweh is already at work providing for new, godly leadership for his people. There are no slogans, no campaigns, no speeches. It is all very quiet. Growth seldom makes noise, and Yahweh is growing his new leader. Eli's sons dominated the picture. All Israel suffered under the arrogant, cynical, immoral priesthood, clergy who savored prime cuts over teaching godliness, who much preferred having a woman in bed than interceding for Yahweh's flock. It must have seemed to many like there was no hope of improvement, no exit from the night. But in the middle of it all the text keeps whispering, "Don't forget Samuel—you see how Samuel is serving." That is Yahweh's manner—quietly providing for the next moment even in the middle of the darkest moments.

Several years ago *Leadership,* a ministry journal, included a story about a B-17 bombing run over a German city during World War II. Nazi antiaircraft flak hit the gas tanks of the bomber. No explosion. The morning after the raid the pilot went down to ask the crew chief for the shell that had hit the gas tank; he wanted it for a souvenir. The crew chief indicated there were eleven unexploded shells in the gas tank! The shells had been sent to the armorers to be defused. Then Intelligence had picked them up. The armorers had found that the shells contained no explosive charge; they were empty. All but one. It contained a rolled-up note, written in Czech. Finally, Intelligence found someone on the base who could read Czech. Translation: "This is all we can do for you now."

So there were these Czechs who were compelled to work in a munitions plant for the Nazi war effort. They didn't try to blow up the plant or assassinate Hitler. They simply didn't put charges in some of the shells they produced. It was all very quiet and unnoticed but worked "salvation" all the same. Such is frequently God's way for his people. Not all his work is noisy or dramatic. We may be tempted to conclude he has abandoned us because we haven't ears to hear the silent manner of God's work. This is often Yahweh's way in redemptive history and we should mark it. We will not become too discouraged over Hophni and Phinehas so long as we see little Samuel walking around Shiloh.

The Clear Evidence of God's Kindness (2:19-21)

The Samuel-note of 2:18 expands into a little section describing Hannah's annual provision of a robe for her growing lad (v. 19), Eli's blessing asking for additional "seed" to Samuel's parents (v. 20), and Yahweh's gift of three additional sons and two daughters to Hannah and Elkanah (v. 21).

One can't help but observe the stark contrast between verses 19-21 and verses 22-26, a delightful scene set against an ominous one.

Verses 19-21	Verses 22-26
Mother love, 19	Father's sorrow, 22
Eli's blessing, 20	Eli's rebuke, 23-25a
Yahweh's provision (life), 21a	Yahweh's purpose (death), 25b
Samuel's growth, 21b	Samuel's growth, 26

There is a clear parallelism between the two scenes, but the parallels highlight the differences. Here (vv. 19-21) Yahweh is giving life, there he has resolved death.

The keynote of verses 19-21 is Yahweh's generous kindness in giving Hannah five additional children. These, Eli trusted, would be "in place of the request [lit., asking] which was asked for Yahweh" (v. 20). Hannah had asked for Samuel, but she had asked him not for herself but "for Yahweh." And she gave him to Yahweh. Hannah has given and now she receives "grace on top of grace" (John 1:16). That is typical, or, as we might say, "vintage Yahweh." No sacrifice ever seems to impoverish one of Yahweh's servants (Mark 10:28-30). One might find an analogy in a marriage relationship. When I entered into a marriage covenant with my wife, I paid a price. The commitment cost me something; I gave up some privileges and freedoms. Yet I have received far more than I ever sacrificed—genial companionship, devoted affection, daily helpfulness, spiritual (and spirited) discussions, an incarnate antidepressant, and more.

Hannah and her husband now disappear from our story; but they—and their houseful of noisy children (cf. Ps. 127:3-5)— should remain witnesses to us of "the giving God" (James 1:5, Greek).

The Fearful Peril of God's Judgment (2:22-25)

The lad Samuel was growing (v. 21b), but Eli was very old (v. 22a). And Eli heard the bad news about his sons' flagrant immorality (v. 22b). It was common knowledge; all Yahweh's people were talking about it (v. 24). Hophni and Phinehas had turned the tabernacle into a brothel, a place where sin was committed rather than confessed. Eli tried to warn them of their danger—blatant defiance of Yahweh would place them beyond help (v. 25a).[4] "But they would not listen to their father's voice, for Yahweh had decided to put them to death" (v. 25b).

We do well to allow verse 25b to percolate into our minds. It is easy to read it too hastily, as if it said that Hophni and Phinehas did not listen to Eli and, consequently, Yahweh decided to put them to death. But the text does not say that; it says Eli's sons did not listen to him *because* ("for") Yahweh had decided to put them to death. Hophni's and Phinehas' resistance was not the rationale for Yahweh's judgment but the *result* of his judgment. A perfectly just judgment. We cannot divorce verse 25 from the previous account of Hophni's and

---

4. The sense of Eli's statement in verse 25a is that when wrong is done between man and man, God may settle the dispute (perhaps, as some think, through the appointed human judges); "but where the two parties are God and man, what third power is there which can interfere? The quarrel must go on to the bitter end and God, who is your opponent, will also punish you" (R. Payne Smith, *I Samuel*, The Pulpit Commentary [London: Funk and Wagnalls, n.d.], 41). See further, S. R. Driver, *Notes on the Hebrew Text and the Topography of the Books of Samuel*, 2d ed. (1913; reprint ed.; Winona Lake, Ind.: Alpha, 1984), 35.

Phinehas' impudence and immorality. In that light verse 25b says that for their persisting rebellion Yahweh decided to put them to death and that, therefore, they had not listened to Eli's plea. So the text teaches that someone can remain so firm in his rebellion that God will confirm him in it, so much so that he will remain utterly deaf to and unmoved by any warnings of judgment or pleas for repentance. W. G. Blaikie wrote that Hophni and Phinehas

> experienced the fate of men who deliberately sin against the light, who love their lusts so well that nothing will induce them to fight against them; they were so hardened that repentance became impossible, and it was necessary for them to undergo the full retribution of their wickedness.[5]

Be careful of your response to such teaching. Some of you may become Yahweh's prosecutors, alleging he is deficient in mercy. Others may be intellectually curious about the mechanics of hardening—at what precise point in sin's progress does it become impossible to repent? Both the critic and the curious are wrong. Our place is not to question or to comprehend but to tremble before a God who can justly make sinners deaf to the very call to repentance.

---

5. W. G. Blaikie, *The First Book of Samuel,* The Expositor's Bible (Cincinnati: Jennings and Graham, n.d.), 45. We have similar teaching in the New Testament. When Paul discusses the condition of "pagan man" in Romans 1:18-32, he asserts that because of men's ongoing suppression of the truth, "God gave them over" (three times, vv. 24, 26, 28) to the way of life they so eagerly desired, God abandoned them to the lifestyle they passionately wanted to live, God confirmed them in the way they so insistently wanted to go. But Paul contends that man's filthy conduct and depraved attitudes do not merely constitute evidence of man's wickedness but of God's wrath. Romans 1:24 begins with "therefore" and, originally, connects with verse 18: "God's wrath is being revealed from heaven...." God's wrath is not something ready only for the last day but is already functioning (note the present tense, "is being revealed"). God's wrath is not a concept for discussion but a power now operating. Paul wants us to understand that when "God gave them over" God's wrath was acting, confirming men and women in the bondage of the various sins they so cordially crave. Paul is saying that God's wrath may be quietly present, that in it he simply gives you over to wallow in the "freedom" you so trenchantly choose. This doctrine is sometimes called judicial hardening and holds a sobering warning for Christian congregations (cf. Heb. 3:13). John Bunyan portrayed it in *Pilgrim's Progress* in the character of Backslider, the man in the iron cage, who, among other things, told Christian, "I have so hardened my heart, that I *cannot* repent."

The Merciful Meddling of God's Word (2:27-36)
We don't know his name; we don't know where he came from;
we know nothing about him. But, suddenly, out of nowhere, a
"man of God" (v. 27) came to Eli with the word of God.

Eli had at least rebuked his sons for their moral offenses
(vv. 22-25); perhaps—though we can't tell from verses 23-25—
he also reproved them for their liturgical offenses (vv. 13-17).
In any case, he had taken no action to expel Hophni and
Phinehas from the priestly office. Eli might protest, but
his sons suffered no unemployment. There was no church
discipline.

We can follow the flow of the prophet's message if we break
it down according to its structure. The clues for dividing his
speech are its introduction ("This is what Yahweh says," v. 27),
the "why" in verse 29, and the "therefore" in verse 30.

Rehearsal of grace, 27-28
Accusation of wrong, 29
Announcement of judgment, 30-36

The story of previous grace (vv. 27-28) always makes the
present sin (v. 29) appear as lurid as it is. Yahweh had granted
to the "house of your father" (v. 27; probably = Aaron) the
privilege of the priesthood, of serving at the altar, burning
incense, wearing the ephod (see Exod. 28), and enjoying the
food offerings (v. 28). Why then, in light of all these privileges
and gifts, "do you kick at my sacrifice and my offering which
I ordained on account of iniquity, so that you honor your sons
above me by fattening yourselves on the finest cuts of every
offering of Israel, my people?" (v. 29).[6] That is the central
charge. The "therefore" of verse 30 introduces the detailed
announcement of judgment, a judgment that threatens the

---

6. The first verb of verse 29 (Heb. $bā'at$, "kick at," an act of defiance or contempt;
see Deut. 32:15) is second person plural and so includes Eli and his sons; the
subsequent verb, a form of $kābēd$, "you honor (your sons)," is singular, referring to
Eli's action. I have also followed Lyle M. Eslinger (*Kingship of God in Crisis: A Close
Reading of 1 Samuel 1-12*) [Sheffield: Almond, 1985], 133), who follows Horst
Seebass in repointing $mā'ôn$ (dwelling) to $mĕ'āwōn$ (on account of iniquity); then
the prophet is stating that Yahweh commanded sacrifice and offering "on account of
iniquity," that is, as a means of atoning for sin.

decimation of Eli's family line (vv. 30-32, 36),[7] includes a ray of restraining mercy (v. 33),[8] specifies a definite sign by which the truthfulness of the prophecy can be tested (both Eli's sons will die on a single day, v. 34), and promises the rise of a "faithful priest" (v. 35) in place of Eli's family.

Let us return to the center of the prophet's word, the accusation in verse 29. Since Eli allowed his sons' abuse of and contempt for Yahweh's worship to continue, he was honoring his sons above Yahweh.[9] He may verbally reprove them (vv. 23-24) but as judge (4:18) he took no decisive action when they persisted in their offense. He should have at least removed them from the priest's office. Perhaps Eli could not prevent his sons from practicing immorality (vv. 22-25), but he could prevent them from doing it as priests. Hence the man of God rebukes the sin of sweet reasonableness, the willingness to tolerate sin, to allow God's honor to take a back seat, to prefer "my boys" to "my God." For Eli, blood was thicker than fidelity.

Everyone knew the contempt Hophni and Phinehas held for the worship and worshipers of Yahweh (vv. 13-17); their sexual exploits were common scandal (vv. 22-25). Yet still they served as priests of Yahweh. Eli did nothing. "You honor your sons above me." Sweet reasonableness really smells.

There is truth here even for the individual believer. This prophecy against Eli emphasizes that you can end up in grave

---

7. Eli and his sons have forfeited their place in the promised priestly privileges (v. 30). Yahweh's threat in verse 31, "I shall hack off your arm" (Heb.; "arm" as symbol of strength), addresses Eli as representative of all his descendants. In spite of a difficult text, especially in verse 32, the judgment consists of decimating Eli's seed probably by untimely deaths (there will be "not be an old man in your house," vv. 31, 32). This doesn't mean there will be no survivors but that they will be in desperate straits (v. 36) and that the majority will die "as men," in their prime (v. 33b, on which see Driver, *Notes on the Hebrew Text,* 40).

8. Smith translates verse 33a, "Yet I will not cut off every one of thine from my altar, to consume thine eyes and to grieve thy soul," and explains, "that is, thy punishment shall not be so utter as to leave thee with no consolation; for thy descendants, though diminished in numbers, and deprived of the highest rank, shall still minister as priests at mine altar" (*I Samuel,* 56). Instead of "every one of thine" William McKane would render, "There is one man whom I will not cut off," and understand it as a reference to Abiathar (1 Sam. 22:17-20; *1 & II Samuel: Introduction and Commentary,* Torch Bible Commentaries [London: SCM, 1963], 40).

9. Eli himself may have enjoyed the results of his sons' abuse (note v. 29b: "by fattening *yourselves* on the finest cuts"; cf. 4:18, "he was heavy") and therefore have been loath to stop it.

sin by thinking it very important to be nice to people. How easy it is to practice a gutless compassion that never wants to offend anyone, that equates niceness with love and thereby ignores God's law and essentially despises his holiness. We do not necessarily seek God's honor when we spare human feelings.

A final point. I called this section "the merciful meddling of God's word." Let me explain.

There was public, scandalous sin at Shiloh. It was ongoing; it was unchecked. Nothing (beyond verbal exhortations) was being done about it. No surprise that God's people became cynical about worship and sacrifice. Then out of the blue comes a man of God with the word of God. Here is nothing less than the invasion of the word of God, which by announcing judgment on sin and exposing sin protects the people of God from being wholly overcome by its evil. If Hophni and Phinehas threaten to destroy God's people then Hophni and Phinehas will be destroyed to spare God's people. It *is* a work of judgment, it is a harsh word, but it is at the same time a saving word, a merciful word, a protecting word for the people of God. If the true church is to be preserved her false servants must be removed. Hence this is the *merciful* meddling of God's word.

The Stubborn Triumph of God's Purpose (2:35)

Human resistance and disobedience will not stymie Yahweh's purpose. Trenchant rebellion does not send El Shaddai into a state of helpless frustration. Yahweh will rule his people, if not through particular leaders then apart from them and in spite of them. In time Yahweh will remove Hophni and Phinehas by judgment but provide for faithful leadership in their place.

> But I shall raise up for myself a faithful priest;
> he will act in line with what is in my heart and soul;
> and I shall build for him a sure [lit., faithful] house;
> and he shall walk before my anointed all the days.[10]

---

10. As in Hannah's song (v. 10), verse 35 contains an anticipation of the monarchy ("my anointed," i.e., my anointed king). See Eslinger, *Kingship of God in Crisis*, 140.

The major question is: Who is the "faithful priest"? Some have argued strongly for Samuel, certainly a plausible position in view of the immediate context. However, chapter 3 introduces Samuel as the *prophet* par excellence; I have difficulty trimming and forcing that prophetic role into the priestly capacity of 2:35. I think, in light of 1 Kings 2:26-27, 35, that Zadok and his priestly line fulfill the prediction of the faithful priest. When Solomon banishes Abiathar, Eli's descendant, from priestly service, the "word of Yahweh which he spoke about the house of Eli in Shiloh" is fulfilled (1 Kings 2:27). That text only specifies that Abiathar's banishment fulfills the prophecy about the fall of Eli's house—it makes no direct assertion about the identity of the "faithful priest." However, Solomon's elevation of Zadok as sole high priest in place of Abiathar (1 Kings 2:35) implicitly places Zadok in the role of the "faithful priest."[11]

Let us not lose hold on the main thread in the midst of debate. In context, verse 35 is saying: Yahweh's kingdom and people may suffer from arrogant, immoral, unrepentant priests; but Yahweh *will* have a faithful priest; he insists on it; Yahweh has a sort of saving stubbornness that will not turn aside from profiting his people.

My father used to tell about my oldest brother and his broken toys. When Walt was quite small he had a collection of toy cars and trucks in various stages of disrepair. A wheel or two missing—that sort of thing. The problem was that when Walt would "drive" them on the house floor they would dig, scratch, and otherwise deface the floor. Pop at last took action and—probably in Walt's absence—threw the whole junky collection through the lattice work and under the porch. Later—perhaps days' worth—Pop heard little Walt crying. He was under the porch. He'd found his toys. He couldn't get out. Somehow he'd wormed his way under the lattice but couldn't "de-worm" and get back out. His father naturally gave assistance, but before Walt would come out he handed

---

11. Most of the interpretative issues about the "faithful priest" are addressed in C. F. D. Erdmann, *The Books of Samuel*, Lange's Commentary on the Holy Scriptures, in vol. 3, *Samuel-Kings* (1877; reprint ed., Grand Rapids: Zondervan, 1960), 82-84. Erdmann himself argues for Samuel, while C. H. Toy in the translator's notes counters in favor of Zadok and Co.

every single lost, broken, destructive vehicle out to his father. He was determined; he must have those toys.

I am not suggesting any close analogy here but only insisting that stubbornness can be positive, refreshing, and bracing sometimes. That is why Yahweh's stubbornness is so beautiful in verse 35. Israel may suffer under degenerate priests. Yahweh will judge them; "I shall raise up for myself a faithful priest." Yahweh is determined. He *will* have proper leadership for his flock. This may mean that judgment must begin at the house of God (1 Pet. 4:17). Even by that judgment, however, God *will* build his house just as Jesus dogmatizes that he will build his church (Matt. 16:18)—and there's not anything anyone can do to stop it. In that stubbornness God's people find their security; in his tenacity they place their trust.

Study Questions

1. Have you learned to look for God's work in quiet ways, or are you always needing to see him in the dramatic or the noisy?

2. 'Someone may remain so firm in his rebellion that God will confirm him in it.' Do you think there is enough preaching about the urgency of repentance?

3. It is a sobering thought that blood may be thicker than fidelity. Reflect on this in the light of Matthew 10:37.

4. Can we confuse niceness with love? What qualities does Biblical love have that mere niceness lacks?

5. God showed stubbornness in dealing with Israel (1 Sam 2) and the Lord Jesus with his Church (Matt. 16:18). Do you think Philippians 1:6 might suggest this too? If this divine commitment applies to Israel and the Church, does it also apply to individual believers like us?

3

Prophets Profit
(1 Samuel 3:1–4:1a)

The Ecclesiastical Ordinances for the Church of Geneva (1541) specified that

> Each Sunday there is to be a sermon at Saint Pierre and Saint Gervais at break of day, and at the usual hour [nine o'clock].... At midday, there is to be catechism, that is, instruction of little children in all the three churches.... At three o'clock second sermon.... Besides... , on working days there will be a sermon at Saint Pierre three times a week, on Monday, Wednesday, and Friday.[1]

"After darkness, Light" was the motto of reformed Geneva. The preaching schedule reflects the assumption of Calvin and others that light for God's people comes when the word of God has free course among them. Hence six sermons per week.

The Old Testament holds the same assumption. The usual vehicle for Yahweh's word was prophecy, the usual instrument the prophet. It is with the call of Samuel that this usual pattern becomes usual.[2] The contention of 1 Samuel 3 is that Yahweh's

---

1. Thea B. Van Halsema, *This Was John Calvin* (Grand Rapids: Baker, 1959), 143. For the whole text of the ordinances, see J. K. S. Reid, ed., *Calvin: Theological Treatises,* vol. 22 of *The Library of Christian Classics* (Philadelphia: Westminster, 1954), 56-72.

2. Franz Delitzsch (*An Old Testament History of Redemption* [1881; reprint ed., Winona Lake, Ind.: Alpha, 1980]) refers to Samuel's work as the "establishment of a new age." "As Abraham is the father of believers, and Moses is the mediator of the law, so Samuel is the father of the kingdom and the prophetic office" (pp. 82-83).

people find no profit without a prophet and Yahweh is about to prophetably profit them. Quite naturally then we begin by observing...

The Grace in the Prophet's Presence (3:1, 19–4:1a)

"Now the word of Yahweh was rare in those days—there was no vision breaking through" (3:1b). A "vision" (Hebrew, *ḥāzôn*) was one of the ways Yahweh communicated his word to a prophet.[3] Yahweh was not speaking his word through prophets except in rare instances (e.g., 2:27-36). A pragmatic American would puzzle over this. His response would be: "No problem; let's just send more fellows to seminary, to Bible college, or open a prophets' vo-tech school." But if the word of Yahweh was rare it means that the word from Yahweh was rare. If a word does not come from Yahweh there will be no word of Yahweh. Man cannot coerce, manufacture, manipulate, or produce that word. Only Yahweh can give it—and turning out more graduates from theological seminaries or religion departments will do nothing to change that. The word of Yahweh is his gift to his people, and in Shiloh time it was seldom given.

We must go on to ask why Yahweh's word was rare. Why was he so silent? Why was he not speaking to Israel? Most likely because Israel stood under his wrath (perhaps because of her corrupted priestly leadership; though cf. 7:3-4). The absence of the word of God was a sign of the judgment of God, of Yahweh's withdrawing the light of his word and allowing Israel to wander in the darkness she apparently preferred.[4]

Other passages support this contention. When Yahweh announced judgment on Israel through Amos (ca. 760 B.C.), he threatened a famine—not a famine of bread or thirst for

---

3. See, e.g., Hosea 12:10, Micah 3:6, Habakkuk 2:1-3; see also Numbers 12:6-8. Proverbs 29:18 ("Where there is no vision, the people perish," KJV) may be oft-quoted because misunderstood. It does not mean that creative, resourceful planners are essential for the survival of an organization or cause; it means that people fall apart when they are left without the word of God to direct them. Compare RSV: "Where there is no prophecy the people cast off restraint."

4. Karl Gutbrod (*Das Buch vom König*, Die Botschaft des Alten Testaments, 4th ed. [Stuttgart: Calwer, 1975], 33) hesitates to go quite this far. He points out that the text (1 Sam. 3) does not specifically say that God's relative silence is to be viewed as his judgment; but he does admit that God's silence seriously hampers and curtails the life of his people.

water but a "famine of hearing the words of Yahweh." People would wander everywhere to seek a word from Yahweh and would never find it (Amos 8:11-12). In Psalm 74 Israel withers under Yahweh's anger, especially displayed in the enemy's destruction of the temple (vv. 3-8) but aggravated by the fact that "there is no longer any prophet" (v. 9). Tragic enough to have Yahweh's sanctuary in smoke; tragic enough when God forces us to walk in darkness—but a silent darkness is unbearable. In Psalm 74 the absence of a prophet's counsel is part of the misery of God's judgment. Later in 1 Samuel, King Saul will attest that the absence of God's word signals the loss of God's presence (1 Sam. 28:6, 15).

The good news of 1 Samuel 3, however, is that Yahweh is breaking his silence; a new era is beginning.

> So Samuel grew, and Yahweh was with him and did not allow any of his words to fall to the ground. All Israel, then, from Dan to Beersheba, knew that Samuel was confirmed as a prophet for Yahweh. Now Yahweh continued to appear in Shiloh, for Yahweh revealed himself to Samuel in Shiloh by the word of Yahweh. And so the word of Samuel continued coming to all Israel. [3:19–4:1a]

Now Yahweh is speaking to Israel on a regular pattern through Samuel. Now Yahweh's silence will be broken. Now his word will no longer be rare and intermittent (cf. Judg. 6:7-10; 1 Sam. 2:27-36). There is an authorized, on-duty prophet speaking Yahweh's word to Yahweh's people. Yahweh has not forsaken his people.

More on these matters later. Presently, we simply note that it is a sign of God's grace when God's word has free course among God's people. That is the teaching of 1 Samuel 3. If contemporary believers have a church where social activities, committee meetings, and nifty programs have not eclipsed the place of the word of God, if the teaching of the word of God stands at the heart of the church's life, if there is a pulpit ministry where the Scriptures are clearly, accurately, and helpfully preached, then they are rich in the grace of God.[5]

---

5. See also J. A. Motyer, *The Day of the Lion: The Message of Amos* (Downers Grove, Ill.: InterVarsity, 1974), 187.

One caution. Some may think, "Yes, but the word of God can't be 'rare' anymore because now the church has his complete word in writing; we have the Scriptures; so we don't need to worry about that." Wrong. What makes the word of Yahweh rare? In Eli's day it was because Yahweh was not giving it frequently. But Yahweh's word can become rare because of problems on the receiving end (Isa. 6:9-10). Several years ago I couldn't get rid of water in my head! My ears, it seemed, wouldn't clear. The fluid in my ear canals (or wherever) just stayed there, sloshed around a little, reduced my hearing capacity, and stirred up my innate irritability. Our friendly doctor hooked me up to some kind of pump or apparatus. You would be aghast at the gunk that can collect in one's head—very slowly, over years and years, until hearing is drastically reduced. That is how the word of God still becomes rare; people have no ears to hear (Mark 4:9). In fact, even the ability to hear must be a divine gift (Mark 4:10-12). We may have the Scriptures but suffer from deafness, and so the word is rare. Starvation may not come from absence of food but from lack of appetite. But God's word—written, preached, welcomed—is the token of God's grace to God's people.

The Kindness of the Prophet's God (3:2-10)

Yahweh's call of the lad Samuel is the keynote of verses 2-10. It takes the Hebrew text a moment or two to strike that note. It begins with a time note in verse 2: "On that day... ," then proceeds to detail where Eli was and the state of his eyesight (v. 2b), to assure that the tabernacle lamp was yet burning (v. 3a), and to locate Samuel's sleeping quarters (v. 3b), and, finally, it gives us the main verb, highlighting the main action of the section—"then Yahweh called to Samuel" (v. 4a). This verb *call* (Hebrew, *qārā'*) occurs eleven times in verses 4-10. No doubt about the theme of this paragraph!

I suppose someone reading this section for the first time might begin to wonder if Yahweh's call will succeed.[6] Apparently Yahweh's call was so clear and audible that Samuel was sure it was Eli—repeatedly so. Young Samuel is willing

6. Lyle M. Eslinger, *Kingship of God in Crisis: A Close Reading of 1 Samuel 1-12* (Sheffield: Almond, 1985), 150.

enough, but why is he so slow to grasp what is happening? Why doesn't he get the point? Verse 7 explains why Samuel was missing the cue: "Now Samuel did not yet know Yahweh, and the word of Yahweh was not yet revealed to him." This statement explains; it does not blame. The connotation is wholly different from that of 2:12, where Eli's sons "did not know Yahweh." The point is that Samuel had not yet had any direct experience with Yahweh, he had had no prior practice at receiving Yahweh's word—so no wonder Yahweh's call baffled him. Samuel was on untraveled ground. When the light dawned on Eli, however (v. 8b), all fell in place.

But what use do verses 2-10 hold for us? For contemporary believers do not stand in Samuel's position: we are not being called to receive direct divine revelation as Samuel was. We are in no way prophets as Samuel was (to be) a prophet. Someone might say that we should at least imitate Samuel's attitude toward the word of God (v. 10). That may well be so, but it does not bring the bulk of verses 2-10 home to us.

Let us then try a different approach. Instead of asking, How might verses 2-10 apply to us? let us ask, How do verses 2-10 reveal our God? Once we see what Scripture reveals about God we usually will see how it applies to us.

I have already suggested my own answer in the heading of this section: verses 2-10 display the kindness of the prophet's God. Let us not look too closely at the experience of Samuel but at the character of Yahweh. And what do we see? We see the kindness and gentleness of Yahweh. Here is a new step for Samuel and a new point of departure in Yahweh's dealings with Israel. And Yahweh is in no apparent hurry. There is time for Samuel to catch on. God is not heaving an exasperated sigh; he is not ready to berate Samuel for being so dense; he does not launch into a tirade about how Samuel "never gets anything right."

Some matters require time and patience. I remember how in fifth grade I had such an abominable time identifying verbs. I knew the definition of a verb, but I could not apply the definition to the words of a sentence. Whenever I was charged with drawing two lines under the verb in a sentence, it was like playing a grammatical version of pin-the-tail-on-the-donkey (only I, unfortunately, was the donkey). Then a miracle happened. The light dawned. Suddenly, as I recall, and with no apparent explanation. The next year I could identify verbs; there was no mystery about it; it was not difficult. Out of the blue I knew what a verb was. It took time—and trial and error.

Here with Samuel we have a true glimpse of Yahweh. He is willing to give us time to understand him. He is not holding a stopwatch over Samuel, threatening to have done with him if he does not wise up. No, Yahweh moderates his instruction to our condition. So does Yahweh incarnate: "I have many things to say to you, but you are not able to bear them now" (John 16:12); hence they will wait for the Holy Spirit to teach. John Calvin has nicely captured this element of the Lord's character in a couple of lines of his hymn, "I Greet Thee, Who My Sure Redeemer Art":

> Thou hast the true and perfect gentleness,
> No harshness hast thou and no bitterness.

That describes Samuel's Master—and ours. And disciples who tend to cast their God into a mental graven image of a gruff, efficient, impatient sergeant need to know this.

The Tension in the Prophet's Task (3:11-18)

Yahweh communicates to young Samuel an "ear-buzzing" (v. 11) word, confirming that he is about to activate his threatened judgment against Eli's house from start to finish (v. 12), because Eli's sons, whom he has not restrained, keep taking God lightly and treating him with contempt (v. 13);[7] hence they have placed themselves beyond forgiveness (v. 14). A message of judgment, of severe, irreversible judgment— imagine a young lad being given responsibility for that!

Naturally, there would be no problem if Samuel did not have to pass on this word. But Samuel knew better and dreaded having to tell Eli (v. 15b). Understandably so. A deep

---

7. In verse 13 I follow the lead of LXX; the Hebrew is difficult to construe. For explanation, see S. R. Driver, *Notes on the Hebrew Text and the Topography of the Books of Samuel*, 2d ed. (1913; reprint ed.; Winona Lake, Ind.: Alpha, 1984), 43-44, and C. McCarthy, "Emendations of the Scribes," *IDB/S*, 263-64.

affection doubtless bound Eli and Samuel (see Eli's "my son" in vv. 6, 16a). But Eli saved Samuel a good bit of trouble—he placed Samuel under a curse if Samuel did not fully disclose all that Yahweh had spoken to him (v. 17). Under that threat Samuel held nothing back (v. 18a).

Samuel's call, however, highlights the burden, pressure, conflict, and pain of the word of God. No sooner is Samuel called to the prophetic task than he finds how difficult and heart-rending it can be. He is caught in the dilemma only a true prophet knows. The true prophet must speak Yahweh's word (else why is he entrusted with it?); yet the true prophet recoils from speaking judgment (v. 15). He will speak judgment because truth is at stake; he cringes to speak it because compassion moves him.

Andrew Bonar told the story of a Grecian artist who painted a remarkable picture of a boy carrying on his head a basket of grapes. The grapes were painted so realistically that when the picture was put up in the Forum for the citizens to admire the birds pecked the grapes, thinking they were real. The painter's friends heaped their praises on him, but he was far from satisfied. He said, "I should have done a great deal more. I should have painted the boy so true to life that the birds would not have dared to come near!"[8] That is, he should have made it both attractive and repelling.

There is always this tension in the word of God, and any authentic messenger of that word knows and lives in it. If a preacher, for example, never places you under the criticism of God's word, never tells you your sin but only smothers you with comfort, you must wonder if he is a phony. If his preaching contains only the judgment note and seldom offers comfort and encouragement, one must ask if he actually cares for God's people. If one has a high regard both for the truth of God (even if it's judgment) and for the troubles of the church, he will retain the proper tension in the biblical word; he will both afflict the comfortable and comfort the afflicted.

---

8. Marjory Bonar, ed., *Andrew A. Bonar: Diary and Life* (Edinburgh: Banner of Truth, 1960), 466.

The Responsibility for the Prophet's Word (3:19–4:1a)
Samuel as prophet was indeed God's provision for directing
his people through a time of confusion and upheaval.
"Prophet," however, not only spelled God's grace but
Israel's responsibility. When one hears that Samuel was
"confirmed as Yahweh's prophet" (3:20), one immediately
thinks of the prophet promised in Deuteronomy 18:15-19.
He would be a prophet like Moses (vv. 15, 18), who would
speak Yahweh's whole word to Israel, and "whoever will
not listen to my words," said Yahweh, "which he speaks
in my name, I myself will make him give account" (v. 19).
I do not think that Samuel is that prophet like Moses.[9] But
Deuteronomy 18:20-22 assumes that there will also be a line
or succession of prophets until that prophet "like Moses"
comes. And one might almost say Samuel is the father of
that prophetic succession. No more is the prophet merely an
occasional visitor (again, cf. Judg. 6:7-10; 1 Sam. 2:27ff.) but
an established presence. With Samuel there is, we might say,
a prophet in residence. Now Yahweh repeatedly appears
and reveals himself to Samuel "by the word of Yahweh"
(1 Sam. 3:21) and now that word—Yahweh's and Samuel's—
will be coming to all Israel (4:1a). That is both an immense
privilege and a terrible responsibility, both a welcome
benefit and a fearful liability. What if Israel refuses to hear
(cf. Deut. 18:19)? Even worse, what if we refuse to hear God's
final word spoken through his Son-prophet (Heb. 1:1-4;
2:1-4)? Perhaps the Lord himself then gives us the correct
starting point: "But this is the man to whom I will look, he
that is humble and contrite in spirit, and *trembles at my word*"
(Isa. 66:2 RSV; emphasis added).

STUDY QUESTIONS

1. To contemplate times when God has been silent should
   make us value his Word all the more. Does it still amaze
   you that the great and holy God actually has something to
   say to you?

---

9. I don't think there was a prophet "like Moses" in the whole Old Testament
period—at least not as Deuteronomy 34:10-12 defines the matter.

2. It is a sobering thought that starvation may not mean lack of food but of appetite. Is your appetite for God's Word still keen? Do you read it at home and hear it in church as often as you once did - and do you still obey it?

3. If it is true that 'once we see what Scripture reveals about God we usually will see how it applies to us', does this suggest that, before asking how any Bible passage applies to me, I ought always first of all to seek what it says about God?

4. Some of God's attributes need time for their revelation. Patience is certainly one of these. Can you think of others? What about faithfulness, for instance?

5. If true preaching afflicts the comfortable and comforts the afflicted, which are you needing most just now, and are you ready to receive it?

4.

Rabbit-Foot Theology
(1 Samuel 4:1b-22)

Our writer draws a heavy line across the page after chapter 3. Actually, 4:1a is the concluding remark of chapter 3: "And the word of Samuel continued to come to all Israel."[1] Period. We'll hear no more of Samuel until chapter 7. Throughout chapters 1–3 Samuel had been increasingly the focus of attention. After 4:1a there is an abrupt shift; his literary light goes out. The writer will relate the eliminating of the old regime (ch. 4) before returning to the new leadership (ch. 7), and Yahweh will teach Israel some lessons in "Arkeology" (ch. 5-6) before they come to repentance under Samuel. Samuel is suddenly eclipsed; for three chapters the ark of the covenant takes the spotlight.

Chapter 4 falls into two main sections, verses 1-11 and 12-22. The first reports the battle(s) and concludes with a notice of two deaths (i.e., of Hophni and Phinehas; actually, there were numerous Israelite deaths in the battle but these are the two significant ones for the writer). The second section relates the news of the battle and also closes off with a report of two deaths (those of Eli and of the wife of Phinehas). The focus

---

1. At the beginning of 4:1b LXX has, "In those days the Philistines gathered together for war with Israel." This clause could have dropped out of the Hebrew text (see NEB). However, LXX also pads 3:21 with a note about Eli and his sons; I doubt that it is original. In any case, the difficulty of the text at 4:1 does not alter the fact that Samuel suddenly drops out of the narrative.

of the chapter is the ark of the covenant (mentioned twelve times). We might set out the overall structure and content in terms of the ark:

> Arrival of the ark, 1-11
> > Battle, 1b-2
> > > "Taking" the ark, 3-4
> > > > Response to the ark's arrival:
> > > > > by Israel, 5
> > > > > by Philistines, 6-9
> > Battle, 10
> > Taking the ark, 11
> News of the ark, 12-22
> > Double report:
> > > to town, 12-13
> > > to Eli, 14-17
> > Double response/result:
> > > Eli's fatal fall, 18
> > > Daughter-in-law's fatal birth, 19-22

A geographical note before diving into the teaching of chapter 4. Aphek (where the Philistines assembled, v. 1) was located on the coastal highway north of the Philistine cities and about twenty-two miles—as the crow flies—west of Shiloh. We don't know the precise location of Ebenezer (v. 1; cf. 7:12); perhaps the battle occurred a little to the east of Aphek.[2]

The Fallacy of Yahweh's People
So far, so bad. Israel was "struck down" in the first engagement with the Philistines. Not that Yahweh had not been active; he

---

2. According to verses 2 and 10, Israel lost a total of thirty-four thousand fighting men in these battles. The matter of the "large numbers" in the Old Testament lies beyond the scope of our discussion, but the interested reader can begin investigating the matter in Ronald B. Allen, "Numbers," *The Expositor's Bible Commentary*, 12 vols. (Grand Rapids: Zondervan, 1990), 2:680–91; William Sanford LaSor, David Allan Hubbard, and Frederic William Bush, *Old Testament Survey: The Message, Form, and Background of the Old Testament* (Grand Rapids: Eerdmans, 1982), 166–70; John W. Wenham, "Large Numbers in the Old Testament," *Tyndale Bulletin* 18 (1967): 19–53, as well as Wenham's condensation, "The Large Numbers of the Old Testament," in David and Pat Alexander, eds., *Eerdmans' Handbook to the Bible* (Grand Rapids: Eerdmans, 1973), 191-92.

had been, but in a "wrong" way.[3] He had "struck down" Israel (v. 3a). The elders asked the right question: "Why did Yahweh strike us down today before the Philistines?" (v. 3). They answered too quickly. They should have allowed the question to hang and bother them for a while. Then perhaps the threats of Leviticus 26:17 and Deuteronomy 28:25 would have come to mind. Instead they had their brainstorm: "Let us take to us the ark of the covenant of Yahweh from Shiloh; and let it come among us and save us from the hand of our enemies" (v. 3b).

The ark of the covenant was that sacred, gold-covered, portable box, 3 ¾ feet long by 2 ¼ feet wide and high, which — unless ancient Israel was on the march in the wilderness — sat behind the thick veil in Israel's worship center in the area called the Most Holy Place (Exod. 25:10-22; 37:1-9). The ark of the covenant suggested Yahweh's rulership (it was called "the Ark of the Covenant of the Lord of Hosts Enthroned on the Cherubim" [1 Sam. 4:4 NJPS]; the cherubim were representations, attached to the lid of the ark, of winged, suprahuman creatures), revelation (for the ark contained copies of the Ten Commandments and Yahweh also promised to speak there to Moses with additional direction for Israel), and reconciliation (for the lid of the ark, called, traditionally, the "mercy seat," was sprinkled yearly with the blood of sacrifice; see Lev. 16).[4] So the ark pointed to Yahweh, the ruling, speaking, forgiving God.

The ark was also the sign of Yahweh's leading his people, not least against their enemies in battle (Num. 10:35). Perhaps this came to mind as the elders pondered Israel's defeat that dark day near Aphek. Perhaps they remembered how central the ark had been at the Jordan river-stopping (Josh. 3-4) and at the destruction of Jericho (Josh. 6). Perhaps they decided they needed to return to the old ways, to the old "faith," in order to experience one of Yahweh's old-time deliverances. In any case they had decided: "Let us take to us the ark of the covenant of Yahweh from Shiloh; and let it come among us and save us" (v. 3).

---

3. A point rightly made by Lyle M. Eslinger, *Kingship of God in Crisis: A Close Reading of 1 Samuel 1–12* (Sheffield: Almond, 1985), 166, though I do not agree with all of his comments on 4:3.

4. For further study see Marten H. Woudstra, *The Ark of the Covenant from Conquest to Kingship* (Philadelphia: Presbyterian and Reformed, 1965).

Actually, the elders' words can be translated a bit differently. Their last sentence can be rendered: "Let him [Yahweh] come among us and save us." I have translated it as though the reference was to the *ark* ("Let it..."). The Hebrew allows either translation. But, whatever we make of the words, the thinking is the same. Their assumption is: if we bring the ark to battle, Yahweh will be forced to deliver us to protect his honor. Should something happen to the ark, it would make Yahweh the loser—and, naturally, he would not allow that to happen. He'll have to save us now—his honor's at stake. They now have God under pressure because they have the sign of his presence; hence he dare not allow them to lose. To have God's furniture is to have God's power. The ark is their religious ace in the hole.

When I was eight or nine years old I remember learning a lesson that was taught to my older brother. He seemed to have a practice of asking a girl for a date and making plans for the evening, then, on the given evening, perhaps an hour or two beforehand, he would go in and ask his father for the car, indicating that he had a date. Now I was only an indirect observer and was always in another room, but I didn't need good ears. "Ya don't go getting a date and making plans and then come in here to ask for the car. I don't go for those high-pressure tactics. Ya ask for the car first, then ya get your date!" Saved me a lot of trouble a few years later. But Pop knew about high-pressure tactics. If my brother made all his plans, then asked for the car but was refused—why, then, who's the bad guy? What kind of Dad is that? So, my father smelled an underlying assumption by his son: "I have all these plans made and if you don't come through on your end, your reputation will hit zero."

Israel seemed to hold a similar assumption. Here was a pressure tactic, a way of—if you'll pardon the expression—twisting God's arm. That is not faith but superstition. It is what I call rabbit-foot theology. When we, whether Israelites or Christians, operate this way, our concern is not to seek God but to control him, not to submit to God but to use him. So we prefer religious magic to spiritual holiness; we are interested in success, not repentance.

In spite of Israelite enthusiasm (v. 5; in Israel's view God is always good for morale) and Philistine alarm, the scheme flopped. In view of all the hype one expects more than the laconic entry of verse 10: "So the Philistines fought and Israel was struck down, and each man fled to his tent." Not only that, but Yahweh's ark was captured (v. 11). The people who read the papers and listened to the newscasts could draw only one conclusion: Yahweh had suffered defeat; he was unable to deliver the goods for Israel. Not only Israel but Yahweh was the loser.

The text forces two important implications upon us: Yahweh will suffer shame rather than allow you to carry on a false relationship with him; and Yahweh will allow you to be disappointed with him if it will awaken you to the sort of God he really is.

Contemporary believers must beware of thinking they are immune from this rabbit-foot faith. What is behind a church's twenty-four-hour prayer vigil? Is it a desire to be in earnest with God, to plead with him in some matter? Or is there some thinking that if we simply organize and orchestrate such coverage, God will be forced to grant whatever we are praying about? Perhaps individual Christians have observed that "things go better with prayer." But what then is the drive behind their daily devotional exercises? Is it delight in meeting with God or with "things" going better? Whenever the church stops confessing "Thou art worthy" and begins chanting "Thou art useful"—well, then you know the ark of God has been captured again.

The Fulfillment of Yahweh's Threat

It's only a hint at first. Israel's counselors had hit upon the inspired idea for victory. They sent to Shiloh to requisition the ark, and the writer matter-of-factly notes that the ark was in the care of Eli's sons, Hophni and Phinehas (v. 4). This fact is important to the writer. Naturally, Eli's sons accompanied the ark into battle. When the writer summarizes the results of the battle in verse 11, he places the deaths of Hophni and Phinehas in the last and perhaps climactic position.[5] All his

---

5. See Eslinger, *Kingship of God in Crisis*, 174.

readers immediately realize that here is the fulfillment of Yahweh's word, of his decision (2:25) and his threat (2:34). Here then is the irony in verses 1-11: Israel plans the bringing of the ark as the key to victory, but Yahweh uses it to carry out his purpose to put Hophni and Phinehas to death.

The irony goes deeper. There was no doubt about how the press and the media would interpret the event: Even with the very sign of Yahweh's presence among them Israel's troops were decimated; in Israel's defeat Yahweh was defeated; he was unable to give Israel victory. Yahweh—to his shame—was a loser. But if we've listened to the story from the first, we know that the strange twist is precisely here. We know (on the basis of 2:12-17, 22-25, 29-30) that on this day that seemed to dishonor Yahweh, Yahweh was in fact beginning to protect his honor and to restore it. Yahweh may be despised in Philistia (for a while) but he will no more be despised in Shiloh.

One must be careful not to miss the way God is working here. It is so easy to be wrapped up in the bloodiness of Israel's defeat, in the tragedy of the ark's capture, in the blot on Yahweh's reputation, that one becomes blind to the fact that in the middle of all this Yahweh is clearly but quietly fulfilling a word he had spoken. Indeed, though in fulfilling this word he acts in judgment, he nevertheless acts in grace, for in his judgment he is removing false shepherds who caused his people to go astray.

With the death of Eli (v. 18) a whole era will pass away; the slate of the old leadership will be cleared for Samuel, the man Yahweh has called.

The Tragedy of Yahweh's Departure

He was a pitiful sight. An old man, quite heavy (v. 18), sitting on a seat by the side of the road (v. 13). He looks but he does not see; blank stares are all the blind man can muster now (v. 15). It takes no divining to see he is deeply agitated; perhaps he is visibly trembling—certainly his heart is (v. 13). He seems to know disaster has come; only he cannot weep because it is not yet confirmed. He may hear the rapid pounding of feet but cannot see the torn clothes or soiled head of the messenger (v. 12). He won't know until someone tells him the news. And it seems that it takes forever (vv. 12-16) before the messenger speaks to him. But he heard the commotion in town (v. 14), and when he asked about it the answer came: Israel fled... a great slaughter... both your sons died... the ark of God captured (v. 17). That was the fatal blow: not Hophni's and Phinehas's deaths but the capture of the ark. His heart was already trembling over the ark, but this was too much. Eli fell backward, his neck snapped, death (v. 18).

And the news was too much for Phinehas's wife. She was pregnant and soon to deliver. When she heard the report about the capture of the ark of God, and that her father-in-law and her husband had died, she gave birth, for her labor pains had begun (v. 19). But there was more death than life in her bedroom. Not even the well-meaning encouragement of her female friends could cut the gloom (v. 20). She died in childbirth. Her last act and words sum up that dark day (vv. 21-22). Probably she taught more theology in her death than Phinehas had done in his whole life.[6]

Whether the baby's name, Ichabod (v. 21), means "no glory" or "where is the glory?" does not matter. Phinehas's wife explained what she meant: "The glory has departed from Israel," or better, "has gone into exile from Israel" (v. 22)—this because the ark of God had been taken.

H. L. Ellison asserts that the story of Phinehas's wife (vv. 19-22) is "one of the most touching in the Bible,"

> but she was wrong. The glory of God had indeed departed, but not because the ark of God had been captured; the ark had been captured because the glory had already departed.[7]

I think Ellison is right. In any case, Ichabod and I Samuel 4 teach us that sometimes God must depart from us in order that we might seek him rightly. And in the meantime we do well to ponder what a tragedy it is when the presence of God no longer abides among the people of God. Could "Ichabod" be justly written over many of our church sanctuaries?

---

6. By the report of Eli's death and the words of Phinehas' wife the writer clearly shows that the real tragedy is the loss of the ark, not the deaths of Eli or of his sons. See Antony F. Campbell, *The Ark Narrative (1 Sam 4–6; 2 Sam 6): A Form-Critical and Traditio-Historical Study*, SBL Dissertation Series 16 (Missoula: Scholars, 1975), 83.

7. H. L. Ellison, *Scripture Union Bible Study Books: Joshua–2 Samuel* (Grand Rapids: Eerdmans, 1966), 51.

STUDY QUESTIONS

1. God does not exist for us, we exist for him. Can you think of other Biblical examples of attempts to put pressure on God beside the example in 1 Samuel 4.

2. What is the difference between basing a prayer on God's promises and trying to force God's hand? It is important to think this through.

3. Can you think of examples in your own experience or that of others where God has acted both in judgement and in grace at the very same time?

4. Think about the quotation from H.L.Ellison on pp 45, 46. Why is it of crucial importance that we rightly understand 1 Samuel 4:22?

5

Arkeological Discoveries

1 Samuel 5:1–7:1

A shdod. Northernmost of three Philistine coastal cities. Perhaps at the time the premier city of the Philistine pentapolis. Three miles in from the Mediterranean coast.[1] The scene of the Philistines' first "arkeological" discovery.

The Supremacy of Yahweh (5:1-5)

The Philistines had captured the ark of Yahweh and had placed it before the image of their god Dagon in Dagon's shrine.[2] One needn't be perceptive to get the point: here, in the gospel according to the Philistines, was Yahweh (represented by the ark), the defeated god, brought in before Dagon, the victorious god. However, before Wheaties time the next morning, "Dagon had fallen face downward on the ground before the ark of Yahweh" (v. 3). Now Dagon bows before Yahweh! The masterstroke is in the next line—and I think the writer probably had tongue in cheek, twinkle in eye, and acid in ink when he wrote most matter-of-factly: "So they took Dagon and put him back in his place."[3] It doesn't sound

---

1. Ashdod is approximately thirty-five air miles west of Jerusalem, which may help a modern reader with location but would be senseless to a Philistine or an Israelite whose miles were filled with wadis and hills to be negotiated.

2. Dagon was probably a vegetation or grain deity; he was widely worshiped throughout Mesopotamia, as well as at Ugarit. See H. A. Hoffner, Jr., "Dagon," *ZPEB*, 2:2.

3. There is a little more force in 5:3b, "they took [*lāqaḥ*] Dagon," if one reads it in light of the six occurrences of *lāqaḥ* in chapter 4, referring to the ark being "taken,"

like a punchline. But imagine: a god—and they have to stand him back up! What kind of god is that? How would a godly Israelite respond upon hearing this story? With the only pious response: holy uproarious laughter.

It became worse. Next morning Dagon's head and hands came off when he tried to bow before Yahweh's ark (v. 4). A regular Humpty-Dumpty situation with no Elmer's glue. Dagon is simply getting the godness knocked out of him. Indeed, the Philistines themselves will soon admit that Yahweh has "out-godded" their god (v. 7). So the "defeated" God defeats the "victorious" god on the latter's home turf. What biting humor in verses 1-5: scenarios of Dagon's "homage" (vv. 1-3a), Dagon's helplessness (v. 3b), and Dagon's "destruction" (vv. 4-5).

Yahweh, however, intends for his people to think, not merely to laugh—to realize that, unlike a battered Dagon, Yahweh doesn't have to have someone come and set him up again. He can fight the Philistines by himself. He doesn't need his people to cheer him on; he will bring back his ark all by himself. Humor, yes; but didactic humor, teaching the self-sufficiency and supremacy of Yahweh. And solemn humor: don't begin to think, Israel, that you can manipulate the living God like a lucky charm for your own convenience (1 Sam. 4); and don't begin to think that he needs you to support and carry him; if any carrying is to be done, he will carry you (cf. Isa. 46:1-4).

It is axiomatic in paganism that the gods are dependent upon man. Part of the old Babylonian *Gilgamesh Epic* contains a flood story. Utnapishtim, who survives the flood in a boat, offers a sacrifice at the end of the ordeal. He relates how the gods smelled the aroma of his sacrifice and drink offering and how "the gods gathered like flies over the sacrificer."[4] If gods and goddesses did not have food and drink (supplied by the sacrifices of their devotees), they, like anyone, began to languish. But with the destruction of mankind during the

---

and in light of 5:1, 2, where the Philistines "take" the ark. Now they must "take" Dagon and reshelve him.

4. Alexander Heidel, *The Gilgamesh Epic and Old Testament Parallels* (Chicago: Phoenix Books, 1963), 87.

flood and with Utnapishtim marooned in the boat for the duration, it had been weeks since the divinities had had a proper meal. Hence their greedy response to Utnapishtim's sacrifice. That is conventional paganism. Note its assumption: the gods depend on man to sustain them.

First Samuel 5:1-5 is meant to counter such thinking in Israel. Not only does the episode teach the Philistines the supremacy of Yahweh over Dagon but it instructs Israel that such supremacy is utterly independent of his people. Yahweh is not like Dagon (and his kind), a helpless god needing to be cuddled, protected, and sustained by his worshipers.

The danger is that contemporary Christians may think that they are not dim-witted pagans and so, naturally, such matters of humorous and historical interest have nothing to do with them. But the church has its own paganizing mind. What are we to say of songs that croon, "Somehow, he needed me"? What about poetic ditties that speak of God's having "no hands but our hands," "no feet but our feet" to do his will? I know there's an element of truth in such sentiments but it's largely buried. What of the lyrics of our hymns?

> Rise up, O men of God!
> His kingdom tarries long;
> Bring in the day of brotherhood
> And end the night of wrong.

Very stirring, and, probably, too cocky.[5] I am not saying we should cease serving Yahweh with all our might but that we must beware of Christian arrogance that casts Yahweh in Dagon's image. The God of the Bible does not need us—and that is good news (see, again, Isa. 46:1-4)! Note: I did not say he does not want us.

The Severity of Yahweh (5:6–6:16)

This was no tame God the Philistines had "conquered." The ark had fallen into their hands but they had now fallen into Yahweh's hand: "Now the hand of Yahweh was heavy upon

---

5. For the basis of my criticism, see George Eldon Ladd, *A Theology of the New Testament* (Grand Rapids: Eerdmans, 1974), 103.

the Ashdodites—he devastated them" (5:6).[6] Yahweh struck the people of Ashdod and its surrounding areas with tumors (5:6b),[7] which brought terror, suffering, and death (vv. 9, 11-12). Since we hear of "rats that are ruining the land" in 6:5, some scholars think the tumors may have been the swellings in the armpits, groin, and sides of the neck that are symptomatic of bubonic plague, of which rats are carriers.[8] (LXX, followed by NEB, mentions the rats in 5:6.) In any case, Yahweh was assaulting the Philistines, whether by bubonic plague or some other means. The Ashdodites confessed that neither Dagon nor they could stand up to Yahweh (5:7).

After official consultation the ark arrived in Gath; so did plague and panic (vv. 8-9). Gath sent the ark to Ekron but the Ekron Jaycees met the transport party at the city limits with their "Oh no, you don't!" (v. 10).[9] The Philistines were clear about some things. They now knew that it was not because the men of Ashdod were greater sinners than other Philistines that its funeral directors were so busy. No, there was enough evidence: the presence of the ark had brought disease and death to Ashdod, Gath, and Ekron. This was nothing but the "hand of God" striking the Philistines. And his hand was heavy—very, very heavy (v. 11b).

The ark's tenure in Philistia proved to be, for the Philistines, a very long seven months (6:1). The consensus was clear: send the ark back to Israel. The question: How to do that? Naturally,

---

6. The verb (be heavy, *kābēd*) in 5:6 and 11 is cognate to the noun *kābôd* (glory) in 4:21-22. ("To be heavy" or "weighty" is not so far removed from "glory" as it may seem. A weighty person in society would be one who is honorable or glorious. A few years ago one might hear an American teenager say, "That's heavy." That is, the matter or the object alluded to has real significance.) Though the *kābôd* had departed from Israel, it was certainly *kābēding* the Philistines.

7. The word in the Hebrew text (*'ōphāl'm*) seems to indicate swellings of some sort; hence many translate "tumors" (RSV, JB, NEB). The Hebrew scribes have supplied the word *ṭĕḥōr'm* in the margin, suggesting that it be read instead of *'ōphāl'm*. Some think this marginal reading is meant to explain *'ōphāl'm*, i.e., hemorrhoids (NASB, NJPS); others think the scribes were supplying a more polite term. Those fascinated with such matters may begin by consulting the major commentaries.

8. See R. K. Harrison, *Introduction to the Old Testament* (Grand Rapids: Eerdmans, 1969), 714-15.

9. The location of Gath is disputed. If it is identified with Tell es-Safi it would be approximately ten miles east/southeast of Ashdod; then Ekron, if identified with Tell el-Muqenna', would be five miles north of Gath (Tell es-Safi). See A. F. Rainey, "Ekron," and "Gath," *ISBE*, rev. ed., 2:47-48, 410-13.

the lords of the Philistines don't know; one must turn to the clergy for the answer (6:2). Their priests and diviners tell them that it is imperative for a guilt or a reparation offering to accompany the ark on its return. We have the priests' instructions in full in 6:4b-9.

Since there are five "lords of the Philistines," the ark must carry back five gold tumors and five gold rats (though on the latter cf. v. 18), that is, the Philistines are to make gold images of their tumors and rats. What an exercise in creativity! (How would you like to make an image of your tumor, and which one would you choose for your model?) Yet the Philistines were not amused by the exercise. They were under a triple stroke (v. 5b—their bodies, their gods, their land), and, above all, they dare not become dense and thick as the Egyptians did at the exodus (6:6).[10] They must not resist Israel's God only to crumple under the mockery of his judgment.

All is nearly ready: there's a new cart, to be pulled by two cows that are suckling calves, cows that have never been under a yoke before (v. 7a). The ark is to be placed on the cart; the golden rats and tumors are in a box beside the ark; and the Philistines are ready for the moment of truth (v. 8).

The diviners have structured the situation so that the Philistines can tell whether it was indeed Yahweh who ravaged them. They will know it was really Yahweh who had brought disaster on them if the cows pull the cart, ark and all, straight on up the road to Beth-shemesh in Israel; but if the cows don't do that, then they will know it "just happened" and had nothing to do with "his [Yahweh's] hand" (v. 9). They want to know beyond doubt whether they had received a bad break or a divine judgment.

Hence, in their view, they have provided the opportunity for Yahweh to write his signature across their circumstances. And they made it as difficult as possible for him to do so! Even city boys should know that any cows in their right maternal minds would naturally go back to their sucking calves that had been penned up at home (v. 7b). One certainly wouldn't

---

10. The Philistines' knowledge of Yahweh's exodus deliverance may be a bit garbled (see 4:8), but they had apparently heard the story. That should not surprise us in light of Exodus 15:14, for, according to the biblical record, none of it was done in a corner (cf. Acts 26:26).

expect them, contrary to nature, to go walking off toward Israel as if in the grip of an invisible hand. If the cows did what no normal cows would do, then the Philistines would know, unmistakably, that Yahweh had stricken Philistia.[11]

"Now the cows went straight on the road in the direction of Beth-shemesh; they went along on the same highway, lowing as they went; they did not turn to the right or to the left" (v. 12). Here was Yahweh's cow-revelation to the Philistines; perhaps we could say he spoke in a "low" —but clear—voice.

The Philistines witnessed what occurred (6:9, 12, 16). Yahweh had spoken to them. To be sure, he spoke through cows rather than prophets. He did not give them the whole torah but he did give them some truth. And they were responsible for rightly responding to the truth they did receive. Yahweh had stooped to show them, in terms they could understand, that he himself had destroyed their god, their land, and their bodies. Now what will they do with that revelation? Should they not turn and at least begin to serve or fear this obviously real and living God? Or will they go back to Ashdod and take Dagon to the local image shop for repairs? Maybe they will lobby the five lords to fund the research and development of rat and mice pesticides. Some of the elite may slap "Survivor of the Plague of 1070" bumper stickers on their chariots. Perhaps the majority simply sighed, "Glad that's over!" It is so easy for us sinners—Philistine or otherwise—to respond only to the pain and not to the truth of a situation. Our immediate fears are alleviated but our heads are no wiser, our hearts no softer. Perhaps the Egyptians (6:6) have no corner on denseness.

Yet even in this judgment there is a ray of hope for us. For, limited and restricted as it may be, if Yahweh stoops to reveal himself even to the enemies of Israel, to this noncovenant people, perhaps we may infer that he may not be totally adverse to some day bringing near those who are far off by the blood of the Messiah (Eph. 2:13).

---

11. The situation is somewhat like the god-contest between Yahweh and Baal on Mount Carmel in 1 Kings 18. When Elijah orders the sacrifice, altar, and trench deluged with water (vv. 33-35), he has made it as impossible as possible (to human minds) for Yahweh to answer by fire. If Yahweh nevertheless does so, he will have proved himself beyond doubt the real God (vv. 38-39). The greater the difficulty the greater the clarity and certainty.

The Sanctity of Yahweh (6:13–7:1)

The return of the ark to Israel marks a major transition in our narrative, though the theme of Yahweh's severity continues. Now Israel discovers the severity of Yahweh. Yahweh's stroke will fall on both pagan Philistines and covenant people, especially when that covenant people violates the holiness of their God.

Our primary focus centers on verse 19, which is also our primary problem. There are signs that the Hebrew text of verse 19 has been disturbed in the process of transmission. We will simply have to wade through the difficulties.

First, how many did Yahweh strike down? The traditional Hebrew text records 50,070 (see NASB), or, literally, "seventy men, fifty thousand men." However, since the "fifty thousand men" is missing in some Hebrew manuscripts and since the population of the village of Beth-shemesh could not have been so numerous, it is better to read "seventy men" as do most modern versions.

A second problem: why did Yahweh strike down these seventy men? English versions that follow the Hebrew text almost uniformly render: "because they looked into the ark of Yahweh" (cf. NIV, TEV, RSV, NASB). But the grammatical combination (Hebrew verb plus following preposition) means to "look/gaze at," not "look into."[12] The offense was not in lifting the lid of the ark and looking inside but in looking or gazing at—we might say inspecting—the ark. (Was it not appropriately covered when it arrived and/or did the Levites not cover it? We cannot know.) In any case, the activity flew in the face of the regulations Yahweh had given for the tabernacle furniture in Numbers 4:1-20. Not even the Kohathites (the Levite group entrusted with transporting the holy tabernacle furniture) were permitted to go in and look at the sacred furniture; Aaron and his sons must properly cover it (Num. 4:17-20). After covering the furniture, Aaron and his sons were to assign each of the Kohathites to his specific task. It was all a provision of mercy—Yahweh did not want the Kohathites to die. So (back to 1 Samuel 6) when the Beth-shemesh men violate the sanctity of the ark they suffer the penalty Yahweh had previously announced.

---

12. See BDB, 907-8, sect. 8a, under *rā'āh.*

There's a third problem: what if the men of Beth-shemesh did not gaze at the ark but died for some other reason? The Septuagint reads very differently from the Hebrew text: "And the sons of Jeconiah did not rejoice with the men of Beth-shemesh because [or possibly: when] they saw the ark of the Lord...."[13] Here are "sons of Jeconiah" out of the blue. It is difficult to evaluate the Septuagint here: Had the translator simply been working too late at night or did he have before him a more adequate Hebrew text?

There is something to be said for following the Septuagint at this point. First, "the sons of Jeconiah did not rejoice" carries a tone of originality about it; it is not the sort of detail invented out of whole cloth. Second, the passage has regularly introduced new subjects into the account: the men of Beth-shemesh (v. 13), the cart (v. 14), the Levites (v. 15), the lords of the Philistines (v. 16). The Septuagint's "sons of Jeconiah" would fit this pattern. Third, the nonrejoicing sons of Jeconiah would form a useful contrast to the rejoicing harvesters in verse 13. The ark receives a double response: many rejoice, some don't.[14]

Let's back away from the problems and try to hear the preaching of the text. How does it touch us?

The concern of the text seems to center on Yahweh's holiness (v. 20), his sanctity. Because that has been violated, Yahweh struck down the offenders. But how was Yahweh's sanctity violated? If we follow the Septuagint in verse 19, the answer is: by indifference. We then have the opposite extreme from 4:3. The sons of Jeconiah say, "The ark of Yahweh has come back. So who cares?" If in chapter 4 Israel exaggerates the potency of the ark as the guarantee of Yahweh's presence, here the family of Jeconiah despises the significance of the ark as the sign of Yahweh's presence. That Yahweh seems to be returning to Israel does not move them. They "did not rejoice." Apathy. It may be easy to think, "Surely the fact that God doesn't matter

---

13. It is baffling to note how English versions treat verse 19a. A number of them follow the Hebrew text with no allusion in footnote or margin to the alter-nate LXX reading (so NIV, TEV, RSV, NASB); others simply follow LXX and include no hint that the Hebrew text is different (so NEB, JB, NJB)!

14. I am much more willing now than previously to regard LXX of 6:19a as original; in fact, I would give it a slight edge over the traditional Hebrew text here.

to us is not a matter that matters to him"—until seventy men keel over (v. 19b). Too late we may learn that Israel's jealous God is not indifferent about our indifference. Might judgment ever fall on us for the same reason? Not because we commit some blatant act of iniquity but because we lack a passion to adore and delight in God? Perhaps our greatest transgressions are not positive but passive.

If we follow the traditional Hebrew text in verse 19, then the men of Beth-shemesh were struck down for an act of sacrilege—inspecting the ark in violation of the prescriptions and cautions of Numbers 4:1-20. (Who knows how the Philistines handled the ark? But they are pagans without Yahweh's written law; Israel, however, has that law and is therefore held accountable for it.)

The men of Beth-shemesh certainly respond to the disaster Yahweh inflicted. Their response, as noted in verse 20, consisted of two questions. The first was entirely proper: "Who is able to stand before Yahweh, this Holy God?" The second was off track: "And to whom will he go up away from us?" (literal trans.). The New English Bible catches their mood: "No one is safe in the presence of the LORD, this holy God. To whom can we send it, to be rid of him?" Much later, the Gerasenes will try the same solution. They will be afraid of the power of Jesus that restores people and destroys pigs. The only option they will see is to beg Jesus to leave (Mark 5:1-20). So at Beth-shemesh. No self-examination. No searching of hearts. The ark—and the power of Yahweh with it—must be removed.

God's people today no longer have the ark of the covenant, but we can fall into the same Beth-shemesh mode of thinking. We can forget that Yahweh is holy, in a word, different, and that he does not conform to our expectation of an easygoing God.

Our culture does not help us to smash our graven image of the casual God. Our culture proclaims that God must be the essence of tolerance; he is chummy rather than holy, the "man upstairs" rather than my Father for Jesus' sake. So long as our novelty license plates declare that "God is my co-pilot" we can be sure that we have not yet seen the King, Yahweh of hosts. As Jonathan Edwards noted, it is the absence of "godly fear" that signifies a lack of the knowledge of God.[15]

We need to share half of the attitude of Beth-shemesh's citizens; there is a sense in which it is dangerous to be in the presence of God. But we must not want him "to go up away from us." We must regard his presence as our supreme joy *and* our supreme peril. This does not mean we cannot be intimate with God; it means we cannot be familiar with him. Intimacy is able to call him "Father" and tremble at the same time—and as it trembles know that it is loved!

Whichever way we take verse 19 we will find it searching us.

Back in the fifties when professional baseball's Dodgers were in Brooklyn, several of the Dodgers were stopped by a police officer for speeding. Since shortstop Pee Wee Reese was driving, he had to handle the public relations. He apologized to the officer, identified himself as Pee Wee Reese of the Dodgers, then turned to point out Duke Snider, Carl Erskine, and Rube Walker. The officer was properly delighted and waved them on without a ticket.[16] They eluded the penalty because they were, after all, members of the Brooklyn Dodgers.

One might expect Yahweh to function in the same way, bringing his judgment on the pagan Philistines (5:1–6:12) but exempting his Israel from any such scourge. But he does not (6:19–7:1). His severity falls upon both Philistia and Israel. The men of Beth-shemesh do not elude Yahweh's judgment because they are Israelites. They too stand under it. The steadfastness of Yahweh's love for Israel does not compromise the justice of his judgment. There is a word in this for Presbyterians—and other sinners.

The study of arkeology in 1 Samuel 5–6 is not fruitless, for the discoveries we make enable us to destroy our false images of Yahweh. When we discover the supremacy of Yahweh (5:1-5) we see he is no helpless God; we see in the severity of Yahweh that he is no hidden God but one who clearly proves he is at work, even if he must use noisy cows to make his point;

---

15. See Iain H. Murray, *Jonathan Edwards: A New Biography* (Edinburgh: Banner of Truth, 1987), 259.

16. Duke Snider with Bill Gilbert, *The Duke of Flatbush* (New York: Zebra, 1988), 117.

and as we discover the sanctity of Yahweh, we may realize that the casual god we have been worshiping does not exist. If arkeology destroys our graven images it is a useful science indeed.

STUDY QUESTIONS

1. How can we strike a balance between two facts: that God is totally self-sufficient and that he graciously uses us in his service?

2. The Philistines had evidently heard what had happened to the Egyptians at the Exodus and it made them fearful. Do you ever tell others of a judgement to fear as well as of God's willingness in grace to forgive when we come his way?

3. God spoke to the Philistines through the cows. Can you think of another time when he spoke through an animal? Try the Book of Numbers.

4. 'Perhaps our greatest transgression are not positive but passive.' Could this sometimes be because we want to be thought nice? See Chapter 2, Question 4.

5. What is the difference between intimacy and familiarity in our dealings with God?

6

New Mercies
(1 Samuel 7:2-17)

Perhaps you have not missed him. You may have been so caught up in the story that you have not thought about him. Yet now he appears again; Samuel is preaching to Israel (v. 3). This is the first mention of Samuel since 4:1a. We have had almost three Samuel-less chapters. As Samuel's appearance in chapter 3 was a sign of fresh grace to Israel, so his presence in chapter 7 coincides with new mercies Israel desperately needs. Here Samuel as prophet and intercessor seeks to restore to repentance the Israel that has been so severely judged (ch. 4–6). So we trace Yahweh's mercy in Samuel's ministry.

The Preparation for God's Mercy (7:2-6)

Life would be unbelievably drab and listless without emotions and feelings. Never getting high blood pressure over anything may be a sign that one has health—or lacks vitality. There were some signs of spiritual vitality in Israel during those twenty years the ark was in safekeeping in Kiriath-jearim. "All the house of Israel went lamenting after Yahweh" (7:2).[1] Samuel addressed his preaching (v. 3) to Israel in her longing and remorse. It is quite likely that verse 3 condenses Samuel's activity; he may well have preached in various places over

---

1. I take the verb as coming from the little used n`H`H, "to wail, lament"; see BDB, 624, and its cognate noun(s) there.

some period of time until he could see that Israel's repentance appeared genuine (v. 4) and that the time was ripe for Israel to "go public," officially and corporately renewing covenant relations with Yahweh (vv. 5-6).

It is well to have tears and sobs and sorrow over sin (v. 2). Repentance frequently begins with such grief and a consciousness of one's misery. But true repentance consists of something more substantial. And it is proper to express repentance in public rites and ceremonies (v. 6), so long as such rites represent realities and are not mere religious charades.[2]

During World War II a worker in the French underground was able to enjoy auto travel all over France with no hindrance from the Germans. Some loyal French policemen put handcuffs on him. The German patrols always thought him a prisoner and paid no attention to him. Repentance can sometimes masquerade like that; we take the tears or distress as infallible signs of repentance. Yet people can be moved without being changed.

Samuel's preaching (v. 3) was meant to counter any frothy repentance; he pressed Israel to go beyond a merely emotional response:

> If it is with all your hearts [emphatic phrase] that you are turning back to Yahweh, put away the foreign gods from among you, along with the Ashtaroth, make your hearts steadfast toward Yahweh, and serve him alone, and let him deliver you from the hand of the Philistines.

Genuine repentance, Samuel says, is a *tangible* repentance. It does not stop with tears and weeping but moves to concrete action: "put away the foreign gods from among you" (see the same demand by Jacob in Genesis 35:2-4 and by Joshua in Joshua 24:14-15). True repentance will meet Yahweh's demand for exclusive allegiance with whatever it takes to

---

2. No one seems to know exactly what the water pouring (v. 6) signifies. Is it a "symbolical representation of the temporal and spiritual distress in which they were at the time" (C. F. Keil, *Biblical Commentary on the Books of Samuel* [1875; reprint ed.; Grand Rapids: Eerdmans, 1950], 73; so too Erdmann [in Lange's Commentary]; cf. Josh. 7:5, Ps. 22:14; Lam. 2:19)? Does it reflect the self-denial of the occasion— Israel is depriving herself of even this necessity of life (Robert P. Gordon)? Does it signify the washing away of communal guilt (Joyce Baldwin)?

obey it.[3] Samuel's demand is simply the reassertion of the
first commandment (Exod. 20:3). It is the same demand that
one first-century Jew had the audacity to make: "Anyone who
loves his father or mother more than me is not worthy of me;
anyone who loves his son or daughter more than me is not
worthy of me; and anyone who does not take his cross and
follow me is not worthy of me" (Matt. 10:37-38, NIV). (What
are we to make of a Man who goes around demanding the
devotion required by the first commandment for himself?) It
is the demand upon the Christian who should lose his life in
and to the mercies of God (Romans 12:1 in context). It is the
ongoing need of the church (Rev. 2:4-5) as she discovers the
Christian life is a life of such ongoing, continual repentance.

Samuel is also calling Israel to a *difficult* repentance. They
are to put away the foreign gods along with the Ashtaroths,
that is, they are to renounce both the male and the female
deities of the prevailing fertility worship. Canaanite religion
exerted a powerful appeal with the sexual rites that were part
of its worship.[4] Most fun-loving Canaanites doubtless found
the combination of liturgy and orgy highly congenial, not to
speak of the convenience of having chapel and brothel at one
location. It was no easy task to peel Israelites out of the grip
of a cult that both asked for and approved of the offering their
glands as a living sacrifice to Baal and Asherah—which was
their "reasonable service" if they wanted their crops to grow.[5]
One might just as well try to relieve poison ivy by scratching.
No super-ficial—only a super-natural—repentance would
break such bondage. And only steadfast hearts ("make your
hearts steadfast toward Yahweh"; cf. Psalm 51:10) will keep
them in the way of repentance.

Genuine repentance is the proper preparation for God's
mercy. Not that repentance coerces such mercy. There is no

---

3. We could also say such repentance is a strange repentance. Only Yahweh lays
this either-or, all-or-nothing demand on his people. The other gods and goddesses
of the ancient Near East were not so picky and intolerant. A pagan devotee was
welcome to address multiple gods and goddesses in prayer simultaneously. It is only
in Israel that we meet this jealous God (which means he loves his people too much to
tolerate their cuddling up with rivals).

4. See my *Such a Great Salvation: Expositions of the Book of Judges* (1990, rpt.
Christian Focus, 2000), 31-33, for an explanation of Canaanite fertility worship.

merit in such repentance, but there is no saving help without such repentance. Repentance is not the cause but only the condition of Yahweh's deliverance. The one who truly repents always knows his only hope rests in the "Who knows...?" of divine mercy (please see Joel 2:14 and Jonah 3:9 in context). But genuine repentance will always move beyond wet eyes and moved feelings and stirred emotions; it will cast down idols and cling to the only God. Perhaps William Cowper expressed such repentance best in his hymn, "O For a Closer Walk with God":

> Return, O holy Dove, return,
> Sweet Messenger of rest!
> I hate the sins that made thee mourn
> And drove Thee from my breast.

But when our congregation sings this hymn, it is this stanza that rises up and strikes me down:

> The dearest idol I have known,
> Whate'er that idol be,
> Help me to tear it from Thy throne,
> And worship only Thee.

The Experience of God's Mercy (7:7-10)

The Philistines heard. Philistines always hear; Philistines always know. And, as usual, Philistines come (v. 7). For them the Mizpah assembly spelled revolt rather than repentance— and they may not have been totally mistaken.[6] In her emergency Israel can only plead with Samuel: "Do not hold back from crying out to Yahweh our God, and let him [or: that he might] save us from the hand of the Philistines" (v. 8).

Israel's plight is admittedly pathetic, but she occupies much firmer ground than in the crisis of chapter 4. One can't help noticing the contrast between an Israel that thinks she has coerced Yahweh's power by having his furniture (ch. 4) and an Israel who sees her helplessness and can only resort to desperate prayer (ch. 7).

---

5. Cf. W. G. Blaikie's comments on the attraction of pagan religion (The First Book of Samuel, The Expositor's Bible [Cincinnati: Jennings and Graham, n.d.], 88-89).

6. Mizpah is probably to be identified with Tell en-Nasbeh, eight miles north of Jerusalem, on the main north-south watershed road.

Chapters 4 and 7 are meant to stand beside one another; there is a formal parallel between them, a parallel that sets off the contrasts. Note the following:

Chapter 4	Chapter 7
Israel "struck down"	Philistines "struck down"
(Hebrew, n`G^P)	(Hebrew, n`g^P)
by Philistines,	by Israel,
2, 3, 10	10
Manipulation	Repentance
"Let it save," 3	"Let him deliver/save," 3, 8
Philistines hear,	Philistines hear,
6	7
Result: "Ichabod"	Result: "Ebenezer"
21	12

Here in chapter 7 Israel is not dabbling in religious magic (ch. 4) but walking by sheer faith. They dangle by the mere mercy of Yahweh. They see no recourse, but, taking their cue from Samuel (v. 3c), they share his position ("Let him [Yahweh] save us from the hand of the Philistines," v. 8). Their only weapon is prayer,[7] their only hope that Samuel might place his hand upon the throne of the Lord for them. And even Samuel is reduced to a cry of distress on their behalf (v. 9).[8] Desperation, however, is never in trouble when it rests on omnipotence. Yahweh blasted the Philistines with his thunder and threw them into confusion (v. 10b). It's only what he had promised to do (Lev. 26:8; Deut. 28:7).[9] Hannah had known it years ago (1 Sam. 2:10a).

At the heart of Israel's experience of mercy stands her own helplessness and utter lack of resources; prayer is her only recourse. I think Israel's plight more than touches that of the church and of individual believers. The church (denomination or individual congregation) can often be blind to her true

---

7. Hans Wilhelm Hertzberg, *I & II Samuel,* The Old Testament Library (Philadelphia: Westminster, 1964), 68.

8. On the verb "to cry, cry out," z`'^q, see G. Hasel, "z`'^q," *TDOT,* 4:115-16, 119-22. Bible readers can become so accustomed to the *terminology* of God's people "crying out" to Yahweh that we can forget the distress, the desperation, always present in that cry. Biblical prayer is often the cry of a people at the end of their tether. It is easy to lose touch with this fact.

9. Cf. Karl Gutbrod, *Das Buch vom König,* Die Botschaft des Alten Testaments, 4th ed. (Stuttgart: Calwer, 1975), 55.

state. At least in the west the church is so used to developing
new strategies, originating effective gimmicks, or promoting
proven programs that she can dupe herself into thinking that
she lives by her own evangelical cleverness. Yet there is a form
of spiritual warfare that is not really touched by more and
better administration or by brighter and more creative ideas.
But we may not see this except in those times when God takes
our props away and forces us to rely only on his naked hand
for support. This can frequently occur in the believer's personal
life as well. Sometimes the Father may box us in, place us in
a situation in which, one by one, all our secondary helps and
supports are taken from us, in order that, defenseless, we may
lean on his mercy alone. More and more God's people must
walk the way of desperation—prayer. Once we see this, we
will no longer regard prayer as a pious cop-out but as our
only rational activity.

I think it proper to add that in Samuel's intercession on
Israel's behalf (vv. 8-9; see also 1 Samuel 12:23, Jeremiah 15:1)
we see a picture of the office of Christ as our high priest
(see Luke 22:31-32; Romans 8:34). Here is the true secret of
our steadfastness: we rely on the prayers of Another whose
prayers are always effectual. Nothing is quite so moving as
knowing that I am a subject of Jesus' intercessory prayer.

The Memory of God's Mercy (7:11-14)

In the wake of Israel's rout of the Philistines (v. 11),
Samuel sets up a monument (probably somewhere west of
Mizpah),[10] calls it Ebenezer (the stone of help), and explains
its significance—"Up to this point Yahweh has helped us"
(v. 12). Samuel certainly intends to commemorate Yahweh's
contemporary help. But he means much more, for in his "up to
this point" (KJV's "hitherto") there is a whole chain of mercies
remembered. Samuel's statement goes back into the past and
gathers its gratitude (perhaps he remembers the provision for
Abraham & Co., the liberation from Egypt, the preservation

---

10. Verse 12 says Samuel set up his Ebenezer, literally, "between Mizpah and
the tooth/crag." The latter was perhaps the name for some rock outcropping or
topographical landmark well-known to the locals. Also, we do not know the location of
Beth-car in verse 11, except that it is west of Mizpah, where the Philistines scrambled
through the hills for home.

in the wilderness, the subjugation during the conquest; see, e.g., Psalm 105). At the same time he looks to the future and marshals its hope, for his "up to this point" implies that what Yahweh has been for his people he also will be.

Perhaps we should pause to ask how the events of 1 Samuel 4 fit into all this—or do they? It sounds nice to say "Up to this point Yahweh has helped us," but how, if at all, was Yahweh helping Israel when the ark was captured and the Philistines were butchering Israelites and seizing plunder? W. G. Blaikie has contended:

> All that Samuel has considered well. Even amid the desolations of Shiloh the Lord was helping them. He was helping them to know themselves, helping them to know their sins, and helping them to know the bitter fruit and wo[e]ful punishment of sin.... The links of the long chain denoted by Samuel's "hitherto" were not all of one kind. Some were in the form of mercies, many were in the form of chastenings.[11]

So Yahweh's help came even in the darkness; it includes the events of 2:11-4:22 as well. Surely that too was "help," when Yahweh eliminated ungodly leadership in order to give his people a shepherd after his own heart.

Samuel, then, with his Ebenezer monument seeks to rivet Israel's memory to the past and most current of Yahweh's mercies. He knows that it is memory that keeps gratitude fresh and that gratitude keeps faith faithful.

When my wife and I began dating during college years, I would often offer her half a stick of gum. (I always had a pack of gum with me because I had a paranoia of bad breath. Yet it was poor etiquette to partake without offering some to one's companion. Hence we both masticated our respective half sticks of gum.) Unknown to me at the time, Barbara always kept her gum. Years later I saw how. She has two or three sheets of eight-by-twelve inch posterboard on which she had stuck each brownish-gray blob. Underneath each chunk she entered the date on which it was received and chewed. She might have "March 11, 1963," for example, and above it the

---

11. Blaikie, *First Book of Samuel*, 104.

respective wad of gum. She could get maybe twenty such entries on a sheet. It was her own way—however unique—of remembering our early courtship. One does not need to pluck off each ossified wad and chew it again in order to resurrect the memory. Fortunately, seeing is sufficient! But her gum boards do stimulate memories and memories stir up love and produce appreciation.

That is what monuments to Yahweh's deeds should do for the faith of Yahweh's people. Indeed, sometimes that is all that sustains you. You may be tempted to despair, pressed too close to the limit, almost too tired to care, upset because even the light of God's presence seems withdrawn. You know what the pit is like. Yet you punch faith's replay button. You can hear the authorized version, that is, the biblical story, which, to a great degree, is a record of the trouble of God's people. In that story you hear again of that people's God:

> In all their affliction he was afflicted,
>   and the angel of his presence saved them;
> in his love and in his pity he redeemed them;
>   he lifted them up and carried them all the days of old.
>   [Isa. 63:9 RSV]

Or you can review the experiential version—the string of Yahweh's providences and mercies over the years to you and to the "church in your house." Itemize them. Are there not any number of Ebenezers along the way? As you see, then, in Bible and experience, Yahweh's repeated supply and deliverance lead you to begin to ponder all these things in your heart (cf. Luke 2:19). Surely, you think, God has not given goodness and mercy all the way through merely to desert and abandon me at this point. "Up to this point Yahweh has helped us." That "up to this point" gives confidence for the future, unknown and unlit as it is.

Some may berate us for living in the past. I think the Bible would tell us that we could do a lot worse. There is a sense in which the saints must live in the past if they are to remember Yahweh's mercies and be able to sing, "O to grace how great a debtor, daily I'm constrained to be." We can put it this way: we stand in the present but dwell on the past in order that we can be steadfast for the future.

Some months ago I proposed a change at our celebration of the Lord's Supper. Our communion table, like many others, bears the legend of Christ's words, "This do in remembrance of me." I suggested that perhaps we should screw in two hooks into the bottom edge of that inscription and hang another appropriately carved dictum beneath it. The one I proposed was (traditionally translated): "Hitherto hath the Lord helped us." It would be fully proper. Where is there a more decisive "hitherto" than when God did not spare his own Son (Rom. 8:32)?[12]

Summary (7:15-17)

Verses 15-17 draw a line across our narrative, momentarily wrapping up Samuel's career. Samuel traveled an annual circuit consisting of sites/sacred places in Benjaminite territory.[13] Three times we are told that "Samuel judged (v'P^f) Israel" (vv. 15, 16, 17).[14] Although the verb can certainly connote the idea of administering justice (see RSV on v. 17), I do not think we can sever the uses of v'P^f in verses 15-17 from its earlier use in verse 6. The latter is an occasion of mourning, confession, and repentance, where "Samuel's 'judging' of

---

12. A comment or two on verses 13-14, especially 13. The contention that "the Philistines were subdued and no longer came into the territory of Israel" (v. 13a) seems difficult to reconcile with the situation in chapter 13 (to name no other). Note, however: (1) The author or editor of 1 Samuel surely had as much sense as we do and would have recognized the contradiction if he viewed it as such (cf. Gutbrod, *Das Buch vom König,* 55-56). Apparently he saw no major conflict. (2) Verse 13b qualifies 13a, for "the hand of Yahweh was against the Philistines all the days of Samuel" assumes that there was ongoing conflict. (3) Verses 13-14 have the character of a summary statement and should not be pressed in details. (4) A statement like 13a can be intended in a relative rather than an absolute sense; this may be the case between, for example, 2 Kings 6:23b and 24 (A. F. Kirkpatrick, *The First Book of Samuel,* Cambridge Bible for Schools and Colleges [Cambridge: Cambridge University Press, 1896], 90). (5) If we take "all the days of Samuel" (v. 13b) strictly (i.e., as referring to his activity throughout his whole life and not merely to his work prior to Saul's kingship), then chapters 13–14 constitute an instance of how the hand of Yahweh was against the Philistines all the days of Samuel. Hence chapters 13–14 do not contradict but explicate 7:13. One could argue that in 7:13-14 our writer wants us to realize how important Samuel was. He was really the shield of Israel. Samuel, he might be saying, was far more responsible for the safety of Israel than was the soon-to-be-desired king, Saul (cf. D. F. Payne, "1 and 2 Samuel," *The New Bible Commentary: Revised* [Grand Rapids: Eerdmans, 1970], 290).

13. I take Gilgal to be the Gilgal near Jericho and the Jordan. Bethel, Mizpah, and Ramah are all up on the Central Benjamin Plateau.

14. The same root will be used five times at the beginning of chapter 8 (vv. 1, 2, 3, 5, 6).

Israel is a religious activity that combines ritual and spiritual direction."[15] Samuel's ongoing work then did not consist of merely deciding legal disputes but of reproof, instruction, and counsel for living under Yahweh's lordship.[16]

It is instructive to have glimpses of Samuel in both a major crisis and routine duties. The Lord's servant usually has both, but frequently far more of the latter. Crucial breakthroughs (vv. 3-6) are exciting but patient consolidation (vv. 15-17) is necessary if their impact is to be preserved. Fresh commitment requires plodding instruction to sustain it. The circuit through Benjamin is never as glamorous as revival at Mizpah, but it is the road for many of us. Yahweh has his altars there as well.

Study Questions

1. If repentance must move to concrete action, can the same be said also of faith?

2. Is the idea that repentance is supernatural new to you? But how else could it be real, given that you and I are sinners?

3. How central is prayer in your whole approach to life with God?

4. Ebenezer is a helpful reminder of the value of recalling God's past deeds of grace for us. Why not make a list of them?

5. For the Christian it can be true that 'every common bush' is 'aflame with God'. Seek today to see God in many ordinary things and His grace in humble duties.

---

15. Moshe Garsiel, *The First Book of Samuel: A Literary Study of Comparative Structures, Analogies and Parallels* (Jerusalem: Rubin Mass, 1990), 66–67.

16. Cf. Joyce G. Baldwin, *1 & 2 Samuel*, Tyndale Old Testament Commentaries (Leicester: InterVarsity, 1988), 81; and Matthew Henry, *Commentary on the Whole Bible*, 6 vols. (New York: Revell, n.d.), 2:319.

Part 2

A King in God's Place

1 Samuel 8–14

7

The King Thing
(1 Samuel 8)

I was cleaning out and rearranging our storage room at the back of the carport. Houses in Mississippi (where we then lived) normally do not have basements, so, lacking a true garage, all extra items must go into the storage room. Naturally, it was hot, sticky, and dirty in there. Of course, I had stuff all around on the floor. Surely, whenever I would turn to pick up something I would bump something else and down it would go. Perhaps the reader knows the feeling. You realize you are right near the edge; in your refined depravity (which we prefer to call frustration) you really *dare* (and almost hope) someone to speak to you so that verbal leveling can occur. Ah, then I heard this female voice calling my name. That was my cue, and I didn't miss it. In a nasty, crabby dialect I both growled and hollered, "What?!" Imagine my surprise when I went out to the carport to find the "voice"—the nice Baptist lady who lived next door. One can't lie, but the truth hurts. I had to admit I thought it was my wife calling me! Which is even worse—a pure admission that I liked to be nice to neighbors but didn't mind crabbing at the dearest person in my life. What hurt the most, however, was the fact that I was exposed. My neighbor saw the real me; there was no place to hide.

The Bible does that. True, it is a revelation of God, but it is also a revelation of God's people. The Bible reveals not only

God but us. That is the function of 1 Samuel 8; it is Yahweh's analysis of his people, of Israel and of us. Such exposure, however, is easy to avoid: simply become engrossed in the historical problem of kingship in Israel and you will easily miss the primary blow the text means to strike. Let us, however, hold to the more painful way. This chapter then reveals...

Our Passion for Substitutes (8:5-8)

"Appoint for us a king to judge us like all the nations" (v. 5c). That was the elders' request/demand. It seemed plausible: Samuel had become old and a transition was certainly coming (v. 5a); and Samuel's sons, like Eli's, were scoundrels, and no one wanted to be stuck with them (vv. 2-3, 5b).[1] The solution: a new form of government. Up with monarchy.

Yahweh evaluates the king request in verses 7-8. If we are to hear this text, we must not fudge over Yahweh's analysis. "It is not *you* [= Samuel] they have rejected, but they have rejected *me* from being king over them" (v. 7b, emphasis in Hebrew). Israel has a longstanding tradition of such behavior: "In line with all their doings from the day I brought them up out of Egypt up to this very day—they abandoned me and served other gods; that's what they are doing to you [Samuel] as well" (v. 8). The king is not merely a substitute for Samuel but for Yahweh. What we have here is simply the old idolatry with a new twist.

We must insist that the demand for a king was not wrong in itself. If it was not perfectly permissible it was nevertheless permissible according to Deuteronomy 17:14-20 (I date Deuteronomy pre-Samuel). Moses had indicated that the time might come when Israel would want a king and that would be all right provided they heeded certain strictures. Occasionally scholars claim that the fault in the elders' request was their wanting to be "like all the nations" (1 Sam. 8:5). There is some truth to that (and we will come back to it) but Deuteronomy 17:14 finds no fault in Israel's desire for a king "like all the nations that are around me." Ironically, however, the rest of Deuteronomy 17 makes sure Israel will not have a king "like all the nations," for he must be a man of Yahweh's

---

1. The threat of military attack was another plank in their argument; see 12:12.

choosing (v. 15a), a brother Israelite, not a foreigner (v. 15b), without the customary royal perks—military machine, multiple wives, and massive wealth (vv. 16-17), and subservient to the rule of Yahweh's law (vv. 18-20). So the fault (in 1 Sam. 8) was not in the fact of the request but in the motive for the request. It was not the request itself but what was behind the request that tainted it.[2]

If we cheat and run to 1 Samuel 12, we will find the verdict of 8:7-8 confirmed. There as Samuel accuses Israel he rehearses Yahweh's saving deeds in Israel's distresses. Exhibit A: Israel was in Egypt in slavery; they cried out to Yahweh; Yahweh sent Moses and Aaron as deliverers (12:8). Exhibit B: Israel forgets Yahweh, who subjects them to various oppressors in the time of the judges; Israel cried out to Yahweh, confessing sin and pleading for deliverance; Yahweh sent Jerubbabel et al. to deliver them (12:9-11). Exhibit C: Israel sees Nahash the Ammonite flexing his military muscles against them, "then you said to me, 'No, but a king must reign over us'—but Yahweh your God is your king" (12:12). In the current emergency, there was no crying out to Yahweh for deliverance but a demand for a king. A clear if subtle substitution. Their help now was not in the strong name of Yahweh but in a new form of government. It is not monarchy but trust in monarchy that is the villain (see Psalms 118:8-9; 146:3).

---

2. There has been a mammoth debate about the alleged conflicting views of kingship within 1 Samuel 8–12. Even Samuel himself seems ambivalent, vigorously opposing it (8:6) yet enthusiastically supporting it (10:24). For an excellent survey of the critical debate, see J. Robert Vannoy, *Covenant Renewal at Gilgal: A Study of 1 Samuel 11:14–12:25* (Cherry Hill, N.J.: Mack, 1978), 197–239; note Vannoy's own contribution on pp. 227–32. I have long thought that the Old Testament text never opposes kingship as such but is only concerned with the kind of kingship exercised. It is refreshing to see studies supporting this position; e.g., David M. Howard, Jr., "The Case for Kingship in Deuteronomy and the Former Prophets," *Westminster Theological Journal* 52 (1990): 101–15 (a review of Gerald Eddie Gerbrandt's *Kingship According to the Deuteronomistic History* [Atlanta: Scholars, 1986]). First Samuel is no nastier in its portrayal of kingship than it is of other forms of leadership. Leadership by priesthood failed—when it came to Hophni and Phinehas. Judgeship did not succeed—at least when it was entrusted to Samuel's sons (cf. Moshe Garsiel, *The First Book of Samuel: A Literary Study of Comparative Structures, Analogies and Parallels* [Jerusalem: Rubin Mass, 1990], 62–64). If someone wanted to put down kingship, one would expect him to make a better case by white washing the alternatives!

Let us stop at this point to put chapter 8 in perspective. I have shown above how chapter 12 is an *explication* of chapter 8; it shows how Israel's demand for a king was a rejection of Yahweh. We must also note that chapter 7 poses a *contrast* with chapter 8; there Israel in her emergency and in her helplessness (and her kinglessness) had leaned in repentance, prayer, and hope upon her Help in ages past (7:12) and found deliverance. There was no mighty king; only a faithful intercessor. If chapter 7 forms a contrast to chapter 8, chapter 4 provides a *parallel*. Note: after chapter 7 with its proper focus on repentance and deliverance, where her only weapon is prayer, Israel turns around and in chapter 8 makes the same error as in chapter 4; that is, trusting in some mechanical provision for her security. There it appeared as superstition ("the ark among us"), manipulating God; here it is political ("a king over us"), substituting for God. But it is the same idolatry. Wisdom has not yet conceived.

Israel's situation is full of instruction for us; it reveals Israel and us and Yahweh's way with us. We would be wrong not to pause and ponder:

1. We have a tendency to assess our problems mechanically rather than spiritually. Our first impulse is to assume there is something wrong in our techniques. The need is for adjustment, not repentance; there is something wrong in the system that needs doctoring. How easy for even energetic evangelicals to look for a new gimmick rather than cry out for a new heart.

2. Instead of looking to God for help we are more interested in prescribing what form God's help must take. Our attention is not on God's deliverance in our troubles but on specifying the method by which he must bring that deliverance (therefore, we trust the method). We are not content with seeking a saving God but desire to direct how and when he will save.

3. Yahweh will sometimes give us our request to our own peril (8:7a, 9). God's granting our request may not be a sign of his favor but of our obstinacy. Sometimes God's greatest kindness is in not answering our prayers exactly as we desire (see Psalm 106:15).

4. In light of the current situation (8:1-3, 5a) and danger (cf. 12:12), Israel's request for a king was perfectly rational; yet

Yahweh viewed it as rejecting his kingship. Our proposals and solutions then can be completely reasonable, clearly logical, obviously plausible—and utterly godless.

It all reminds me of the time my brother offered me a teaspoon of vanilla extract. When our parents were out, the kitchen belonged to my brothers, and they often whipped up some dessert, whether pudding or divers and sundry other experiments. Whatever was in the works one evening, vanilla was required. Jim offered me a taste. He let me smell the stuff; I liked the smell. I knew it was used in other concoctions I very much liked. Everything said yes, and so did I, until I swallowed it! It seemed so reasonable.

Because some of our idolatry is so sophisticated and appears so reasonable, it can be extremely difficult to detect. But Yahweh's eye penetrates the fog (vv. 7-8). "Samuel experiences what Moses, the prophets, and even Jesus experience: 'We do not want this man to reign over us' (Luke 19:14)."[3]

Our Aversion to Holiness (8:5, 19-20)

By our "aversion to holiness" I simply mean that we do not like to be different for God's sake. We do not like to be distinct; we would rather blend. So with Israel. I noted above that in itself Israel's desire for a king, even a king "like all the nations," was permissible according to Deuteronomy 17:14ff. (though, as noted, Deuteronomy 17:15-20 lays down strictures to prevent Israelite kingship from being an ape-job of pagan kingship). However, for Israel "like all the nations" is more than an expression; it becomes a passion. After Samuel had solemnly warned Israel about what life under a king would be like, Israel refused to budge: "No, but a king must be over us, and we—we too—shall be like all the nations..." (vv. 19b-20a). With a king, Israel says, we will fit, we will belong, we will, at last, get up to speed. After all, this *is* the Iron Age, and we must have structures compatible with the demands of a new era.

Yet Israel was unique by definition. Read Deuteronomy 4:32-40. When since the beginning of time had any nation ever heard God speaking real verbs and adjectives and

3. Hans Wilhelm Hertzberg, *I & II Samuel, The Old Testament Library* (Philadelphia: Westminster, 1964), 72.

imperatives out of the middle of fire and still come away alive? Has there ever been a god who took his own nation out of the clutches of another nation by bludgeoning its hard-headed, hard-hearted oppressors into submission by raw power and sheer terror? Israel could not escape being different. But they could try. "And we—we too—shall be like all the nations."

True, we are a people under command. "You shall be different because I, Yahweh your God, am different" (Lev. 19:2; the usual translation uses "holy" rather than "different," but you get the point). But Israel and the rest of us prefer to keep in step with our culture and fit into the molds of our society. Who wants to stand out in the middle of a crooked and perverse generation? Why should the church or Christians individually have a different definition of success? Why should there be a certain detachment in our outlook (à la Heb. 11:13-16)? Why a winsome purity in our conversation? Why faithfulness in marriage? Or chastity before it? Why a seeking of justice for the helpless or a flowing of compassion to the neglected? Why a passion for worship over entertainment? Why prefer to enjoy God than to wallow after fulfillment?

Alexander Maclaren has put it well: "One of the first lessons which we have to learn... is a wholesome disregard of other people's ways."[4]

Our Immunity to Wisdom (8:11-18, 21-22)

"Listen to them but testify against them" (v. 9). Those were Samuel's orders. He was to spell out for Israel what having a king would be like. So he did (vv. 11-18).

Samuel's disclosure of the king's ways (vv. 11-18) does not depict the extraordinary abuses of kingship but simply the usual practices of kingship (which, admittedly, could be or become abusive).[5] Israel must know what monarchy will cost her.

Samuel's summary of a king's ways is simple: "He will take... he will take...." Four times he uses the verb (Hebrew, lāqaḥ; vv. 11, 13, 14, 16). He also places emphasis on the direct

---

4. Alexander Maclaren, *Expositions of Holy Scripture: Deuteronomy, Joshua, Judges, Ruth, and First Book of Samuel* (reprint ed., Grand Rapids: Baker, n.d.), 295.

5. Kenneth A. Kitchen, *Ancient Orient and Old Testament* (Chicago: InterVarsity, 1966), 158–59.

objects of the verb,[6] in order to make the people see what precious possessions a king will requisition for himself.

It is as if Samuel said: Think of your sons! The king will draft them for his charioteers and horsemen, for platoon commanders, for farm labor, and for weapons production. What about your daughters? You think they'll stay at home? No, the king will want them for perfume-makers, cooks, and bakers. Government work. Don't think your property is secure. The king will filch your finest fields, vineyards, and olive groves for his favored servants. And if he doesn't pilfer your land, don't think even your crops are your own. Ever hear of taxes? Royal officers and lackeys have to eat, you know, so you'll have to tithe your grain and grape crops to the king. He'll even want to use *your* servants and livestock for his work. There's a word for it—slavery; and you'll cry out as if you were in Egypt again.[7]

"The people refused to listen to the voice of Samuel" (v. 19). If Samuel's words never fell to the ground (3:19), then surely his words should be heeded as God's word. But Israel will not allow wisdom to lure them away from the folly they so eagerly want to commit. Hence Samuel is to listen to their voice (v. 22) while they refuse to listen to his (v. 19).

Israel's muleheadedness should instruct us. It teaches us, for example, that knowledge or information or truth does not in itself change or empower. (Our society has not learned this. Watch television news clips that discuss some contemporary social or moral problem. Interviewers ask an expert what needs to be done. Usually the answer is that we must get or use funds to educate people about the harmful effects of

---

6. S. R. Driver, *Notes on the Hebrew Text and the Topography of the Books of Samuel,* 2d ed. (1913; reprint ed., Winona Lake, Ind.: Alpha, 1984), 67.

7. It used to be customary for scholars to argue that 8:11-18 must be very late, no one could have spoken this way unless he had lived through some (later) fiascos of Israelite and Judean kingship. Then, so this view runs, this critical view was placed into Samuel's mouth in order to give it more punch and authority. But Samuel's description of the king's ways does not require extended experience under kingship. Kingship was the norm all around, and without doubt Samuel knew how various Canaanite kinglets functioned in their city-states. There is no reason to question the authenticity of Samuel's description. See the well-known study by I. Mendelsohn, "Samuel's Denunciation of Kingship in the Light of the Akkadian Documents from Ugarit," *Bulletin of the American Schools of Oriental Research* 143 (1956): 17–22.

the current villain. It is the education fallacy, and the fallacy assumes that if people only know that something will destroy them they will leave it alone. It never reckons with intrinsic stupidity.) Education may clarify; it cannot transform.

When our oldest son was a mere one year old we had a problem with his splashing and playing in the toilet bowl. Granted, it's not a moral issue, and (usually) it was only water. But then parents have the mess as well as certain hygienic standards. So we forbade him to play in the potty. And he knew he should not—he received some muffled whumps through his diaper to move him toward compliance. One day I caught him exiting the bathroom, hands deliciously wet, shaking his head from side to side, saying to himself, "No, no, no!" He knew what was verboten but that did not change his action. There is a difference between having the truth and loving the truth (2 Thess. 2:10); only the latter leads to obeying the truth.

Israel then hears God's wisdom but does not submit to it; God gives her instruction but she is not teachable. Which should lead God's current people to cry out for a soft heart, for a teachable spirit, for preservation from the arrogance of our own stupidity. "The way of a fool is right in his own eyes, but a wise man listens to advice" (Prov. 12:15, RSV).

There is another lesson Israel's resistance teaches: Since Yahweh will sometimes give us our requests to our own peril (vv. 7, 9, 22), we should not be too upset if he does not give us what we wanted. How many mercies may hide there. His refusals are not indifference but may be kindness.

First Samuel 8 is your mirror; it reveals Israel and you. How easily you misplace your trust; how ashamed you are to be different; how resistant to any word that does not agree with your opinion. There—you are revealed.

Study Questions

1. 'No mighty king; only a faithful intercessor.' Which is the more important?

2. Consider how blessed Christians are in having One who combines the offices of King and Intercessor.

3. Have you come to expect God's answers to your problems always to take the same kind of form? Why is this wrong?

4. Is there a temptation for us to avoid being different – even different for God?

5. Can you think of times when God has said 'No!' to your prayers and you have discovered afterwards what a good answer that was?

8

Lost and Found
(1 Samuel 9:1–10:16)

So far as anyone knew it was only another day on the farm. Saul is still in a bit of a grog as he hovers over his All-Bran trying to fortify himself for the day. Kish comes back from the shed a bit animated with the news that the donkeys had run off.[1] Could Saul take a man and go look for them? It looks like simply another chapter in "Minor Irritations in Life on the Farm." Lost asses, fruitless search, a servant's suggestion, a prophet's hospitality, sacred oil. Who could've known? That day on Kish's farm it just looked like the usual, ordinary, routine, run-of-the-mill sort of bump-along life most of us have. But Samuel's ear had heard what was really up: "tomorrow about this time I will send you a man. . . " (9:16). Yahweh frequently magnifies the minutiae of our lives into channels of his mercy. But we are getting ahead of our story.

Introductions first. First, we meet Kish, Saul's father (9:1): a rather wealthy farmer with a solid Benjaminite pedigree. Then Saul (9:2), Kish's son. What a handsome fellow! People would have voted him Mr. Israel had there been such a contest. A shame they didn't have basketball at Gibeah High School; with his height Saul would have been a star center.

---

1. We don't know how many wandered off. Most contemporary western readers probably have no great affection for and even less need of donkeys, and may therefore think Kish's loss trivial. But such livestock constituted a significant chunk of Kish's wealth and property. It would be akin to an urban reader missing several paychecks or a farmer losing his haywagons or pick-up.

The writer passes on into his story; but you must keep in mind this description of Saul in 9:1-2, his ideal appearance and his physical impressiveness. File it away; it will prove important much later in our story. In order to digest 9:1–10:16 I will divide the passage into four sections each summarized by a key word.

Providence (9:3-27)

"Providence" is God's way of *provid*ing for the needs of his people. That's not all of it, but some of it. When I use "providence" here I mean that wonderful, strange, mysterious, unguessable way Yahweh has of ruling his world and sustaining his people, and his doing it, frequently, over, under, around, through, or in spite of the most common stuff of our lives or even the bias of our wills.

Here was common stuff all right: looking for lost asses, asking dozens of local folks ("Have you happened to see...?"), making a thorough tour of the central hill country (9:4-5a),[2] deciding to give up the fruitless search (v. 5b), urging an inquiry of the man of God (v. 6), happening to find a fourth shekel's weight of silver for a prophet's fee (vv. 7-8). It is all so natural and ordinary. As Alexander Maclaren has put it:

> Think of the chain of ordinary events which brought Saul to the little city,—the wandering of a drove of asses, the failure to get on their tracks, the accident of being in the land of Zuph when he got tired of the search, the suggestion of the servant; and behind all these, and working through them, the will and hand of God, thrusting this man, all unconscious, along a path which he knew not.[3]

It all seems so casual; who would know it was planned? It looks like we are dealing simply with what appears rather than with what is ordained. How do we know losing the asses and finding a kingdom was God's doing?[4] Because of an "intrusion" into our story.

---

2. We cannot be sure of exact locations for areas/places mentioned in 9:4-5; but check Yohanan Aharoni and Michael Avi-Yonah, *The Macmillan Bible Atlas*, rev. ed. (New York: Macmillan, 1977), 59 (map 86), for a helpful reconstruction.

3. Alexander Maclaren, *Expositions of Holy Scripture: Deuteronomy, Joshua, Judges, Ruth and First Book of Samuel* (reprint ed., Grand Rapids: Baker, n.d.), 300–301.

4. "Asses Sought, a Kingdom Found" is Ralph Klein's rubric for 9:1–10:16 (*1 Samuel*, Word Biblical Commentary [Waco: Word, 1983], 80).

That intrusion occurs at 9:15-17. I call these verses an intrusion because they are. If you read the story through verse 14 and then go immediately to verse 18, you will find the story connects perfectly, the narrative never missing a beat. So, in one sense, verses 15-17 are not necessary for the flow of the story—only for understanding it. The emphatic "Yahweh" at the first of verse 15 clues us that something of great import is being said.

> Now *Yahweh* had uncovered Samuel's ear the day before Saul's coming, saying, "At this time tomorrow I will send you a man from the land of Benjamin, and you shall anoint him as leader over my people Israel; and he shall save my people from the hand of the Philistines; for I have seen my people; for their cry for help has come to me." Now Samuel saw Saul, and *Yahweh* answered him, "Look! The man I told you about; he will govern my people."

Now we hear the secret of what Yahweh is doing. "I will send you a man." That puts an entirely different face on matters! What has so far appeared as a lackadaisical, happenstance affair is very much under Yahweh's direction. This is not another episode of "As the Cookie Crumbles"; Saul is sent, designated, disclosed by Yahweh. Sometimes it helps to be in on the secret.

However, we might ask: Does Yahweh's providence only operate in the affairs of major figures in salvation history (Saul in this case) or does his (mostly) invisible wisdom follow my path as well? Does Yahweh direct only major episodes in his kingdom or does his sway extend to the individual lives of his subjects? Surely the latter. Wisdom testifies to it: "A man's mind plans his way, but the Lord directs his steps" (Prov. 16:9); and "A man's steps are ordered by the Lord; how then can man understand his way?" (Prov. 20:24, RSV). So Yahweh's strange and baffling providence is not the exclusive privilege of some kingdom elite; it extends to each of his people no matter how apparently common. However, unlike 1 Samuel 9, he may not let you in on the secret. You may see traces of what he has been doing much later as you look back, but in the present you may be just as much in the dark as Saul was. If so, you must simply go on looking for the lost asses—or whatever task God has given you to do.

We must, however, fasten on to this intrusion, especially in verse 16. Note that Yahweh's providence is in the service of his pity. He is sending Saul to Samuel because Saul is the one who will "save my people from the hand of the Philistines, for I have seen my people; for their cry for help has come to me." Some look at 9:16b and call it pro-monarchical, whereas texts like 8:7-8 are viewed as anti-monarchical. But it is not so simple as that. Actually, 9:16b is pro-merciful.

I think we should back away from this text for a moment and look at the larger picture, that is, all of chapters 8–14. These chapters taken as they stand depict three distinct assemblies of Israel, each of which is followed by an action narrative:

Assembly	8
Action	9:1–10:16
Assembly	10:17-27
Action	11
Assembly	12
Action	13–14

In some way each assembly-section accuses Israel (see 8:7-8; 10:19; 12:12, 17);[5] yet each action-section shows Yahweh's mercy in providing for or delivering his people (in setting apart a future deliverer in 9:1–10:16, in bringing deliverance from Nahash through Saul in chapter 11 or from the Philistines through Jonathan in chapters 13–14). Israel's rejection does not paralyze Yahweh's providence. Although Yahweh sees Israel's idolatry in her cry for a king (8:7-8), he also hears her distress in her cry for relief (9:16). Israel's stupidity cannot wither Yahweh's compassions.

Separating so-called pro-monarchical and anti-monarchical sections only keeps us from seeing the paradox of biblical truth. No, we must not trivialize Israel's sin, but neither dare we minimize Yahweh's mercy. Not only is 9:15-17 the key for

---

5. In 1 Samuel 8 the primary accusation does not come directly from Samuel to Israel but is stated by Yahweh to Samuel (vv. 7-8). Since working out the structural scheme, I discovered that Dennis J. McCarthy had already proposed a similar one, though he did not pull chapters 13–14 into the scheme (cited in V. Philips Long, *The Reign and Rejection of King Saul: A Case for Literary and Theological Coherence*, SBL Dissertation Series 118 [Atlanta: Scholars, 1989], 175).

interpreting all of 9:1–10:16, but it is also the lens for magnifying Yahweh's mercy in light of chapter 8. These foolish, stubborn people do not cease to be objects of Yahweh's compassions. Again, let no sin be glossed over; let no one excuse its God-denying wickedness. But surely, if you are a child of God, you rejoice to see that your God is "mule-ish" on mercy, that your sin does not dry up the fountain of his compassions, that his pity refuses to let go of his people. "As the height of heaven above earth, so *strong* is his faithful love for those who fear him" (Ps. 103:11 NJB, emphasis added).[6]

"For I have seen my people; for their cry for help has come to me." (Note the similarity with Israel's bondage in Egypt, Exodus 2:23, 25; 3:7.) W. G. Blaikie has summed it up well:

> God speaks after the manner of men. He needs no cry to come into His ears to tell Him of the woes of the oppressed. Nevertheless He seems to wait till that cry is raised, till the appeal is made to Him, till the consciousness of utter helplessness sends men to His footstool. And a very blessed truth it is, that He sympathizes with the cry of the oppressed. There is much meaning in the simple expression—"their cry is come up to Me." It denotes a very tender sympathy, a concern for all that they have been suffering, and a resolution to interpose on their behalf. God is never impassive nor indifferent to the sorrows and sufferings of His people.[7]

So... providence, but a warm providence—moved by pity.

Assurance (10:1-9)

With Saul's servant out of earshot, Samuel anoints Saul. I think a section of 10:1 has dropped out of the Hebrew text somewhere along the line; a good case can be made for following the Septuagint in verse 1, in which case Samuel says:

---

6. Such is the proper translation of Psalm 103:11; the verb (*gābar*) carries the idea of might or strength. The psalmist introduces the dimension of immeasurable distance in line 1 only to transmute it in line 2 into the category of unguessable strength.

7. W. G. Blaikie, *The First Book of Samuel*, The Expositor's Bible (Cincinnati: Jennings and Graham, n.d.), 136

Has not Yahweh anointed you leader over his people, over Israel? And you will govern the people of Yahweh, and you will save them from the hand of their enemies; and here is the sign for you that Yahweh has anointed you as leader over his inheritance....[8]

Note Samuel's reference to the sign. In fact, there will be several signs (see vv. 7, 9). Samuel gives Saul a sketch of the signs that would come about; it would be a most unusual day! First, near Rachel's tomb on the border of Benjamin[9] Saul will meet two men who will tell him that Kish's asses have been found and that, as Saul has guessed (9:5), his father was worried sick about the persons, not the beasts. Next, near the oak of Tabor (somewhere in Benjamin on the way to Bethel) Saul will meet three men on their way to worship at Bethel, toting along all the materials for sacrifice—three young goats, three loaves of bread, and a skin of wine, respectively. These men will inquire about Saul's welfare and give him two loaves of bread (10:3-4). Finally, when approaching Gibeah (v. 5, cf. v. 10) he will encounter a group of prophets fresh from the high place, strumming their guitars, playing their pipes, exulting in God;[10] Yahweh's Spirit will "rush" upon Saul; he will join in their "prophesying"; indeed, he will be turned into "another man" (vv. 5-6).[11]

All these signs came about as Samuel had predicted (v. 9b). It is precisely because they are so uncanny that they are so

---

8. See S. R. Driver, *Notes on the Hebrew Text and the Topography of the Books of Samuel*, 2d ed. (1913; reprint ed., Winona Lake, Ind.: Alpha, 1984), 78. The NIV and NASB stick with the Hebrew text; RSV, rightly, in my opinion, follows LXX.

9. Genesis 35:16, 19-20 does not counter this location. That text does not say Rachel was buried near Ephrath (i.e., Bethlehem) but on the road to Ephrath from Bethel. Contemporary travelers may be shown "Rachel's tomb" on the Jerusalem-Bethlehem road about a mile north of Bethlehem (the present structure dates from the Crusaders; see *IDB*, 4:5). There is an explanation: "Rachel's tomb" is not Rachel's tomb.

10. On these prophets see E. J. Young, *My Servants the Prophets* (Grand Rapids: Eerdmans, 1952), 85–87; and A. A. MacRae, "Prophets and Prophecy," *ZPEB*, 4:891–93.

11. Saul is turned into "another man" (10:6), given "another heart" (10:9). I do not think we should construe this change as equivalent to regeneration of the Ezekiel 36 or John 3 variety. In verse 6 the change comes as a result of Yahweh's Spirit "rushing" (*ṣālaḥ*) upon him. The verb is used of the Spirit "rushing" upon Samson, in each case not regenerating but giving power to meet a crisis, such as knocking off Philistines (Judg. 14:6, 19; 15:14). The same is true of Saul in 1 Samuel 11:6. Cf. David in 16:13. The "rushing" of the Spirit indicates his equipping for the tasks of leadership. In this sense Saul is another man, receiving what he had not had before.

significant. They are not bland generalizations like the little quips from a fortune cookie. They are detailed: two men meet you at a precise location (near Rachel's grave) with a very particular message (asses found, etc.); or three men come upon you at the oak of Tabor, one having three young goats, one with three loaves of bread, one with a skin of wine, and the bread man gives you two of his loaves! Samuel may have been a sharp prophet but such signs are beyond mere human foresight. Such minutiae can come only from Yahweh. Therefore these signs should *signify* to Saul that he does have Yahweh's authorization for kingship (v. 1) and Yahweh's presence (v. 7) to carry out the demands of kingship. The signs are meant to assure.

However, we should properly balance this note of assurance. Saul is to receive both the power of the Spirit (vv. 6-7) *and* the direction of the word through Samuel (v. 8). A good deal of debate rages around verse 8. It may form part of a plan for striking a decisive blow against the Philistines. But this much is clear: Saul the king, who is promised Yahweh's power, is to submit to Samuel the prophet who brings Yahweh's word. "I shall make known to you what you are to do." Yahweh's Spirit gives power; but that power is to be exercised in obedience to Yahweh's word. The Spirit and the Word must never be separated. What right have we to think we can enjoy the Lord's power and presence when we deny his lordship by trampling on his word (Luke 6:46)? One cannot help but think this union of word and Spirit is a word in season for the contemporary church. Many crave dramatic signs of the Spirit's power but have little enthusiasm for common obedience to the Lord's word.

Equipment (10:10-13)

We are assured in verse 9 that all three signs Samuel had depicted actually happened to Saul on his return trip. The writer, however, does not give a line-upon-line, blow-by-blow description of their fulfillment. The summary of verse 9 is enough—except for the third sign. He chooses to narrate it in detail (vv. 10-13). He must have had a special reason for doing so; perhaps he wanted to include the reaction of the people, or perhaps he wanted to underscore that Saul really was equipped with Yahweh's power for his coming task.

You can imagine the stir it caused. Apparently what startled the home folks was seeing this shy, retiring country boy caught up in the singing and proclaiming of these prophets. It was so out of character. "What has come over the son of Kish? Is even Saul among the prophets?" (v. 11).

A question often debated is whether the townspeople here view the prophets and/or Saul positively or negatively. Their comments seem ambiguous to us. I don't care to amass the positive and negative votes; the reader can open other commentaries and tally the opinions. Suffice it to say that I think the locals' primary reaction is surprise, a generally positive surprise.

The astonishment over the change in Saul was so memorable that the folks coined a proverb: "Is even Saul among the prophets?" (v. 12b). That is, whenever at some later time, someone in Gibeah saw, heard of, or experienced something utterly unusual or unexpected, they might remark, "Well, is even Saul among the prophets?" An American might say, "Wonders never cease"; but around Gibeah they exclaimed, "Is even Saul among the prophets?" It refers to a marvel that seems beyond explanation.

One citizen, however, seems to have had an explanation. He piped up and said, "But who is their father?" (v. 12a). That is, "Consider the source." I doubt he was referring to Samuel. Was he suggesting that if *Yahweh* is the one who inspires the prophets in their praises, then surely he is able so to grip Saul and cause him to do the same?[12]

We arrive then at a familiar biblical contention: Yahweh frequently defies human expectations and gives the most unlikely people all they need to serve him effectively. So he equips Saul. No matter how unlikely in men's eyes, Yahweh is able to make him able.

In one of George MacDonald's novels he depicts the journey of Thomas Wingfold, curate of the local Anglican

---

12. Cf. C. F. D. Erdmann, *The Books of Samuel,* Lange's Commentary on the Holy Scriptures, in vol. 3, *Samuel-Kings* (1877; reprint ed.; Grand Rapids: Zondervan, 1960), 155–56.

church in Glaston, toward the truth as it is in Jesus.[13] Strangely enough the human instrument used to set Wingfold upon this quest and to guide him along the way was Joseph Polwarth, gatekeeper of the manor park, a man with no social stature at all. Polwarth was a dwarf, a deformed one at that, riddled with asthma and familiar with grief. Who would have thought someone like that would be the one to open the kingdom to the local clergyman? But that is not merely the stuff of a novel. That's the way it so often is in the true story of Yahweh's kingdom. He may not choose the most natural; instead he may choose the most unlikely and equip them to do what he wills. "Who is their father?"

Concealment (10:14-16)

The narrative closes with a little conversation with Saul's uncle. Where have you been? Looking for the asses; we couldn't locate them so we went to Samuel. Ah, what did Samuel tell you? "He just told us that the asses had been found" (v. 16 NJPS). End of conversation. "But he did not tell him what Samuel had said about the matter of the kingdom" (v. 16b). The narrative ends with a secret. Saul's uncle is in the dark.

But then everybody is. One of the fascinating marks of this whole section is that hardly anyone knows what is really going on. It's as if there's a conspiracy of mystery. Samuel knows—because Yahweh told him (9:15-17); but Kish and Saul and the servant simply think they are looking for erring livestock. Samuel's remark (9:20) certainly stirred Saul's curiosity but still must have left him puzzled. Folks at the feast could infer there must be some reason for the special honor paid to the tall stranger, but they hadn't the ghost of a clue about the matter (9:22-24). Saul's servant can't tell us anything, because he was ordered beyond eyesight and earshot (9:27). Of course, he would be suspicious—what was the fragrant oil doing all over Saul's head? (Even if Saul's head was covered, smell would detect what sight could not.) What had Samuel said to him? He could wonder; but he didn't know. Saul's joining the prophets' songs (10:10-13) certainly made waves, but

---

13. George MacDonald, *The Curate's Awakening*, ed. Michael R. Phillips (Minneapolis: Bethany House, 1985).

aside from trying to figure out what had come over Saul, no one knew the secret. Then there's Saul's uncle at home by the corral. "What'd Samuel tell ya?" "Oh, he just told us that the asses had been found," Saul replied, as he pointed to the guilty critters inside the corral. But not a word about the kingdom.[14]

In light of all this secrecy it is interesting to observe that the verb *māṣā'*, (to find) occurs twelve times in our section. Saul and his servant did not find the asses (9:4, twice); the servant "found" the prophet's fee (9:8), Saul and his servant find (i.e., meet) girls going out of town to draw water (9:11), who urge them to hurry so that they can find (= meet) the seer (9:13, twice). Samuel assures Saul that the asses have been found (9:20), as do the two men Saul "finds" near Rachel's grave (10:2; hence twice). Three men will find (meet) Saul near the oak of Tabor (10:3). With God's power upon him Saul will "find" opportunities, presumably to put down Israel's enemies (10:7). Then the word for uncle: Samuel told us the asses had been found (10:16).

Now *māṣā'* is a rather common verb so I do not want to press this point. But it does strike me as ironic to see the repeated use of this verb in a story about a secret. Livestock, people, money, and opportunities are "found" —so is a kingdom, but hardly anyone knows it. Yahweh is actively at work but few see what it is he is doing.

I remember once reading a story about a catcher for a minor league baseball team located in one of our northwestern states. He decided he would have a little fun, so, when the umpire called the next pitch a ball rather than a strike, the catcher jumped up with an irate look, turned to the umpire, and with typical vehemence exclaimed, "You're right! That pitch was a ball!" The ump was nonplussed. The catcher continued his "tirade." The crowd naturally thought he was disputing a bad call and began to hoot and boo the umpire. When the ump threatened to throw the catcher out of the game for trying to rouse the masses against him, the catcher retorted

---

14. For additional discussion of mystery and secrecy in this narrative, see Karl Gutbrod, *Das Buch vom König*, Die Botschaft des Alten Testaments, 4th ed. (Stuttgart: Calwer, 1975), 70–72, and Robert Polzin, *Samuel and the Deuteronomist* (San Francisco: Harper and Row, 1989), 90–91.

(as he kicked dirt and continued to carry on) that the umpire couldn't do that because he, the catcher, was *concurring* with the umpire's call. His words uttered with angry look in the ump's face were something like: "I'm not arguing with you— I'm agreeing with you. I said that pitch was a ball. You made an excellent call!" By this time the crowd was caught up in its partisan uproar against the hapless umpire. The people were there and they thought they knew exactly what was going on down at home plate, but, actually, they didn't have a clue. Something entirely different was happening than what appeared to be happening.

Yahweh frequently seems to manage his kingdom that way. No, I don't mean like a prankster baseball catcher. But I mean that often his real work is concealed. He is working for the deliverance of his people but we do not see it. He works secretly. We can clearly see surface matters like lost asses, and perhaps that is all we discern. Yahweh often maintains his kingdom in an undercover way, surreptitiously. And his true servants will always find the most bracing encouragement in that.

STUDY QUESTIONS

1. Have there been times in your own life when you have seen God's providence in the way quite ordinary things have come together into a wonderful providential pattern?

2. Why is it irreverent to expect God always to explain his ways to us when we do not understand them? What should we be doing instead?

3. 'The Spirit and the Word must never be separated.' When they are sometimes things happen that even get into the news and bring dishonour to the Lord's Name. Can you think of such instances? What lessons can we learn from them?

4. Can you think of unlikely people in Scripture and your own experience who have been greatly used by God? Who would have thought a Baby born in a stable would turn out to be the King of the universe?

5. 'We can clearly see surface matters like lost asses, and perhaps that is all we discern.' How does God's Word enable us
   to see more deeply into things, and do we prayerfully seek
   such discernment as far as the events of our own lives are
   concerned?

9

A Lost King?
(1 Samuel 10:17-27)

Solemn occasions can become memorable because of some unexpected wrinkle. Family tradition has it (and it is doubtless true—all our traditions are true) that once while my grandfather was preaching a mouse ran up his leg and was smooshed with a hard, downward blow of Grandpa's hand. Not your normal church service. The same sort of thing occurred at the convocation in Mizpah for the public presentation of Israel's king.[1] The king was selected—and missing. Kish's son seemed as lost as his father's asses had been. No one ever forgot the panic over the absent king nor pulling him out of the baggage once they found him. We now inquire about the teaching in this episode.

How Relentless God's Word Is
First, note that Yahweh's word simply will not quit. Samuel keeps hammering Israel with Yahweh's reproof, seeking to stir her into acknowledging her sin.

> Here's what Yahweh, God of Israel, says: 'I, I brought Israel up from Egypt; and I delivered you from the hand of the Egyptians and from the hand of all the kingdoms that were oppressing

---

1. I prefer (as noted before) to identify Mizpah with Tell en-Nasbeh, eight miles north of Jerusalem on the north-south road; see A. F. Rainey, "Mizpah," *ISBE*, rev. ed., 3:387–88. I do not think that 10:17-27 duplicates 9:1–10:16; that passage speaks of a private anointing, whereas 10:17-27 deals with a public selection that confirms the preceding private action.

you.' But you, today you have rejected your God, the one who saves you from all your miseries and adversities, and you have said, 'No, but you must set a king over us'; well now, take your place before Yahweh by your tribes and divisions. [vv. 18-19]

But Samuel had already made his point in 8:6-22. The assembly at Mizpah was a special, formal occasion for selecting or discerning who was to be king over Israel. It was a historic moment. Why did Samuel kick it off on such a negative note? Why sour the hour? Even if it was Yahweh's word, couldn't it be communicated with a little more finesse and with a bit more sensitivity to the circumstances?

There was a grievous injustice in the Church of Scotland in the late eighteenth century. The General Assembly (national body) would impose a minister upon a parish even if the people were opposed to him and even though the presbytery (regional body) would not approve him. On one such occasion in 1773 the General Assembly ordered a presbytery and all its minister members to be present and to induct Mr. David Thomson as minister of a parish near Stirling. The formal task fell to Robert Findley, presbytery moderator. However, instead of preaching as was customary, Findley called Mr. Thomson forward and addressed him in a way seldom if ever done in such situations. He told him that they were met by the authority of the General Assembly, which was acting as if it were superior to any parliament. Findley reminded Thomson that he had been opposed by six hundred heads of families, sixty heritors, and all except one of the elders of the parish. He admitted that Thomson had maintained a good character—until within the last seven years he had obstinately persisted in trying to settle in the present parish. Findley then appealed to him to "give it up" (back down from seeking installation). Mr. Thomson, in a low voice, directed Findley "to obey the orders of your superiors." Findley then, without any of the usual formulas or posing of questions to the candidate, simply concluded by saying: "I, as moderator of the presbytery of Stirling, admit you, Mr. David Thomson, to be minister of the parish of St. Ninian's, in the true sense and spirit of the late sentence of the General Assembly, and you are hereby admitted accordingly." Without praying for the local parish, the minister, or the presbytery, and after singing a few lines of a psalm, Findley dismissed the congregation.[2]

Why, you just don't do that! Not if you care about etiquette and decorum. But sometimes truth must come before propriety. Sometimes the Robert Findleys and Samuel-ben-Elkanahs know that they must be faithful rather than cordial. If Israel really has rejected the God who saves them (v. 19) and has not seen that or repented of it, can we expect Samuel to smile blandly and croon with outstretched hand, "So good to see all of you here today for this happy occasion that brings us together"? Israel's God may love us too much to be nice. His word may pursue us relentlessly until we hear it. He may even ruin a nice occasion if it will get your attention and lead you to repentance.

How Clear God's Choice Is

Samuel walked Israel through the process of the lot; he began with all the tribes until the elimination narrowed down to one man: Saul (vv. 20-21). Yahweh used the lot to disclose his will (Prov. 16:33). What Yahweh had disclosed privately to Samuel (9:15-17) he now declared publicly to Israel (10:20-21). Saul's secret anointing is now confirmed in his public selection.[3] What God had done in secret he now declares from the housetops.

This public confirmation was, of course, an absolute necessity. Matthew Henry long ago pointed this out:

> [Samuel] knew also the peevishness of that people, and that there were those among them who would not acquiesce in the choice if it depended upon his single testimony; and therefore, that every tribe and every family of the chosen tribe might please themselves with having a chance for it, he calls them to the lot....

2. Thomas M'Crie, *The Story of the Scottish Church from the Reformation to the Disruption* (1875; reprinted., Glasgow: Free Presbyterian, n.d.), 503–4.

3. "In the general context, the choice by lot seems to be a miraculous confirmation of the revelation given to Samuel in ch. 9 and of the secret anointing which followed it" (Hans Wilhelm Hertzberg, *I & II Samuel,* The Old Testament Library [Philadelphia: Westminster, 1964], 88).

4. Matthew Henry, *Commentary on the Whole Bible,* 6 vols. (New York: Revell, n.d.), 2:334. Henry also included a redemptive-historical observation: "When the tribe of Benjamin was taken, they might easily foresee that they were setting up a family that would soon be put down again; for dying Jacob had, by the spirit of prophecy, entailed the dominion upon Judah" (he refers to Gen. 49).

By this method it would appear to the people... that Saul was appointed of God to be king.... It would also prevent all disputes and exceptions....[4]

So Yahweh's choice was clear, necessarily so. It was also unusual in that before or with Saul the tribe of Benjamin was "taken." Saul was probably not *all* modesty when he called Benjamin "the smallest of the tribes of Israel" (9:21), for Benjamin had been nearly annihilated in her civil war with Israel early in the period of the judges (see Judg. 20–21, especially 20:42-48).[5] Yet, again, Yahweh chose what was weak to shame the strong. All in character.

How Dependent God's People Are

I am wary about pressing the significance of verses 21c-24. Perhaps no special meaning (such as the heading suggests) is intended; perhaps the text only means to inform us that they couldn't find Saul, that the Lord told them where to look, that they pulled Saul out and acclaimed him king. However, I'm not sure it's that simple. You will form your own judgment, but let me explain why I think we have more than mere information here.

First, I find the last words of verse 21 fascinating. "He was not found." The lot had zeroed in on Saul; they looked for him; but "he was not found." I wouldn't think much of this except that the same verb ($m\bar{a}\dot{s}\bar{a}$') kept appearing (twelve times) in the preceding narrative (9:1–10:16). There it was used in several ways, not least of which involved the quest to find the lost asses. When I read $w\breve{e}l\bar{o}$' $nim\dot{s}\bar{a}$' (and he was not found) at the end of verse 21, I can hardly help thinking of the repeated use of $m\bar{a}\dot{s}\bar{a}$' in 9:1ff., especially of the asses that they "did not find" (9:4). Is a subtle irony intended? On her own Israel will be no more successful finding her king than Saul and his servant had been in finding the asses.

Moreover, the structure of verses 17-27 places the hinge of the story in these verses:

---

5. The date rests on the fact that Phinehas, Aaron's grandson, was still high priest at the time (Judg. 20:27-28).

Convocation, 17
  Accusation, 18-19
    Selection, 20-21b
      Frustration, 21c
        Revelation, 22
      Discovery, 23
    Acclamation, 24
  Direction, 25a
Dismissal, 25b-27

Is verse 22 meant to be the focal point of the episode? Are the people so dependent on Yahweh that he must even disclose to them where they can find Saul? The rest of the section keeps describing Samuel's activity (vv. 17, 18a, 20a, 24a, 25a, 25b); so when verse 22 highlights Yahweh's disclosure it may well be significant.

I propose then that verses 21c-24 mean to depict how Israel is utterly dependent upon Yahweh, even to the point of finding their king once he has been chosen. Israel cannot manage apart from Yahweh even in the simplest matters. We may find some theological spillover in that point (John 15:5).[6]

How Necessary God's Law Is
"Then Samuel told the people the rights and duties of the kingship" (v. 25a RSV). "Rights and duties" properly translates the Hebrew *mišpaṭ* here. Samuel wrote this *mišpaṭ* down on a scroll and placed it in the sanctuary. We cannot help contrasting this with "the *mišpaṭ* of the king" in 8:9, 11. There Samuel was to warn Israel of the usual manner of a king, of the rights they claimed, and of the way kings customarily ruled. But here (10:25) "the *mišpaṭ* of the kingship" (or, kingdom)

---

6. Who really knows what moved Saul to hide himself? Many commentators chalk it up to modesty and humility (e.g., Keil, Kirkpatrick, Gordon), and there is something to be said for that (cf. 1 Sam. 15:17 NASB/NIV). Or was Saul manifesting timidity, even a subtle resistance to the appointed task? (see V. Philips Long, *The Reign and Rejection of King Saul: A Case for Literary and Theological Coherence*, SBL Dissertation Series 118 [Atlanta: Scholars, 1989], 215–18, who also cites McCarter). Karl Gutbrod asks whether the combination of Saul's hiding himself and his external impressiveness (vv. 23b-24) is not meant to suggest that for Israel the trappings of kingship must always be united with humility and—between the lines—to question whether Saul will remain in this "humble majesty" and in this "exalted lowliness" (*Das Buch vom König, Die Botschaft des Alten Testaments*, 4th ed. [Stuttgart: Calwer, 1975], 76–77).

stands opposed to "the *mišpaṭ* of the king" in 8:9, 11. Here the *mišpaṭ* of the kingship consists of a document that prescribes how kingship is to function in Israel, so that Israel's king will not go "mispatting" in any way he likes. The "*mišpaṭ* of the kingship" is Yahweh's law regulating how the king is to conduct himself.[7] I should think it contained provisions very much like those in Deuteronomy 17:14-20. Israel's king is not actually a king but a vice-king, himself under the law of Yahweh, Israel's true King. Royal submission to that law should eliminate tyranny and abuse.

It was this idea that even royalty is subject to divine law that led John Knox to call for charges of murder and adultery to be brought against Queen Mary Stuart. At the time (1560s), most believed the sovereign to be the law. Knox, however, had this strange notion that a sovereign was under law, subject to trial by law and judgment by the people.[8]

By extension of principle all God's people are in Saul's position; we are a people under God's law, and we need to be.[9] Israel came under Yahweh's law at Sinai. And that was not a

---

7. J. Robert Vannoy has stated this matter very well in his *Covenant Renewal at Gilgal: A Study of I Samuel 11:14–12:25* (Cherry Hill, N.J.: Mack, 1978), 231 (I transliterate his Hebrew script): "In this action [i.e., v. 25] Samuel takes the first step in resolving the tension which existed between Israel's improper desire for a king, as well as their misconceived notion of what the role and function of this king should be, on the one hand, and the stated fact that it was Yahweh's intent to give them a king on the other. It is clear that the purpose of the *mišpaṭ hammĕlukāh* is to provide a definition of the function of the king in Israel for the benefit of both the people and the king-designate. This constitutional-legal description of the duties and prerogatives of the king in Israel would serve to clearly distinguish the Israelite kingship from that known to the Israelites in surrounding nations. In Israel, the king's role was to be strictly compatible with the continued sovereignty of Yahweh over the nation, and also with all the prescriptions and obligations enunciated in the covenantal law received at Sinai and renewed and updated by Moses in the Plains of Moab. In short, it was Samuel's intent to see that the *mišpaṭ hammĕlukāh* [10:25] would be normative in Israel, rather than the *mišpaṭ hammelek* [8:9, 11]."

8. Otto Scott, *James I: The Fool as King* (Vallecito, Calif.: Ross House, 1976), 49.

9. Some will doubtless dispute this. If that is so, they will say, why did Paul say all those nasty things about the law in Romans and Galatians? Paul was primarily opposing the way people were (mis)using the law; he was battling a misconception about the function of the law. The law can never be in any way to any degree a standard you can meet and so earn salvation. The law can show you how you fail to be or to do what God requires, but it cannot absolve you of the guilt incurred in breaking the law. The law can accuse you but cannot justify you. The law is like your back-porch thermometer—it will show you how hot or cold it is outside, but it does not have the power to raise or lower the temperature. That's why my only hope is Jesus, the Law-keeper who suffered the law-breaker's judgment (Gal. 3:10, 13). On

sad mistake. You will never view the law incorrectly so long as you remember that Exodus 20:2 comes before Exodus 20:3-17. Yahweh says, I have set you free from bondage; it was not your doing; only my power decimated Pharaoh, my lamb protected you from ruin, my hand split open the sea; now that you are free, here is how a free people is to live—my commandments. You don't keep them in order to earn freedom—that has been my gift; you keep them in order to *enjoy* freedom, to preserve and maintain it, to avoid becoming slaves again to anyone else.

In my car I keep a booklet of maps—maps of Baltimore City and County. There are fifty or sixty pages of them. Very detailed, precise, and exact. If I must go to some hospital, I can see at a glance the location and the streets and the roads that will take me to it. In their way those maps are very restricting, confining, and picky. But I have never had a map rebellion. For though the maps severely limit my (sane) options they nevertheless preserve my freedom. They keep me free from wandering all over the place trying to find my destination, free from trusting my uninstructed feelings, free from wasting large amounts of time, free from frustration that comes from wasting time, and so on. In their own way the maps are laws and commandments, but submitting to them makes for freedom rather than bondage.

Back to 1 Samuel 10. Saul is under a law governing kingship, not to destroy his kingship but to allow it to function properly. And God's people are under Yahweh's law and commandments, not to inhibit and sour the Christian life but to order it and protect it from an alien bondage. Look at the material in Romans 12–15, Galatians 5–6, Ephesians 4–6, Colossians 3–4, or the Epistle of James. What is it largely but applications of the commandments to the Christian life? The intent of such teaching is to keep a people free in purity of life, holiness of desires, winsomeness of speech, absence of bitterness; to maintain balanced relationships, spiritual warfare, and concrete compassion. For Christ's people the law

the Christian and the law, see J. Knox Chamblin, "The Law of Moses and the Law of Christ," *Continuity and Discontinuity: Perspectives on the Relationship Between the Old and New Testaments*, ed. John S. Feinberg (Westchester, Ill.: Crossway, 1988), 187–201.

should no longer be dreadful curse but glad obedience—if we prize our freedom.

How Divisive God's Servant Is

Sometimes what happens after the meeting is as significant as what happens at the meeting. We heard those outbursts of acclamation (v. 24); but now as folks straggle home we see two distinctly opposite reactions to the newly chosen king. There were some "mighty men whose hearts God had touched" (v. 26b). What a support and encouragement this contingent must have been (cf. Luke 22:28). But then there were the no-goods (lit., "sons of Belial," v. 27), who kept asking, "How can this fellow save us?" What can this country bumpkin, this hick Benjaminite farmer, do for us? The point should not be lost: the king causes division; the king suffers rejection even within Israel.

Perhaps you cannot help but see an analogy to our Lord Jesus Christ. And I think there is a legitimate analogy here, not because Saul is some sort of type of Christ but on the basis of the appointed *office* (kingship) they share. The local scoundrels were rejecting Saul not merely as a person but also in his office as Yahweh's appointed king through whom he willed to save his people.

Indeed Jesus so much as said that it was his mission to bring division (see Luke 12:51 in context). And there were those in Israel who said, "How can this fellow save us?" "Isn't this fellow Jesus, the son of Joseph—we know his father and mother; how does he now say 'I have come down from heaven'?" (John 6:42). What is so special about him?

It goes on. Men and women still despise Yahweh's appointed Servant and King. What, after all, can a Jew, executed as a criminal two thousand years ago—what can he have to do with how I face the last judgment? My marriage? My fears? My disasters? "How can this fellow save us?"

STUDY QUESTIONS

1. 'His word may pursue us relentlessly until we hear it.' Has God ever had to speak to you twice – or even uncountable times – before you have been willing to hear his Word? If so, what does that tell you about him and about yourself?

2. The commentary mentions John 15:5. What stories from the ministry of Jesus give us examples of this spiritual principle in the experience of the disciples?

3. If you think the Law is irrelevant for a Christian, read Ephesians and see how many of the Ten Commandments are there, in one guise or another.

4. Why do we sometimes resent legitimate authority, even when it is benign? What does this tell us about ourselves?

10

A Hopeful Beginning
(1 Samuel 11)

Istill remember those first days of school in grades 1–8. Things were fresh. Two new pairs of blue jeans for the school year; they weren't faded as they would be by April. Maybe a new shirt or two. New supplies: the teacher passed out new, long yellow pencils. This was the first day, before the erasers were chewed off those pencils, before one had gnashed his teeth on the metal band that held the eraser in place. But, for now, there was hope. It was a new beginning.

And in 1 Samuel 11 we breathe the air of a new and hopeful beginning for the nascent kingdom. Saul's military debut kindles hope. The theme of the chapter is salvation. Words derived from the root *yāša'* "to save, to deliver," occur three times (vv. 3, 9, 13). The appointed king brings salvation/deliverance to Yahweh's people. Here is a retort to the debunkers who had despised Saul, badmouthing, "How will this fellow save us?" (10:27). Answer: By the power of God's Spirit (ch. 11).

Let us now trace the teaching of the chapter.

The Arrogance the World Shows (11:1-3)
Trouble is brewing east of the Jordan. Nahash, the Ammonite king, has besieged Jabesh-gilead, a fortified town about twenty miles south of the Sea of Galilee and two miles east of the Jordan on the Wadi Yabis.[1] In fact, Nahash may have been

---

1. See H. G. May, "Jabesh-gilead," *IDB*, 2:778–79.

on a binge of terror among all Israel east of the Jordan. One of the Dead Sea Scrolls (4QSama) includes additional material before what would be 11:1 in our Bibles:

> Now Nahash, the king of the Ammonites, had been oppressing the Gadites and the Reubenites grievously, gouging out the right eye of each of them and allowing Israel no deliverer. No men of the Israelites who were across the Jordan remained whose right eye Nahash, king of the Ammonites, had not gouged out. But seven thousand men had escaped from the Ammonites and entered into Jabesh-gilead.[2]

Perhaps this material dropped out of most texts at some point in their transmission, but we do not know if that was the case.

The men of Jabesh-gilead, however, could not sit around and calmly contemplate textual problems. They had to face Nahash. They asked for treaty terms as his vassals (11:1). He gave them. They would be spared, but Nahash would scoop out all their right eyes (v. 2). That meant never-ending subservience, for it made most men unfit for military service. The left eye was normally covered by the shield in battle.[3] With the right eye gone... well, you can't fight what you can't sight. But Nahash wasn't primarily interested in producing disabled veterans. His delight was in heaping disgrace upon Israel (v. 2b)—it was such a thrill for him slowly to turn the screws of humiliation on Israel. He was so sure of himself and so enjoyed watching Jabesh-gilead sweat that he consented to their frantic request to allow them to send for help—if they could get it. Nahash was having such fun with his game.[4]

---

2. The translation is that of P. Kyle McCarter, Jr., *I Samuel*, The Anchor Bible (Garden City, N.Y.: Doubleday, 1980), 198. Josephus in his *Antiquities* (6.68–70) seems to presuppose such a Trans-jordanian rampage by Nahash.

3. Claus Schedl, *History of the Old Testament*, 5 vols. (Staten Island, N.Y.: Alba House, 1972), 3:64.

4. That Nahash should relish cruelty should not surprise us. Nor is it the relic of an ancient, barbarous age. Compare Joseph Stalin's quip: "To choose the victim, to prepare the blow with care, to slake an implacable vengeance, and then go to bed... there is nothing sweeter in the world" (Robert Leckie, *Delivered from Evil: The Saga of World War II* [New York: Harper and Row, 1987], 87). We can hardly expect otherwise from a race of depraved sinners. Most of us are far less bloody and far more refined in the kind of cruelty we inflict on others.

One can debate whether Jabesh-gilead was in the right by knuckling under (seemingly) so readily to Nahash (v. 1b).[5] But there is no doubt about Nahash's intention; he wants to heap "disgrace" (or scorn, mockery; Hebrew, *ḥerpāh*) upon all Israel (v. 2b).

> His words reveal his consciousness of the inferiority of Israel, indeed he even allows the men of Jabesh seven days to look for help among their kinsmen. This is the lowest ebb of pre-exilic Israelite history. Such is the intended meaning.[6]

Such is the arrogance of the world for God's people.

This arrogance, this hatred, never ceases. Nahash may become historical furniture, but the "Ammonite mind," that is, to maim, destroy, and strangle God's people, is always with us. I shan't take space to multiply additional historical or contemporary illustrations. "If the world hates you," Jesus said (and he did not mean "if it should" but "if—and it will"; see 1 John 3:13), "you know that it has hated me before it has hated you" (John 15:18). What a new light this warning must have shed on Jesus' previous words: "You are my friends if you keep doing what I command you.... I have called *you* [emphatic] friends" (John 15:14, 15). That makes a difference. One can face the arrogance of the world so long as he has the friendship of Jesus.

The Difference the Spirit Makes

The messengers of Jabesh-gilead come to Gibeah of Saul with their dire emergency (v. 4).[7] They told (v. 3) Nahash they'd send word throughout Israel's territory. But they came to Gibeah. They may have come to Gibeah first—there were folks around there who had roots in Jabesh-gilead (see Judg. 21:8-14). When Saul came in from his farm work and heard the alarming news, "the Spirit of God rushed upon Saul" (v. 6a)—and that

---

5. W. G. Blaikie argues that Jabesh-gilead's submission was tantamount to rejection of their covenant with Yahweh (*The First Book of Samuel*, The Expositor's Bible [Cincinnati: Jennings and Graham, n.d.], 170–71).

6. Hans Wilhelm Hertzberg, *I & II Samuel*, The Old Testament Library (Philadelphia: Westminster, 1964), 92.

7. The site of Saul's Gibeah is probably Tell el-Ful, about three miles north of Jerusalem.

made all the difference in the world. Saul summoned Israel's militia under dire threat (v. 7), divided his troops, smashed into Nahash's camp between 2:00–6:00 a.m.,[8] surprised the daylights out of the Ammonites, and totally routed them (v. 11).

I would argue that the writer wants to emphasize that Jabesh's situation and Saul's success came about only by the Spirit's power. He does this by placing verse 6 at the center of his narrative. Note the following structure:[9]

The king who oppresses and destroys (Dead Sea Scrolls/4QSama)
Ammon threatens, 1-2
Response of Jabesh:
"We will come out to you," 3
The messengers' bad news, 4
Saul's inquiry and the response to him, 5
The Spirit "rushes," 6
Saul's "message" and the response to it, 7-8
The messengers' good news, 9
Response of Jabesh:
"We will come out to you," 10
Ammon flees, 11
The king who delivers and preserves, 12-13

The difference the Spirit makes is clear in the way he equips a leader. Our writer depicts Saul as a sort of super-judge. He is a second Samson, for the Spirit of God "rushes" (*ṣālaḥ*) upon him (v. 6; also used of the Spirit and Saul in 10:6, 10), just as he had Samson (Judg. 14:6, 19; 15:14). True, the Spirit had equipped other judges (e.g., Judg. 3:10; 6:34; 11:29), but the verb *ṣālaḥ* is not used in these cases. It is used only in connection with Samson and the Spirit's "rushing" upon him, and that three times. Now this verb is used for the third time in 1 Samuel in relation to the Spirit's equipping of Saul. He is Saul but there are shades of Samson about him.

But more. Saul divides his troops into three squads (v. 11), which cannot fail to remind us of Gideon (Judg. 7:16). His hacking up and parcel-posting the pieces of his oxen (v. 7) reminds us of the last episode in Judges (see Judg. 19:29), though Saul's action

---

8. Schedl, *History of the Old Testament*, 3:66.
9. I am including in this structure the material from the Dead Sea Scrolls (4QSama) cited earlier in this chapter. Cf. footnote 2. Its inclusion or exclusion does not vitally affect the centrality of verse 6.

united Israel against a foreign enemy rather than against a fellow (and rebellious) Israelite town or tribe. Moreover, Saul is implicitly described as a "savior" (*môš[.]'a*, v. 3), a term assigned to Othniel and Ehud among the judges (Judg. 3:9, 15).[10] There are more possible judges-connections, but these suffice. This, our writer says, is what God's Spirit does. He takes this shy, hesitating farmer and makes him function as a super-judge. That is the difference the Spirit makes.

The Spirit also makes a difference in the way he reverses a memory. There is a sense in which salvation comes out of Gibeah in this story (v. 4), a striking fact to anyone familiar with Israel's history. Not only striking but ironic and joyful. What a contrast to Gibeah in the early judges' period (though the episode is recorded last in the Book of Judges, chaps. 19-21)! There Gibeah is Sodomburgh (cf. Gen. 19). Sexual perverts abuse a woman through one long night of terror until dawn brings relief in death. There is no sorrow, no repentance in Gibeah—nor indeed in all the tribe of Benjamin. The tribe is so rebellious, so insistent that Gibeah's perverts do *not* receive justice, that a disastrous civil war ensues.[11] But now, in 1 Samuel 11, this place of wickedness and destruction has become the source of salvation and deliverance. Who would have ever thought that anything good could come out of Gibeah? How God brings light out of darkness! That is the difference the Spirit makes.

Israel cannot afford to miss the point: Salvation came not because Israel had a king but because the king had Yahweh's Spirit; it is not the institution of kingship but the power of the Spirit that brings deliverance. Nor can the church afford to miss this point. It is simply Christ's Old Testament way of saying, "Without me you can do nothing" (John 15:5b).

The Renewal the Kingdom Requires (11:14-15)

After the victory over Nahash, Samuel calls Israel to assemble at Gilgal, located very near Jericho and therefore on the

---

10. This last link noted by Ralph W. Klein, *1 Samuel*, Word Biblical Commentary (Waco: Word, 1983), 106.

11. For additional discussion of Judges 19–21, see my exposition in *Such a Great Salvation: Expositions of the Book of Judges* (Christian Focus, 2000), 211–27.

west side of and close to the Jordan River. The text is very Gilgalish—the place name occurs three times and "there" (referring to Gilgal) four times in these two verses. Seven times in two verses—the writer has made his point. Samuel's agenda for Gilgal was to "renew the kingdom" (or, kingship, v. 14). But what did this involve? Does verse 15 provide a partial answer when it states that "they made Saul king there before Yahweh at Gilgal"?[12] Perhaps. But Samuel's objective was to *renew* the kingdom, not (primarily) to complete it. "Renew" implies some degree of prior deterioration.[13] Moreover, whose kingdom or kingship was to be renewed? Saul's? Or Yahweh's?

Robert Vannoy has argued that Samuel refers not to Saul's but to Yahweh's kingship (see 8:7; 12:12) and that his summons to Israel to "renew the kingdom" at Gilgal is a summons "to renew their allegiance to the rule of Yahweh." This is, after all, the burden of the assembly at Gilgal (ch. 12).[14]

Even apart from chapter 12, however, we have clues about what renewing the kingdom might entail. It could mean requiring those who had previously despised Yahweh's chosen king to confess allegiance to him (cf. 10:27; 11:12); perhaps that is why verse 15 specifies that "all the people" made Saul king.[15] To "renew the kingdom" might also mean Israel's fresh commitment to the "*mišpaṭ* of the kingdom" (10:25); that is, to the divine plan for the way kingship was to function in Israel (see comments on 10:25 in the previous chapter). Both of these possibilities, however, implicitly

---

12. I cannot become too exercised over the apparent discrepancies between what occurred at Samuel's lodgings (9:25–10:1), at Mizpah (10:17-27), and at Gilgal (11:14-15) regarding Saul's coming to kingship. The three texts very naturally depict an orderly process of private anointing, public selection, and official installation.

13. See J. Robert Vannoy, *Covenant Renewal at Gilgal: A Study of 1 Samuel 11:14-12:25* (Cherry Hill, N.J.: Mack, 1978), 64–65.

14. Ibid., 67–68, 81–82. Vannoy's argument assumes that chapter 12 describes what took place at the Gilgal assembly (11:14-15); that is, chapter 12 is not a free-standing, place-less piece. He does not neglect to argue this point, and I think he makes his case (pp. 127–30). V. Philips Long, however, sees Saul's kingship as primarily in view; the "renewal" is necessary because of Saul's failure to strike against the Philistines earlier (1 Sam. 10:7) when expected to do so (*The Reign and Rejection of King Saul: A Case for Literary and Theological Coherence*, SBL Dissertation Series 118 [Atlanta: Scholars, 1989], 207–11, 225–28).

15. Cf. Lyle M. Eslinger, *Kingship of God in Crisis: A Close Reading of 1 Samuel 1–12* (Sheffield: Almond, 1985), 378–80.

demand renewed allegiance to the rule of Yahweh, and so I find it difficult to quibble with Vannoy's view of what "renew[ing] the kingdom" requires.

We must also keep our finger on the map. It is significant that kingdom renewal takes place at Gilgal. That was the place where Yahweh's power worked for Israel against hopeless odds (Josh. 3-4); it was where a "new" people of God came into being after the rebellious years in the wilderness (Josh. 5:1-12).[16] Perhaps some Israelites saw the contemporary analogies: their utter helplessness before Nahash's reign of terror (1 Sam. 11:1-3, with possible additions from Dead Sea Scrolls) and the obviously new departure in living under the regime of a human king.

I think Christians face substantially the same demand as Samuel placed upon Israel. Again and again, we are to "renew our allegiance to the kingdom" (v. 14 NEB). Is this not the demand that a greater than Samuel places upon us in Matthew 6:33? And if we ask what it means to seek first his kingdom and his righteousness, has he not already spelled that out in Matthew 5:17-6:34? And as we hear those deep, searching, royal demands, don't we begin to realize that we come off no better than Samuel and Saul's Israel? Jesus leaves even our sackcloth in tatters. No wonder they say the Christian life is a life of continual repentance, ever in need of renewing its allegiance to the rule of Yahweh.

Study Questions

1. The commentary does not multiply historical or contemporary illustrations of 'the Ammonites mind'. What illustrations can you find?

2. Think of the big contrast between Gibeah here and in Judges. Are there Gibeahs known to you that you should be praying for?

3. If we are sometimes in danger today of substituting institutions and church structures for the power of the Spirit, are there ways in which we can avoid this danger?

---

16. See my exposition in *No Falling Words: Expositions of the Book of Joshua* (Christian Focus, 2000), 31–49.

4. If I need, in repentance, to renew my allegiance to the Lord, can there be any adequate reason for not doing it at this very minute?

11

Covenant—Accusing and Assuring
(1 Samuel 12)

I had never seen anyone step out of a hospital room with shackles on his ankles. The fellow could walk—there was a short chain between the foot-cuffs—but not easily. A law officer followed to make sure he would have a severely limited liberty. The man was bound, fettered. Some scholars hold that the biblical word for "covenant" (*bĕr't*) comes from an Akkadian term meaning "clasp" or "fetter."[1] Though the derivation is unsure, the image correctly connotes the impact of a covenant. It binds. It fetters the parties, particularly vassals, who accept the terms imposed by the "great king," to the stipulations of the covenant; it binds them to the obligations they have accepted. And for the vassal the primary obligation was always for a total, undivided, exclusive fidelity to his overlord and benefactor.[2] But here Samuel's Israel had failed; in her passion for a king Israel had rejected her only king, Yahweh (1 Sam. 8:7-8; 10:17-19; 12:12, 17). She had broken covenant in asking for a king, and this covenant must be renewed.[3] For that reason repentance and renewal constitute Samuel's agenda at Gilgal. (The fabled New Testament Christian cannot slither out from beneath this text. He or she stands on the same

---

1. Cf. M. Weinfeld, *TDOT*, 2:253–56.
2. Meredith G. Kline, *Treaty of the Great King* (Grand Rapids: Eerdmans, 1963), 14–15.
3. See J. Robert Vannoy, *Covenant Renewal at Gilgal: A Study of I Samuel 11:14–12:25* (Cherry Hill, N.J.: Mack, 1978), 176–81.

covenant turf. What, after all, does the New Testament mean by calling Jesus "Lord" and us "slaves" and by demanding allegiance to only one master [Matt. 6:24]?) Hence, according to 1 Samuel 12, the covenant is both bad news and good news to God's people. Now to the exposition.[4]

The Case Against Us (12:1-15)

This section easily divides itself into three subsections, each beginning, or nearly beginning (see vv. 2, 7), with the Hebrew conjunction + particle *wĕʿattāh* ("and now," vv. 2, 7, 13). Hence in summary form we have:

> The "trial" and vindication of Samuel, 1-5
> The accusation and guilt of Israel, 6-12
> The acquiescence and alternatives of Yahweh, 13-15

Samuel's primary burden is to press the case against Israel (vv. 7ff.; see NEB on v. 7); first, however, as a necessary prelude, he obtains Israel's testimony vindicating his own leadership (vv. 2-5). Samuel cannot hide his age or his sons (v. 2), but what of his own leadership? Whose ox or donkey had he taken? Whom had he oppressed or crushed? How many pay-offs had he accepted? Whom had he milked? What accounts had he laundered? Open all the records; play all the tapes; where and how had he acted unjustly? Judge Israel vindicates Defendant Samuel completely (vv. 4-5). There had been no real defect in his character and leadership.

With that, defendant turns prosecutor against Israel the accused. Not only has Samuel been faithful (vv. 2-5) but so has Yahweh. Hence Samuel rehearses Yahweh's "righteous acts" in Israel's history (vv. 7ff.; see discussion in connection with 1 Sam. 8). Samuel points out a pattern throughout Israel's history: crisis, cry for help, deliverance through leadership raised up by Yahweh. Remember, for example, the bondage in Egypt. Israel cried for relief; Yahweh raised up Moses and

---

4. This chapter has attracted a volume of critical debate, which needn't be regurgitated here. Anyone wanting to follow the history of criticism will find a handy digest in Vannoy's *Covenant Renewal at Gilgal*, 95–131, 197–239. On Gilgal as the setting for chapter 12, see Lyle M. Eslinger, *Kingship of God in Crisis: A Close Reading of 1 Samuel 1–12* (Sheffield: Almond, 1985), 383–84.

Aaron through whom he brought deliverance (v. 8). It was the same throughout the Judges' period: oppression by God-ordained adversaries (v. 9), cries for help and deliverance (v. 10), and, in answer, "Yahweh sent" Jerubbaal, Bedan (Barak?), Jephthah, Samuel—whomever was needed (v. 11). Ah, but the most contemporary crisis always seems the worst. In the current emergency the memory of Yahweh's "righteous acts" dissolves in Israelite amnesia. Here comes Nahash (see the previous chapter) wreaking optical destruction—there is no cry for help but a demand for a king. No seeking for deliverance from Yahweh but specifying the method in which deliverance must come. No appeal to the true King. No trust in Yahweh to send adequate leadership as he had always done. Their help, they assume, is not in the proven arm of Yahweh but in a new form of government. "A King—or Bust," not "In God We Trust."

So now they had a king (v. 13). The alternatives were clear for people and king: they could live faithfully under Yahweh's word (v. 14) or they could suffer justly under Yahweh's hand (v. 15). Samuel's emphasis falls, however, on Israel's treasonous unbelief (v. 12):

> When you saw that Nahash, king of the sons of Ammon, came against you, you said to me, "No! But a king must reign over us!"—when Yahweh your God is your king.

We needn't face an Ammonite rampage to slip into a quiet attitude of Israelite unbelief. Whenever the latest crisis comes (sometimes we label it the last straw) we quietly think, "In this he cannot provide; he has no provision for me in this." It is all very silent, private, low-key—and faithless.

The Fear Upon Us (12:16-19)
Samuel gave Israel no time to speak. If Samuel had paused for breath, Israel might only have spouted some religious tripe. But Samuel rushed on:

> Even now take your stand and see this great thing which Yahweh is going to do before your very eyes. Isn't it wheat harvest today? I will call to Yahweh that he may give thunder and rain; so know

and see what a great evil you have committed in Yahweh's eyes by your asking for a king. [vv. 16-17]

Have you ever pressed an argument with your child or parent or friend, an argument that oozes reason and logic and sense, an argument with no loopholes or escapes, only to realize that your airtight case fails to convince? Doesn't penetrate their defenses? Samuel apparently knew this. He knew that he could lay down a solid case in all wisdom and reason (vv. 6 12). But that would not necessarily faze Israel at all. Not likely it would get through the thick barrier. Samuel likely knew that verbal truth without visual aid would leave Israel cold. So he set forth his case (vv. 6-12), laid down the alternatives (vv. 13-15), and ran lickety-split into announcing that Yahweh's thunder and rain could be expected immediately (vv. 16-17). Heavenly booms ought to get Israel's attention.

Granted, a deafening, drenching thunderstorm can certainly terrify and humble folks, but would mere racking thunder and pounding rain cause such fear, such conviction of wickedness (in demanding a king), such urgency for an intercessor, as Israel expresses (vv. 18-19)? Why this sudden "insight"? Because Israel knew this was no *mere* thunder and rain. Samuel had said it was wheat harvest (v. 17), that is, May–June, the beginning of the dry season. Every Israelite knew rain was extremely rare at this time,[5] something like six inches of snow in Miami on Memorial Day. Not impossible, but so unheard of that it tends to make one think. Hence Yahweh got Israel's attention.

If the storm was a sign, what did it signify? It showed Israel "what agencies of destruction God held in his hand, and how easily He could bring these to bear on them and on their property."[6] It showed that covenant curses were not mere official words tucked away in a canonical document

---

5. See *IDB*, 3:622–23; *ZPEB*, 4:579; and George Adam Smith, *The Historical Geography of the Holy Land*, 22d ed. (London: Hodder and Stoughton, n.d.), 65.

6. W. G. Blaikie, *The First Book of Samuel*, The Expositor's Bible (Cincinnati: Jennings and Graham, n.d.), 199. Blaikie continues: "You are gathering or about to gather that important crop [wheat harvest], and it is of vital importance that the weather be still and calm. But I will pray the Lord, and He shall send thunder and rain, and you will see how easy it is for Him in one hour to ruin the crop which you have been nursing so carefully for months back.... It was an impressive proof how completely they were in God's hands."

(cf. Lev. 26:14-46; Deut. 28:15-68) but lively threats of a living God who had the power to impose them at any—even a most unlikely—time.[7] It directly (as opposed to criticisms mediated through Samuel in chapters 8, 10, and previously in 12) displayed Yahweh's estimate of their passion for a king.

At last the point came home. Israel fears she will perish because in addition to all her sins she had added this "evil" of asking for a king. Only when God's people see their sin from his perspective is there hope that they will turn from it.

There was one of those mysterious odors in our kitchen. Not from the refrigerator or the range but from the cabinet where we kept canned and dry goods. A couple cursory examinations yielded nothing. When the odor persisted so did my wonder. One begins to hypothesize. For example, could a rodent be enjoying the advanced stages of his (or her) rigor mortis at our expense? Stench fed determination until I discovered the culprit. There was a can of sauerkraut that looked like it had yielded to internal pressure, had expanded, and begun to seep. Perhaps a food factory defect. But without that obnoxious odor we would not have eliminated the problem.

We seem to have a sauerkraut situation in verses 16-19. How can the living God get you to fear your subtle idolatry, be alarmed by it, be repulsed by it, or even become aware of it, unless he shows you how it smells—to him? And in order to impress this upon his people he scared the liver out of them by a sign of his holy anger. Fear of Yahweh's righteous wrath (v. 18b) seemed to open the way to repentance (v. 19).

Please don't begin to spout any nonsense about how wrong it is to motivate by fear. Why then did Paul write Colossians 3:6 after Colossians 3:5? What matters is whether there is a true basis for fear. If there is reason to tremble, we ought to tremble. Neither the church nor individual Christians should be above truthful terror. If God grants us a sight of our own sin and of his displeasure, we can be sure he does not do so merely to see us tremble but to see us tremble and be restored. In I Samuel 12 we see both the kindness *and* the severity of God

---

7. Vannoy, *Covenant Renewal at Gilgal*, 47; also C. F. Keil, *Biblical Commentary on the Books of Samuel* (1875; reprint ed., Grand Rapids: Eerdmans, 1950), 120.

(Rom. 11:22); Yahweh intends fear as the way to faithfulness
(vv. 20-25). "'Twas *grace* that taught my heart to fear...." That
brings us to our next point.

The Grace Over Us (12:20-25)

What does God do with his people when they have committed
spiritual disaster, when they have charted their own course in
what is, when stripped of all its camouflage, nothing less than
rebellion? What does he say to this people when they have
apparently come to see how ugly their sin really is? He says,
"Don't be afraid"; he says, "You have done all this evil, yet..."
(v. 20). Here is a future and a hope. His full answer, through
Samuel, is:

> Don't be afraid; you have done all this evil. Yet don't turn aside
> from following Yahweh, but you must serve Yahweh with all
> your heart. And you must not turn aside after "zero" gods that
> never profit or deliver because they are "zeros".... Only fear
> Yahweh and you must serve him in fidelity and with all your
> heart.... [vv. 20-21, 24a]

Do you see it? You don't go back and wallow in your guilt,
relive the tragic mistake, the "big one" that has soured your
life. You don't make yourself miserable by bathing your mind
in the memory of your rebellion, punching the replay button
and going over the whole messy episode in lurid and precise
detail as though such misery makes atonement. No, you go
forward in basic, simple fidelity to Yahweh from that point
on. "Only fear Yahweh, and you must serve him in fidelity
and with all your heart" (v. 24).

How can God be like that?[8] How can he say to such people,
"Don't be afraid"? Why will Yahweh still have truck with
folks who've committed treason against him? Because he is
the covenant God. Or, in the words of verse 22, "For Yahweh
will never cast away his people because of his great name; for
Yahweh has been pleased to make you his very own people."

---

8. Perhaps our question really is: How can Yahweh be such a complex God? How
can he burst into white, searing heat over our sins yet cool into warm, tender grace
that refuses to destroy us? Perhaps we cannot answer, only adore. Is this not the
"beauty of the LORD" (Ps. 27:4)?

Yahweh's decision has been to have a people—and he will! He will never go back on that decision. After all, his whole reputation (name) is wrapped up in that.

For some years we have had an unwritten law in our home: Don't flush the stool when someone's in the shower. The rationale behind this law is merciful. Many have had an unexpected, scorching experience. You (to make it personal) are enjoying your cleansing experience when, suddenly and without warning, another family member flushes a toilet stool, which, somehow, monopolizes the cold water and leaves you with only hot water in your shower and livid threats on your lips. I recall such an occasion several years ago. My ten-year-old son suffered temporary amnesia. As soon as he had flushed the stool he was flushed with remorse, but recovered remarkably well, crowing above the din as he made his exit, "You can't beat me up, 'cause you're my father." He meant, "Because of who you are, you are committed to act in a certain way"; that is, there were limits on what I would do to him. That is what Samuel is telling Israel in verse 22: Since Yahweh has been pleased to make you his own people, he will not forsake you. He does not abandon the commitments he makes.

"Yahweh will not forsake his people.... Only fear Yahweh and serve him in fidelity and with all your heart" (vv. 22a, 24a). Here is grace greater than all our sin! You do not try to reverse all the irreversible consequences of your sin but gladly accept the fresh grace from God. You are called to fidelity from this point on. What a word to the downcast! Don't think that the "grand mistake" that has disfigured your life is the first disastrous sin God has seen. Don't think you can silence verse 22. God can make it blink at you in neon if he must. Or make you trip over Romans 5:20b—which is the same thing.

There is then a dual emphasis in verses 16-25: You must see your great evil (vv. 16-19) and yet you must see Yahweh's great steadfastness (vv. 20-25). Only the latter can keep you from despair over the former. It is not only by grace alone that we become God's people but by grace alone we remain his people.

The Man for Us (12:23)

Yahweh also displays that grace (see the previous discussion) in appointing servants who make the welfare of his people their preoccupation. Such was Samuel's stated task (answering Israel's plea of v. 19): "Moreover, as far as I'm concerned, far be it from me to sin against Yahweh by ceasing to pray for you, but I shall teach you the good and right way" (v. 23). If the rejected God refuses to forsake his people, how can his rejected servant do so?

Samuel promises to fulfill a ministry of intercession (pray for you) and instruction (teach you) on Israel's behalf. Perhaps we usually think of intercession in connection with a priest, but in Israel prophets did—or it was assumed that they would—give themselves in intercessory prayer (as Moses in Exod. 32:11-14, 30-32; Num. 14:13-19; Ps. 106:23; Amos in Amos 7:1-6; and Jeremiah in Jer. 7:16; 11:14; 14:11; see also Jer. 15:1).[9] In his priestly intercession and prophetic instruction Samuel filled the offices of both priest and prophet for Israel. (Compare also the apostles' focus on "prayer" and "the ministry of the word," Acts 6:4.)

It is in such offices that we now have a Far Greater than Samuel. And how we need him. No less than Israel. Surely the contemporary church must stifle her arrogance in assuming that only ancient Israel is an unfaithful people. Surely we must confess that we stand—if we do—only because there is a Man who stands in the breach for us before God, One who as our Prophet has called us to take his yoke upon us and *learn* from him (Matt. 11:29; cf. John 15:15b), One who as our Priest always lives to intercede (Heb. 7:25) for his weak, sinful, faltering, and covenant-breaking people.

STUDY QUESTIONS

1. Christians sometimes view Old Testament characters in a rather condescending way, comparing them unfavourably with people of the New Covenant. Can this be justified in the light of Samuel's fine record of integrity in his leadership of Israel?

---

9. I am indebted to Karl Gutbrod, *Das Buch vom König*, Die Botschaft des Alten Testaments, 4th ed. (Stuttgart: Calwer, 1975), 91–92, for helping me see the importance of Samuel's intercessory role.

2. Why is it that, even when God reasons with people in a totally convincing way, they so often fail to accept what he says?

3. We do not like either pain or fear very much. If however pain has its purpose in alerting us to illness or bodily damage, what is fear's God-ordained function?

4. We think of our need of God's grace at the time of our conversion to Christ, but is it not just as true that we need it constantly as we live the Christian life? What do you think?

5. Christ stands as a Prophet addressing us for God and as a Priest interceding for us in God's presence. Is the church of Christian serving Christ, called to functions which are somewhat like this in relation to the world in which we live?

12

Tarnish on the Crown
(1 Samuel 13)

One of my uncles, so the story goes, was moving the china cupboard for his wife. Moved it by himself with the china in it! Didn't quite fit in the new location, so he used a sledge hammer to whack it into its final and proper position. Too bad about the china though. Ruin can come so suddenly.

That is the impression 1 Samuel 13 makes on us. Certainly chapter 12 shatters our giddy optimism about kingship but does leave us with a chastened hope. Hence we come to chapter 13 with positive expectations. We read the customary formula of 13:1, the official introduction to Saul's reign, and—after we stop asking who swiped the numerals from the text[1] —expect at least something decent to come from Saul's rule. We are unprepared for a dark story of royal failure and Israelite helplessness.

Admittedly, chapter 13 does not stand by itself. Chapters 13 and 14 constitute one narrative. However, chapter 13 does bear a significant witness in its own right, and so I have, somewhat artificially, broken it off to consider by itself. In the next chapter I will show its structural unity with chapter 14. In the meantime it may be useful to review the content of chapter 13 via the following structural outline:

---

1. The textual problem of 1 Samuel 13:1 is notorious. For a discussion, see V. Philips Long, *The Reign and Rejection of King Saul: A Case for Literary and Theological Coherence,* SBL Dissertation Series 118 (Atlanta: Scholars, 1989), 71–75.

Setting, 2-7
  Saul's army, 2
    Jonathan's success, 3-4a
  Saul's army, 4b
    Israel's weakness, 5-7a
  Saul's army, 7b
Dialogue, 8-15
  Saul waits
    Samuel's nonarrival, 8
  Saul acts
    Samuel's arrival, 9-10
  Saul's explanation, 11-12
  Samuel's announcement, 13-14
  Samuel's departure, 15a
  Saul's preparation, 15b
Explanation (i.e., how bad it was), 16-23
  Philistine freedom in raiding, 16-18
  Philistine control of weapons, 19-22

With this in mind let us turn to the primary emphases of the chapter.

A Hint of Trouble

There is every reason to cheer when we hear that Jonathan struck down the Philistine governor (see NJB, NJPS) or garrison (RSV, NASB)—whichever it was—at Geba (v. 3). Nothing disturbing about that—not if you're an Israelite and not until tomorrow when the Philistines hear about it.

Jonathan then is the instigator of this initial success. That makes some of us uneasy. Obviously we admire his bravado. But Jonathan is not Saul. He is the king's son, not the king. Why didn't Saul take the initiative? Why didn't the king go out before Israel (8:20)? Of course the press release gave Saul credit for the feat (v. 4), but every Israelite knew who authorized the press releases. It all stirs a question in our minds: Does Jonathan's success point to some lack, some deficiency in Saul? Only chapter 14 can finally answer that.

In the meantime we might observe that God's purposes are not frustrated when his more "authorized" servants prove reluctant. He has others who prove willing in the day of his power. Perhaps there would have been no need for George Whitefield's wild practice of preaching in the fields had Anglicans been preaching the same gospel in their buildings.[2]

A Failure of Obedience

What really matters takes place in the dialogue section, verses 8-15, especially in verses 11-14 (Saul's explanation and Samuel's announcement). The Philistines may be strangling Israel but that pales beside the more crucial issue of royal disobedience.

But can we really fault Saul for his disobedience? Doesn't the penalty seem arbitrary and overly severe? Must we not take Saul's explanation more seriously? Given the facts that Saul had waited seven days (see 10:8), or at least into the seventh day, for Samuel, that his army was evaporating by desertion, that for all he knew the enemy would be upon him momentarily, how can he be blamed or punished for acting as he did? Doesn't he deserve understanding rather than censure? Doesn't he need empathy rather than punishment? The reader can hardly fail to sympathize with Saul in his situation. Whether his explanation vindicates him is another matter.[3]

No question then about the pressure Saul felt. But it is doubtful that the Philistines would have attacked him at Gilgal (v. 12a) near the Jordan. Saul had summoned Israel to Gilgal (v. 4) in line with Samuel's earlier instruction (10:8). But Gilgal was also isolated. Hence Israel could expect to assemble there without undue fear of Philistine attack.[4]

Saul also attempted to shift blame to Samuel: "And *you* [emphatic in Hebrew] did not come at the appointed time" (v. 11). Saul harks back to Samuel's original instructions in 10:8:

---

2. Cf. Arnold A. Dallimore, *George Whitefield: The Life and Times of the Great Evangelist of the Eighteenth-Century Revival,* 2 vols. (Westchester, Ill.: Cornerstone, 1970), 1:334–38.

3. Robert Polzin, *Samuel and the Deuteronomist* (San Francisco: Harper and Row, 1989), 128–31, thinks the narrative also depicts a self-serving Samuel determined to keep Saul on the defensive and subservient to the prophet. Polzin's reading is, in my estimation, overly subtle; if the narrator did not wholly endorse Samuel's position he would not have given his words (vv. 13-14) the dominant position in the narrative.

4. In 1 Samuel 12 Gilgal is the place of covenant renewal; in 1 Samuel 13 it is the place of royal failure.

And you shall go down before me to Gilgal, and I am indeed going to come down to you to offer up burnt offerings and sacrifice peace offerings. Seven days you must wait until I come to you, and I shall make you know what you must do.

Saul seems to have waited into the seventh day but not the whole day—at least that is what 13:10a suggests. But that is not of primary importance. Saul was to wait for Samuel's arrival ("until I come to you"),[5] so that he would receive the prophet's instructions about the conduct of the battle ("I shall make known to you what you must do"). God's prophet would give him God's guidance for the Philistine war. Samuel was the bearer of Yahweh's word, and Saul's task was to wait for it. Instead he proceeded without it. For Saul sacrificial ritual was essential (v. 12b) but prophetic direction dispensable. Saul's was an act of insubordination, a failure to submit to Yahweh's word through his prophet. By his action Saul confessed that certain emergencies rendered Yahweh's word unnecessary.[6] When the chips were down kingship could function on its own.

Kingship is prone to such subtle (or not so subtle) pride. James VI of Scotland was notoriously rude when attending worship services. On one occasion he was seated in his gallery with several courtiers while Robert Bruce preached. In his usual form James began to talk to those around him during the sermon. Bruce paused, the king fell silent. The minister resumed and so did James; Bruce ceased speaking a second time. Same result. When the king committed his third offense Bruce turned and addressed James directly: "It is said to have been an expression of the wisest of kings, 'When the lion roars, all the beasts of the field are quiet': the Lion of the Tribe of Judah is now roaring in the voice of His Gospel, and it becomes all the petty kings of the earth to be silent."[7] Kings

---

5. See Long, *Reign and Rejection of King Saul*, 88–89.

6. I do not think that Saul's offense involved personal intrusion into priestly office (v. 12b). The text probably assumes that he had the sacrifices offered by means of a presiding priest, as both 2 Samuel 24:25 and 1 Kings 3:4 seem to assume for David and Solomon respectively; so A. F. Kirkpatrick, *The First Book of Samuel*, The Cambridge Bible for Schools and Colleges (Cambridge: Cambridge University Press, 1896), 126.

7. D. C. MacNicol, *Robert Bruce: Minister in the Kirk of Edinburgh* (1907; reprint ed., n.p.: Banner of Truth, 1961), 38.

easily forget they are subjects. They can ignore the true King's decrees, either obnoxiously and blatantly—like James, or quietly and subtly—like Saul. In any case, Samuel primarily charged Saul with disobedience to Yahweh (vv. 13a, 14b). Because of this Saul would not enjoy an ongoing dynasty (vv. 13b-14a). Yahweh does not here reject Saul himself (for that see 1 Sam. 15) but a Saulide line of kings.

There is, however, a more immediate, and sadder, loss, a loss easily missed because it is somewhat hidden in a geographical note. "Then Samuel rose and went up from Gilgal to Gibeah of Benjamin; and Saul mustered the people found with him, about six hundred men" (v. 15). Samuel rose and went up from Gilgal. Many Israelites had hidden to save their skins (vv. 6-7); weapons were unobtainable (vv. 19-22); raiders were freeloading throughout Israel (vv. 17-18); the troops Saul did have were demoralized (v. 7). But the worst of Saul's liabilities was that he was without the guidance of Yahweh from his prophet. To be stripped of the direction of God's word is to be truly impoverished and open to destruction. It is one thing to be in terrible distress; it is another to be alone in that distress. Saul had isolated himself from what he needed most—the word of Yahweh for his way. So verse 15 joins 15:34-35a and 28:25b as one of the saddest statements in the book. Saul can number the troops (v. 15b), but that is all he can do; he has lost what matters most. "Samuel rose and went up from Gilgal to Gibeah of Benjamin." Saul is on his own.[8]

An Air of Hopelessness

When Samuel walks away one expects the worst for Israel. Israel now has no direction (vv. 8-15) from Yahweh's word. Saul, the king who is to deliver, has no resources to begin such deliverance. Saul himself contributes to Israel's helplessness; he is part of Israel's hopeless case.

---

8. I cannot help but think that Saul's predicament is very like that of middle- and upper-class churches in our country. A church may provide all the trappings people crave: hyperkinetic programs for all ages of children, fun activities for youth, support groups for diverse needs, counseling services for people in crisis, aggressive visitation, a high-quality music ministry for the talented and/or interested. And yet for all the activities and programs that church is fundamentally alone if it lacks the faithful preaching and teaching of the word of God. The presence of glitz cannot substitute for the absence of the word.

Yet the whole chapter breathes this despair. There was no support from a large number of Israelites—they either hid or fled (vv. 5-7). They did not take Jonathan's victory (v. 3) as a sign of Yahweh's favor and help.[9] There was no defense against Philistine raiders (vv. 16-18). Three Philistine detachments left Michmash, one to the north (v. 17b), one to the west (v. 18a), one to the southeast (v. 18b). No one could stop them; the Philistines dominated at will; and not only in raiding, for there were no weapons available for Israel (vv. 19-22). In spite of the textual and translation problems in these verses (see the grammatical commentaries), the overall picture is clear: Phil-istia keeps Israel disarmed. Israelites even had to go to the Philistines to get their farm tools serviced—for a fee, of course. No doubt about it: Israel is finished. Well, not quite; but only because the Philistine monster has not yet begun to chew the last remnants of his repast.

Chapter 13 then highlights the theme of Israel's helplessness. That is why alert Bible readers are not hopeless about Israel's hopelessness. They have seen it too often before: the total helplessness of God's people proves to be the backdrop for Yahweh's deliverance.

It looked that bleak for the Federal frigate *Minnesota* one Saturday night in 1862 near Hampton Roads. That day the Confederate ironclad, the *Virginia* (formerly the *Merrimac*), had revolutionized naval warfare. The *Virginia* had already sunk the *Congress* and *Cumberland,* and when three additional wooden ships, including the *Minnesota,* had hurried to assist they had run aground. The *Virginia* withdrew for the night since the ebb tide prevented her from coming within effective range of the stranded *Minnesota.* After dawn the next day the *Virginia* steamed toward her helpless prey for a certain kill. Suddenly, something looking like a raft with a boiler on it darted out from behind the *Minnesota* heading for the *Virginia.* It was the *Monitor,* the Federal ironclad commanded by John L. Worden. The *Monitor* engaged the *Virginia* in a four-hour duel that proved a draw. But the *Minnesota* was saved. The

---

9. S. G. DeGraaf, *Promise and Deliverance,* 4 vols. (St. Catharines: Paideia, 1978), 2:93.
10. Shelby Foote, *The Civil War, A Narrative,* vol. 1, *Fort Sumter to Perryville* (New York: Vintage, 1986), 255–63.

Monitor had arrived during the night, put in alongside the *Minnesota,* and had kept her steam up.[10] When it was most hopeless, help came.

That is frequently Yahweh's way with his Israel. That is why the remnant refuses to lose heart. Not that his people enjoy their helpless condition; it is simply that they have seen Yahweh create deliverance out of nothing too many times to give themselves over to total despair.

Study Questions

1. Are our 'explanations' as to why we did not do God's will ever adequate?

2. 'For Saul sacrificial ritual was essential ... but prophetic direction dispensable.' Do the words of Jesus in the last sentence of Matthew 23:23 put this into proper perspective?

3. Consider the departure of Samuel, mouthpiece of God's Word, from Saul and also Amos 8:11-12. Do you think we value sufficiently our constant access to the Word of God?

4. Do you agree that helplessness is not necessarily hopelessness? May it in fact even point us in the direction of real hope?

13

Sad Success
(1 Samuel 14)

Ionce read a story about a baseball game played about the
turn of the century by two Minnesota semi-pro teams. At
the end of nine innings they were locked in a scoreless tie. In
the top of the tenth, however, the team from Benson scored a
run. Willmar, the other team, came to bat in the bottom half
of the inning. Willmar's pitcher, Thielman, smacked a single.
The next batter, O'Toole, smashed a terrific drive deep in the
outfield. The crowd began its customary and proper uproar.
Thielman rounded second base and headed for third with
O'Toole digging after him. As Thielman arrived at third, however, he collapsed. O'Toole daren't pass him in the base path
and so he obligingly half-carried and dragged Thielman the
ninety feet to home plate. Amazingly, the umpire allowed both
runs. Willmar had won! Thielman was the winning pitcher.
Thielman was also dead. He had died of heart failure at third
base.[1] There can be shadows over victory and sadness in success. That is precisely the flavor of 1 Samuel 14.

The writer takes a little time to set the scene for us: here is
the plan (v. 1); here are the leaders (vv. 2-3); here is the place
(vv. 4-5).

Jonathan took his armor-bearer into his confidence. It was
sheer audacity: "Come, let's go over to the Philistine garrison
on the other side" (v. 1). Then the narrator adds a teasing

---

1. *Bill Stern's Favorite Baseball Stories* (Garden City, N.Y.: Blue Ribbon Books, 1949), 7.

bit of intelligence: "But he did not tell his father." We don't know why. Probably Jonathan thought Saul would forbid the venture. Boldness was not Saul's forte these days. Perhaps Jonathan feared Saul would keep them sitting under the pomegranate tree till the cows came home. Jonathan's scheme; Saul's ignorance; this could become dramatic.

Jonathan was moving; Saul was sitting. He was under the pomegranate tree on the edge of Gibeah (v. 2). Here in verses 2-3 the writer depicts the leaders, Saul the king (v. 2) and Ahijah the priest (v. 3). Why does he resurrect Ahijah's family tree? He has his reasons for calling him Ahijah the "son of Ahitub, brother of Ichabod [remember the dark day when "No glory" was born, 4:19-22?], son of Phinehas [the meat-loving, woman-chasing priest of 2:12-17, 22-25], son of Eli [whose line would be judged and excluded, 2:27-36; 3:11-14], priest of Yahweh in Shiloh."[2] The writer may be saying more than appears. "Here are the leaders: sitting there is Saul, whose dynasty has been rejected (13:13-14), assisted by Ahijah, whose priestly line has been rejected. Since Samuel has left Saul has no authorized prophetic direction; he has a rejected priestly line instead. What help can such a king and such a priest give?"

Finally, the writer insists that a little topography is good for the understanding. Hence he describes the location of Jonathan's venture:

> Between the passes where Jonathan tried to cross over to the Philistine garrison there is a rocky crag on the one side and a rocky crag on the other. The name of the one is Bozez and the name of the other Seneh. [v. 4]

He adds that the one is on the north in front of Michmash, the other to the south in front of Geba (v. 5). Their names, roughly equivalent to Slippery (Bozez) and Thorny (Seneh), hardly invite hikers. And between these rock outcroppings the Wadi

---

2. V. Philips Long, *The Reign and Rejection of King Saul: A Case for Literary and Theological Coherence*, SBL Dissertation Series 118 (Atlanta: Scholars, 1989), 105-6, citing David Jobling, and J. P. Fokkelman, *Narrative Art and Poetry in the Books of Samuel*, vol. 2, *The Crossing Fates (I Sam. 13–31 & II Sam. 1)* (Assen/ Maastricht: Van Gorcum, 1986), 48–49.

Suwenit cuts its deep trough toward the Jordan with steep banks on either side. One might infer from verses 12 and 13 that most sane folks considered the point impassable.[3] That fact could prove an advantage.

So much for the setting. Our writer has been rather brisk: Here is the plan (which is secret); here are the leaders (who are rejected); here is the place (which is impossible). Now, he says, here is the secret (v. 6).

The Imagination of Faith (14:6-23)

Jonathan's statement in verse 6 deserves billboard status:

> Come, let's go over to the garrison of these uncircumcised fellows; perhaps Yahweh will act for us, for nothing can keep Yahweh from saving by many or by few.

We can hardly claim that Jonathan's faith was a product of his environment. A quick look back at 13:5-7, 8, 17-18, 19-22 should convince us that there were no grounds for optimism there. The circumstances did not stimulate optimism. But this is not optimism. It is faith. Some people are naturally optimistic—they don't know any better. But faith can arise even when no reason for optimism exists.

Reason for faith may exist. Jonathan clearly indicates the basis of his. Faith arises in such a situation because it looks not to circumstances but to God. Note again his words: Clear conviction about God ("for nothing can keep Yahweh from saving") produces great expectation of God ("perhaps Yahweh will act for us") and recognizes God's "normal" manner of working ("by many or by few," i.e., through his servants). Jonathan is not trusting his own daring scheme. He does not say, "Perhaps Yahweh will act for us, for we are rather clever." If anything, his daring is an expression of his trust in Yahweh, a trust rooted in truth about Yahweh.

Yet the beauty of Jonathan's faith is its imagination ("Come, let us go... perhaps Yahweh will act for us"); and the beauty of that imagination is its balance ("perhaps"). It is as

---

3. On the location, see S. R. Driver, *Notes on the Hebrew Text and the Topography of the Books of Samuel*, 2d ed. (1913; reprint ed., Winona Lake, Ind.: Alpha, 1984), 106.

if Jonathan says, "God *can* do mighty works with very small resources, and God *may* be glad to do it in this case; and how can we know, dear armor-bearer, unless we place ourselves at his disposal?" How refreshing to hear Jonathan's "Who knows"—who knows what Yahweh will do? There is no limit to how he can save! He has no need of at least six hundred trembling men!

And how refreshing to hear Jonathan's "perhaps." "Perhaps Yahweh will act for us." Many in our own day think otherwise. They think that to say "perhaps" cuts the nerve of faith, that if faith is faith it must always be certain, dogmatic, and absolutely positive. Faith, however, must not be confused with arrogance. Jonathan's "perhaps" is part of his faith. He both confesses the power of Yahweh and retains the freedom of Yahweh. Faith does not dictate to God, as if the Lord of hosts is its errand boy.[4] Faith recognizes its degree of ignorance and knows it has not read a transcript of the divine decrees for most situations. All this, however, does not cancel but enhances its excitement. Who knows what this omnipotent God may be delighted to do against these uncircumcised Philistines!

Speaking of Philistines, we had better return to the Wadi Suwenit. Jonathan had proposed a sign to know whether Yahweh would have them venture or not; if the garrison called them to come up, that would be Yahweh's green light and assurance of victory (vv. 9-10). The Philistines spotted the two Israelites and wisecracked about Hebrews coming out of their holes. It is difficult to know precisely what their invitation meant, which literally runs: "Come up to us, and let us make you know something" (v. 12). The latter clause may be a challenge—we'll "teach you a lesson," as the New International Version and the Tanakh (NJPS) take it. Jonathan didn't care. They had said, "Come up to us." That's all he needed to hear.

---

4. I am reminded of the anecdote in John Whitecross, *The Shorter Catechism Illustrated from Christian Biography and History* (reprint ed., London: Banner of Truth, 1968), 105: "A minister, praying for a child apparently dying, said, 'If it be Thy will, spare this child.' The wretched and distracted mother interrupted him with the words, 'It *must* be God's will; I will have no *ifs.*' The child, to the surprise of many, recovered, but lived to break his mother's heart, and was publicly executed at the age of twenty-two."

The garrison obviously did not see any threat. One easily supposes the Philistines were back at their poker and beer momentarily. In any case, the outpost probably could not have seen Jonathan and his companion as they climbed the north wall of the wadi. Jonathan and his armor-bearer clambered their way up the high, steep bank, negotiated old "Slippery," and hit the Philistines before they could call Dagon to the rescue! Jonathan led the attack; his armor-bearer followed and finished off those Jonathan had flattened (v. 13b). There were now twenty men who would never teach a Hebrew another lesson (v. 14).

This sudden, initial attack produced two results: terror and confusion. The Tanakh nicely retains the thrice-repeated Hebrew root *ḥrd* (be terrified; terror) in verse 15:

> Terror broke out among all the troops both in the camp [and] in the field; the outposts and the raiders were also terrified. The very earth quaked, and a terror from God ensued.

Another (somewhat) threefold repetition emphasizes the confusion. In verses 16 and 19 the writer refers to the *hāmôn*, which can mean either "multitude" (v. 16) or "confusion" (v. 19; i.e., what multitudes frequently cause). In verse 20 he summarizes the Philistine panic by using *měhûmāh*, a relative of *hāmôn*, in the last phrase — "very great confusion." Fairer-weather friends appeared in abundance (vv. 21-22) and the rout was on. But the bottom line (v. 23a) carries the whole truth: "So Yahweh *saved* Israel on that day." Jonathan was right: "Nothing can keep Yahweh from saving by many or by few" (v. 6b). This salvation, however, did not begin in royal mathematics (13:15b; 14:2) but with imaginative faith, faith that was willing to say, "Perhaps Yahweh will act for us."

The Air of Tragedy (14:24-46)

There are, however, clouds over this victory. Israel wins but can hardly celebrate. The writer explains why in verses 24-46.

Our writer has closed off the first segment of his story with verse 23: "So Yahweh saved Israel on that day." He follows with a supplementary account (something Hebrew narrative often does) giving the rest of the story in verses 24-46. However, he pits the opening line of his supplementary narrative in deliberate and direct contrast to the summarizing statement of the previous section. One shouldn't miss it:

So Yahweh saved Israel on that day. [v. 23]
But the men of Israel were hard pressed on that day. [v. 24][5]

He goes on to explain why Israel was "hard pressed": Saul placed a curse on any troops who ate food before evening and, apparently, total victory. This led to both military exhaustion (vv. 25-31)[6] and ritual transgression (vv. 32-35; cf. Lev. 17:10-14; Deut. 12:15-16, 20-25)—and nearly to the destruction of the savior (vv. 36-46)![7] The writer packs irony into his verb, for here in verse 24 he uses *niggaś* (be hard pressed), which also appeared in 13:6. There Israel is "hard pressed" because of massive Philistine pressure; here, the Philistines are defeated but Israel is *still* hard pressed because of Saul! Saul shows a strange ability to turn deliverance into distress.

For the moment, I want to back up and look at all of chapters 13 and 14. By doing this one can more readily see the vivid contrast our writer paints between Jonathan and Saul. We must see this in order to appreciate the sense of tragedy hovering over the story. I needn't go into profuse detail if the

5. Against Driver (*Notes on the Hebrew Text*, 112) and Klein (*1 Samuel*, Word Biblical Commentary [Waco: Word, 1983], 130, 132) I do not accept the reading of LXX at the end of verse 23 (it adds two sentences to what stands in the Hebrew text). This Septuagintal padding loses the direct contrast in the Hebrew text between verses 23a and 24a and also drops the *niggaś*-clause from 24a with all its loaded irony in the light of 13:6. The translation of verse 24 is not the problem some think it is; 24a simply functions as the heading or subtitle of the whole following section, while 24b picks up the narrative flow, explaining why Israel's troops were "hard pressed." We may translate: "But the men of Israel were hard pressed on that day.... Now Saul put the troops under oath...."

6. Aijalon was approximately twenty miles west of Michmash, and the terrain is not flat like western Kansas. It is no miracle that Israel's troops were faint. "Aijalon lies at a point where the hills give way to the plain, so that the hill country may be considered to have been cleared of the Philistines" (Hans Wilhelm Hertzberg, *I & II Samuel*, The Old Testament Library [Philadelphia: Westminster, 1964], 115).

7. Cf. Ellison's pungent comment: "Saul's oath (24) belongs to those superstitions which think that God is more likely to listen if men indulge in unnecessary self-denial. If God withheld His answer (37), it was because He often takes our stupidities as seriously as we mean them" (H. L. Ellison, *Scripture Union Bible Study Books: Joshua–2 Samuel* [Grand Rapids: Eerdmans, 1966], 58). Klein (*1 Samuel*, 143) observes: "Paradoxically, the troops' redeeming of Jonathan put Saul under the curse of his own oath of v 44."

reader will take the time to consider chapters 13–14 in light of
the structure proposed below:

Success of Jonathan 13:2-4	Success of Jonathan 14:1-15	Wisdom of Jonathan 14:27-30
Fear of Israel 13:5-7	Deliverance of Israel 14:16-23	Offense of Israel 14:31-35
Folly of Saul 13:8-15	Folly of Saul 14:24	Folly of Saul 14:36-44
Distress of Israel 13:16-23	Distress of Israel 14:25-26	Intervention of Israel 14:45-46

Several observations: (1) Although it would not be wise to
press details, a look at each vertical column shows that the
whole narrative repeats the same pattern three times. (2) There
are three positive pictures of Jonathan set in contrast to three
"follies" of Saul.[8] (3) In light of such contrast, it is interesting
to note that chapter 11 used the root *yāšaʿ* (to save) three times
in reference to Saul's activity (11:3, 9, 13) while chapter 14
uses the same root three times in connection with Jonathan's
deeds (14:6, 23, 45; see also v. 39). Not Saul but Jonathan has,
in human terms, become the savior of Israel.[9]

Any reader who really gets dirty in the ink of the text
instinctively senses that Jonathan is royal material. What

---

8. The initiative (13:3-4), imagination (14:6-14), and insight (14:27-30) of
Jonathan stand opposed to the insubordination (13:8-15), stupidity (14:24), and
remorselessness (14:36-44) of Saul. At last Israel must pit her counteroath against
Saul's oath in order to save her savior (14:44-46)!

9. A Saul-Jonathan contrast has often been observed in chapters 13–14; see
e.g., Moshe Garsiel, *The First Book of Samuel, A Literary Study of Comparative
Structures, Analogies and Parallels* (Jerusalem: Rubin Mass, 1990), 85–87, 92.

a splendid king he would make! But that is where the tragedy comes in: Jonathan will never get such an opportunity. To be sure, he is crown prince. But Jonathan has already been rejected as king in the rejection of Saul's dynasty (13:13-14). Jonathan is eminently suited for a kingship he can never have.[10] Our questions fly thick and fast, all our "Whys?" and "What ifs?" Why could not Jonathan have been king instead of Saul? Why does he only get to play John the Baptist to David? Why did Jonathan have to be eliminated? Why must Jonathan's opportunities be squelched by Saul's choices? It is as if the text asks us: What do you suppose God is doing? Why does he work this way? Why are we meeting Yahweh's "unsuccessful ways" again? Why this waste?

Such questions are normal. They are also revealing. They reveal us: twentieth- to twenty-first-century citizens of the western culture we have imbibed. In our minds self-fulfillment is a right. If we've ingenuity and discipline our efforts should be crowned with success. Should we be of a religious bent we happily acknowledge that "God and/or Jesus" assists us in our quest. One can always use such help. But Jonathan seemed to know better. The kingdom was not Saul's or Jonathan's; it was Yahweh's kingdom. For Jonathan, then, the kingdom was not his to seize, not his to rule, but his to serve. I think the rest of 1 Samuel will support my point. Maybe a tragic life isn't tragic if it's lived in fidelity to what Christ asks of us in the circumstances he gives us.

The Judgment of History (14:47-52)

We have now come to the summary section of the second major division of 1–2 Samuel (see the structural comments in the Introduction). Here is a wrap-up of Saul's reign. (Saul's story will continue in chapters 15ff. but more as a foil for David than as king of Israel.) And what surprises us about this summary is that it is so positive. It is pro-Saul. Verses 47-48 are enough to prove this:

---

10. "Jonathan, the 'given man,' cannot be this man. The reason for that lies not in him but in Saul. Saul stands as the great hindrance in the way of Jonathan's succession to the throne. Saul pulls the shining hero down with himself in his collapse" (Karl Gutbrod, *Das Buch vom König*, Die Botschaft des Alten Testaments, 4th ed. [Stuttgart: Calwer, 1975], 103).

Saul consolidated his rule over Israel and made war on all his enemies on all fronts: on Moab, the Ammonites, Edom, the king of Zobah and the Philistines; whichever way he turned, he was victorious. He did great deeds of valour; he defeated the Amalekites and delivered Israel from those who used to pillage him. [NJB]

This catches us by surprise. We've just heard an extended story depicting Saul in negative tones (and we know that the rest of the story will intensify that negativism)—and now we hear such a positive assessment! Whom to believe?

If we want the truth, we must believe both. Verses 47-48 constitute what we may call the judgment of history. By that I do not mean that any other judgments are unhistorical or inaccurate. By the judgment of history I mean that way that people have of assessing a man's achievements, contributions, and relative success (or lack of it). History's judgment is that external human calculation of a person's life and work. It's what folks can observe. By such a standard, Saul had made his mark and made it well. Whether he turned east (Moab, Ammon), southeast (Edom), northeast (Zobah), or west (Philistines), he succeeded in war, he defeated enemies, he delivered Israel.

But Judge History does not have the decisive verdict. (We tend to deify history as we do nature, e.g., Mother Nature). The vital assessment cannot come from the applause of men within history but only from the God who reigns over history. What matters then is not success (whether political or military) but covenant. Yahweh is not looking for winners but for disciples. That is the reason for the negative undertow in chapters 13–14. Saul has begun to fail at the point of the covenant in that he did not submit to the covenant God. And for the Bible covenant obedience matters far more than vocational achievement.

We have then these two estimates of Saul, the historical and the covenantal. Both are true. Saul was, looking at the whole picture, a courageous and militarily successful king. No need to deny that; no reason to hide it. Let us, as 1 Samuel 14 does, readily and thankfully acknowledge it. Two assessments; both true. But only one matters. One can be a historical success and a covenant failure. Like Mary, we should ponder these things in our hearts.

STUDY QUESTIONS

1. If you have read a number of Christian biographies, can you find in them or in Christians you know illustrations of a faith that makes people daring for God. How daring is your own faith?

2. 'Faith does not dictate to God.' How can it, in fact, if it is basically trusting God in all circumstances?

3. Jonathan was a wise son of a foolish father. Can you find examples in the Books of Kings of monarchs who, by God's grace, made good when their fathers had been anything but good?

4. Are you prepared to play second fiddle when you feel you could be the orchestral leader if God so ordains that the former is his place for you?

5. 'For the Bible covenant obedience matters far more than vocational achievement.' Think that through. How much of a reversal of the world's values is it?

Part 3
A Man after God's Heart

1 Samuel 15-31

14

Rejecting the Chosen
(1 Samuel 15)

Chapter 15 begins a new section of the Samuel materials; our writer closed off Saul's reign with the official summary of 14:47-52. In chapter 15 (and the following chapters) Saul and his reign form the foil and backdrop for David's rise. All three major sections of 1 Samuel (see Introduction: Where Shall We Cause Division?) begin with a crisis situation loaded with potential disaster for Israel: the Hophni-Phinehas scandal (ch. 2, furnishing the necessity for raising up new leadership, ch. 1), the royalmania of chapter 8, with its implicit rejection of Yahweh's kingship, and, here, Saul's rejection. Samuel certainly viewed this last as a major disaster for both Saul and Israel—otherwise why be so upset (vv. 11, 35)?

Samuel strikes the keynote of the chapter in verse 1: "Listen," he orders Saul, "to the voice of Yahweh's words."[1] The verbal root šāmaʿ (listen, hear; obey) occurs eight times (vv. 1, 4 [not discernible in English translation], 14, 19, 20, 22 [twice], 24). That is a covenant king's first priority: he must submit to Yahweh's will. That is the matter that matters in this chapter.

Since the chapter is long, it will be useful to catch the flow of the text at a glance. Hence the structural outline:

---

1. See Robert Alter, *The Art of Biblical Narrative* (New York: Basic, 1981), 93–94.

Prophetic direction to Saul, 1
    Vengeance on Amalek, 2-3
    Saul's unfaithful success, 4-9
        The word of Yahweh, 10-11a
            Samuel's response, 11b [narrative, 12]
                Saul's profession, 13
                Samuel's question, 14
                    Saul's explanation, 15
            The word of Yahweh, 16a
                Saul's response, 16b
                    Samuel's accusation, 17-19
                        Saul's protest, 20-21
                            Samuel's announcement, 22-23
        Saul's superficial repentance, 24-31
    Vengeance on Agag, 32-33
Prophetic separation from Saul, 34-35

Now we will attempt to outline the teaching of the chapter.

The Comfort of Vengeance (15:1-9, 18, 32-33)

I intend to punish what Amalek did to Israel—laying a trap for him on the way as he was coming up from Egypt. Now, go and crush Amalek; put him under the curse of destruction with all that he possesses. Do not spare him, but kill man and woman, babe and suckling, ox and sheep, camel and donkey. [vv. 2b-3 NJB]

That was the word of Yahweh of hosts (v. 2a). Saul was to listen to it and obey it (v. 1).

Some readers, however, are bothered not with Saul's partial obedience but with Yahweh's severe command. The total "curse of destruction"[2] sounds horrid. How can these be the words of the God whose compassion is over all that he has made (Ps. 145:9)? How can we claim this passage as the word of this God?

---

2. NJB's "put them under the curse of destruction" (cf. RSV, "utterly destroy") translates a verb form of *ḥrm*, a root occurring eight times in this chapter (seven as a verb, once as a noun; vv. 3, 8, 9 [twice], 15, 18, 20, 21). This concept, sometimes called being placed "under the ban," meant that people, places, and material were off-limits for Israel's use and were to be "devoted" only to Yahweh by destruction or, in the case of nonflammable precious metals, by placing them in Yahweh's treasury. See Leon J. Wood, *TWOT*, 1:324–25, and Walter C. Kaiser, Jr., *Toward Old Testament Ethics* (Grand Rapids: Zondervan, 1983), 74–75.

To begin a response.... First, it *is* horrid. Second, our claim is only that Scripture is true, not that it is sanitized. Third, Yahweh's vengeance should not be repudiated but praised if it is virtuous vengeance, that is, if it is a just vengeance.

Yahweh contends that his vengeance on Amalek is just. He is punishing them for what they did to Israel when Israel came out of Egypt (v. 2b). Amalek attacked Israel even before Israel arrived at Sinai (Exod. 17:8-16), and Moses remembers it was a dirty attack (Deut. 25:17-19; "how he attacked you on the way, when you were faint and weary, and cut off at your rear all who lagged behind you; and he did not fear God," v. 18 [RSV]). For this Amalek was to be wiped out (Exod. 17:14-16; Deut. 25:19). And lest someone worry that descendants are suffering for their ancestors' sins, 1 Samuel 15 indicates that Amalek had not changed over the years. Note that Samuel refers to the current generation of Amalekites as "sinners" (v. 18) and announces Agag's war crimes as the basis for his execution (v. 33). Is Yahweh not slow to anger when he gives them three hundred years to repent?

It is precisely in God's vengeance that his people find comfort! Yahweh does not forget how his enemies have hated, trampled, and crushed his people. To hear "See! Your God will come with vengeance!" (Isa. 35:4) is to hear good news of great joy, for that means that God will put down and overthrow all who strangle and oppress his people. If he does not do that, what ultimate hope do we have? No vengeance on God's enemies means no deliverance for his people. The "full gospel," the good news in all its completeness, always proclaims both the year of the Lord's favor *and* the day of vengeance of our God (Isa. 61:2). His people enjoy his favor, his enemies receive his vengeance. Perhaps we do not understand this as we should. But God's suffering people always have; it is the bedrock of their prayers (Rev. 6:9-10). How vigilant he is to mark all who despise those under his shelter. Some folks put "Beware of dog" signs on their houses or fences; but the sign on Yahweh's kingdom reads "Beware of flock." Rulers and nations who read it should shudder—especially if they have touched and butchered the sheep of his hand.

The Priority of Obedience (15:10-23)

"I am sorry that I made Saul king, for he has turned back from following me, and he has not carried out my words" (v. 11a). Yahweh's "I am sorry" may sound strange to us. (For the present we must hear it; we will seek to understand it later.) But we must pay attention to Yahweh's assessment of Saul: "He has turned back from following me." Saul's failure to carry out Yahweh's orders signals something deeper than failure—"He has turned back from following me." He would no longer be the follower or the servant of the Lord.[3] If we would hear the testimony of this chapter we must accept Yahweh's assessment of Saul.

And Samuel did. But he did not accept it (as we say) sitting down. "Samuel was angry and cried out to Yahweh all night long" (v. 11b). With whom or what was Samuel angry? At Yahweh? At Saul? About the resulting situation? For whom or what did Samuel plead all night? For Saul, seeking forgiveness for him? For Israel, seeking protection for her? For himself, seeking endurance for the coming confrontation? Could the answer be, "Yes—all of the above"? Possibly. We must not make it too simple. As Joyce Baldwin explains:

> In the first place, Samuel's theology was being put in question. Against his better judgment he had co-operated in king-making, announcing that Saul was the one whom the Lord had chosen (1 Sam. 10:1, 24; 11:15). Now it appeared that the Lord, who 'will not lie or repent' (v. 29), had changed his mind, and Samuel could not come to terms with this challenge to God's sovereignty. In the second place, what was to become of the leadership of Israel? The country was in a worse plight than ever. Last but not least, Samuel was torn within himself by the divine word, and needed to settle his own turmoil before the Lord. The personal cost of ministry is seen in the life of Samuel, and in this passage in particular.[4]

---

3. C. F. Keil, *Biblical Commentary on the Books of Samuel* (1875; reprint ed., Grand Rapids: Eerdmans, 1950), 153.

4. Joyce G. Baldwin, *1 & 2 Samuel*, Tyndale Old Testament Commentaries (Leicester: InterVarsity, 1988), 114–15. Compare J. P. Fokkelman: "We should also realize that the introduction of the monarchy and the anointing of Saul are the greatest acts of Samuel's life and have meant all the more to him because they required considerable self-sacrifice on his part. God had to persuade, and even order him in fact, before he could get involved.... The same Lord who first had to win him over (cap. 8) to the monarchy now flatly announces that he is cancelling it and declares

One thing is clear: "Samuel takes no pleasure in Saul's failure, nor in the task that now confronts him."[5] But his distress is not surprising. Most people who pray "Thy kingdom come..." and mean it get worked up when that kingdom is sabotaged.

Saul, however, is upbeat. His greeting to Samuel sounds almost jaunty: "May you be blessed by Yahweh; I have carried out Yahweh's word" (v. 13).[6] His claim directly contradicts Yahweh's previous disclosure to Samuel (v. 11), just as his (and the people's) actions (v. 9) had contradicted Yahweh's previous orders (v. 3).[7]

Samuel's first question is about the racket he was hearing from the flocks and herds (v. 14). The people, Saul avers, spared that good livestock to sacrifice to Yahweh; but there was compliance—the rest they totally destroyed (v. 15). At the end of his second speech Samuel poses his second question: Why have you not listened to Yahweh's voice (v. 19)? Saul again asserts his obedience: he brought Agag home alive but he totally destroyed Amalek as commanded; the people took livestock but only in order to sacrifice at Gilgal (vv. 20-21). Samuel's third question introduces the climax of the dialogue: Does Yahweh find delight in burnt offerings and sacrifices? Do they excite him as much as obeying his voice? We must linger at verses 22-23.

Samuel's words pick up the theme of listening-obeying introduced in verse 1 and debated by Samuel and Saul (vv. 19-20). If we hear Samuel line upon line we find:

Samuel's life work worthless. At least that is how it appears to Samuel at first sight and of course he is... angry" (*Narrative Art and Poetry in the Books of Samuel*, vol.2, *The Crossing Fates (1 Sam. 13–31 & II Sam. 1)* [Assen/Maastricht: Van Gorcum, 1986], 92). See also Calvin's remarks cited in Keil, *Biblical Commentary*, 153–54n.

5. V. Philips Long, *The Reign and Rejection of King Saul: A Case for Literary and Theological Coherence*, SBL Dissertation Series 118 (Atlanta: Scholars, 1989), 141.

6. Note that Samuel's current encounter with Saul occurs on the way to or at Gilgal (vv. 12, 21). Gilgal then is the place where the kingdom was renewed (11:14-15), where the dynasty was lost (13:7b-15), and now where the king was rejected (15).

7. In verse 9 the narrator seems to stress that Saul's and Israel's contravention of Yahweh's directives was quite deliberate. After stating how they spared Agag and the best of the flocks and herds, that is, the fattest ones (? text problem), the male lambs, etc., the writer clearly states: "And they *did not want* to totally destroy them, but whatever was despised or a 'reject'—that's what they destroyed" (emphasis added). I cannot accept David Gunn's contention that there was no culpable failure on Saul's part. For his reading of 1 Samuel 15, see David M. Gunn, *The Fate of King Saul*, JSOT Supplement Series 14 (Sheffield: JSOT, 1980), 41–56. In answer to Gunn, see Long, *Reign and Rejection of King Saul*, 140, 144–45.

Question
> Does Yahweh find delight in burnt offerings and sacrifices as much
> as in obeying Yahweh's voice?

Assertion
> See! Obeying is better than sacrifice;
> to pay attention is better than the fat of rams.

Comparison
> For rebellion—the sin of divination;
> and arrogance—wickedness and idolatry.

Condemnation
> Because you have rejected Yahweh's word,
> Yahweh has rejected you from being king.

Samuel's question and assertion echo Old Testament orthodoxy
(Pss. 40:6-8; 50:8-15; 51:16-17; Prov. 15:8; 21:3, 27; 28:9;
Isa. 1:11-15; Jer. 6:19-20; Hos. 6:6; Amos 5:21-24; Mic. 6:6-8).
Samuel negates sacrifice not absolutely but relatively; he is
saying that formal worship cannot be substituted for obedient
life, external devotions for internal submission. Your Gloria
Patri, Apostles' Creed, Christian luncheons, and all-star Bible
conferences—none of these matter unless you are keeping
Christ's commandments (1 John 2:3-4). The Berleburg Bible
caught Samuel's reasoning: "In sacrifices a man offers only the
strange flesh of irrational animals, whereas in obedience he
offers his own will, which is rational or spiritual worship."[8]

No one, however, will understand Samuel unless he or she
understands and accepts Samuel's evaluation of Saul's lack of
obedience. Samuel's comparison (v. 23a) is crucial here:

> For rebellion—the sin of divination;
> and arrogance—wickedness and idolatry.

Samuel assumes that sin must be rightly identified (not
listening to Yahweh's voice is not failure or misunderstanding
but rebellion and arrogance) and properly compared (it is in
the same category as sheer pagan idolatry). You may not see
the sinfulness of sin on its surface.

---

8. Cited in Keil, *Biblical Commentary*, 156. The Berleburg Bible dates from 1726–29.

One spring I was wrenching the garden hose around our back yard; I occupied myself for some time watering and spraying. I did not discover until later what was really happening. All that time water was washing down a corner of our basement—over the washing machine, shelves, walls. I had not disconnected the garden hose from the outside faucet that winter; it had frozen and split the pipe (or whatever it was), and when I turned the faucet on that spring—waterfall! But I did not see what was really happening at the time, for outside the house all appeared normal.

If we are to have accurate thinking about sin, Saul's or ours, we must see beyond the polite exterior (that can even talk of holding worship services at Gilgal) to what is beneath the surface or behind the scenes. Saul did not listen to Yahweh's voice; he did not obey Yahweh's clear command. One does not call that an alternate religious understanding, or an expression of theological pluralism, or a quest for finding one's identity. It is rebellion. It is arrogance. It is idolatry. "Because you have rejected Yahweh's word, he has rejected you from being king." To reject Yahweh's word is to reject Yahweh himself, to reject his authority—in a word, to reject his kingship. Since Saul had rejected Yahweh as King over him Yahweh rejected Saul as king over his people. All the smoke and fat on Gilgal's altar would never replace the pleasure God could have had from the living sacrifice of Saul's will.

The Problem of Repentance

Our chapter depicts both Yahweh and Saul repenting, and there is a problem with or in the repentance of each. Yahweh's repentance is paradoxical; Saul's is, in my view, superficial.

Yahweh's repentance. First, the problem with Yahweh's "repentance"—or nonrepentance. The difficulty arises because here in the same chapter one finds two very different assertions about Yahweh's repentance (a "repentance" over his will or deeds, not over some sin):

Verses 11 and 35b:
"I repent that I have made Saul king; for he has turned back from following me...."
And the LORD repented that he had made Saul king over Israel.

Verse 29
And also the Glory of Israel will not lie or repent; for he is not a man, that he should repent.

I have given the texts from the Revised Standard Version because it uniformly uses the traditional rendering each time a form of *nāḥam* occurs in these texts. We may think it unusual that God repents about anything but are doubly puzzled when the text asserts that he both repents and will not repent.

I propose we first listen to the text. It is surprising to read that the everlasting God, the creator of the ends of the earth, whose wisdom is unsearchable and who knows the end from the beginning, repents, that is, regrets or is sorry that he has made Saul king. This verb (*nāḥam*) with God as the subject occurs some twenty-nine times in the Old Testament. Although nuances may vary, it never seems to lose a certain emotional element (e.g., sorrow or regret). One can clearly see this in its first occurrence in the Old Testament:

> The LORD was grieved (*nāḥam*) that he had made man on the earth, and his heart was filled with pain. [Gen. 6:6 NIV]

Frequently the first step, upon hearing such a text, is to wax theological and ask how God could be so grieved over something he, if he's God, must have known would happen. The next step is to introduce the term *anthropomorphism* (attributing human forms or character-istics to God) or *anthropopathism* (attributing human feelings to God) in order to indicate that sometimes the Bible must use the grammar of humanity to communicate the truth about deity, that sometimes Scripture stoops to use human categories to tell the truth about a God far beyond all our categories.

That is all right, but there is a danger that we will dismiss the matter there and not go back to the text! We so focus on the form in which the truth comes that we neglect the truth that comes. Did we really hear the parallel clause in Genesis 6:6, "and his heart was filled with pain" (NIV), and sense the intensity of divine sorrow over human sin? And ought not verse 11 of the present chapter move us beyond the problem of anthropomorphisms? "I am sorry that I made Saul king, because he has turned back from following me...." It is a tragedy when Saul refuses to be Yahweh's disciple; it grieves Yahweh. He is not a "you win some, you lose some" god. Nonchalance is never listed as an attribute of the true God. Verse 11 does not intend to suggest Yahweh's fickleness of purpose but his sorrow over sin; it does not depict Yahweh flustered over lack of foresight but Yahweh grieved over lack of obedience. Samuel was not the only one who mourned. The form (Yahweh repenting) in which the text communicates this truth is a bold one; it was probably meant to be so—to get our attention. We need to know that the God of the Bible is no cold slab of concrete impervious to our carefully defended apostasies.[9]

In verse 29 Samuel seems to be emphasizing to Saul that Yahweh's word about tearing the kingdom from him (v. 28) is no mere threat but an irrevocable decision. Yahweh is not using a political or theological scare tactic designed simply to shake Saul up. The Everlasting One of Israel does not play mind games and, unlike man, he does not vacillate in his purposes. His will is no emotional yo-yo. Verse 29 carries shades of Numbers 23:19, where Balaam assures Balak that if God has decreed to bless Israel, as he has, no highly-paid prophet equipped with the latest and best in sacrificial hanky-panky is going to change that. Yahweh has torn the kingdom from Saul, and that is definite; it is unrepentable. There is no "give" in that word.[10]

---

9. The Westminster Confession of Faith (2.1) asserts that God is without "passions." This does not mean he is devoid of feelings. See the discussion in W. G. T. Shedd, *Dogmatic Theology,* 3 vols. (1888; reprint ed., Grand Rapids: Zondervan, 1969), 1:170–78.

10. Incidentally, the firm word of verse 29 does not mean that Saul is beyond personal recovery; it means his kingship is rejected irrevocably. This was, one might say, Saul's finest opportunity to show genuine repentance. He could have said, "Yahweh's word is firm; I cannot reverse it, I cannot now get things back to 'normal.' But I can confess that Yahweh's word is right, I can bow my back under its rod, I can submit to this hard word and live in obedience to Yahweh from this point on, until he gives the kingdom to the man he has in mind. I may be rejected as king, but I may yet be reconciled as man." The following chapters show that Saul did not do this, but this was his opportunity; he was not the victim of fate. Compare Claus Schedl, *History of the Old Testament,* 5 vols. (Staten Island, N.Y.: Alba House, 1972), 3:102: "Saul's soul could have found a remedy, if he had bowed beneath God's judgment of rejection."

However, the writer will not let us forget the paradox in Yahweh's "repentance," for after verse 29 (= Yahweh will not change his mind [*nāḥam*] about Saul's rejection) he conjures up the emphasis of verse 11 in verse 35b (= Yahweh was sorry [*nāḥam*] he had made Saul king). The paradox tends to split our minds, but a little thought tells us that this God who both repents and does not repent is the only God we can serve. Only in the consistent God of verse 29 and in the sorrowful God of verse 35 do we find the God worthy of praise. Here is a God who is neither fickle in his ways nor indifferent in his responses. Here is a God who has both firmness and feeling. If we cannot comprehend we can perhaps apprehend, at least enough to adore.[11]

Saul's repentance. Verses 24-31 depict Saul's "repentance" in response to Samuel's announcement of Yahweh's rejection in verse 23. There is some evidence that grasping the corner or the hem of someone's robe is a gesture of supplication.[12] If so, verses 24-31 relate three appeals by Saul and three responses by Samuel:

Saul's first appeal, 24-25
Samuel's refusal, 26
Saul's second appeal, 27
Samuel's interpretation, 28-29
Saul's third appeal, 30
Samuel's compliance, 31

We saw that Yahweh's "repentance" was paradoxical—he repents and yet will not repent. With Saul repentance involves facing his sin. That poses a question: Is Saul's repentance repentance? Certainly Saul seems to acknowledge his wrong in verse 24, but when he passes into his request (v. 25: "And now, please forgive my sin, return with me, and let me worship Yahweh") it all seems too easy. I have to agree with Hans Wilhelm Hertzberg: "The description continues in such a way as to show us that Saul has evidently not understood

11. On Yahweh's repenting/not repenting, see Kaiser, *Toward Old Testament Ethics*, 249–51.
12. See Robert P. Gordon, *I and II Samuel: A Commentary* (Grand Rapids: Zondervan, 1986), 146, 345; and Long, *Reign and Rejection of King Saul*, 160–62; but especially Paul A. Kruger, "The Symbolic Significance of the Hem (KANAF) in 1 Samuel 15:27," in *Text and Context: Old Testament and Semitic Studies for F. C.*

the seriousness of the situation."[13] Hence Samuel repeats the severe word of verse 23: "For you have rejected Yahweh's word so that Yahweh has rejected you from being king over Israel" (v. 26); as if to say, "Did you really hear me, Saul? It's hardly a matter of saying, 'O.K., I admit I did wrong; now let's get things back to normal.'"

Verses 27-29 reinforce the finality of Saul's rejection. If grabbing Samuel's robe signified entreaty or supplication, its unexpected tearing provided a parable: so Yahweh had torn the kingdom from Saul (v. 28); and that was final (v. 29).

In response Saul makes his third appeal, which is both understandable and revealing: "I have sinned; now please honor me before the elders of my people and before Israel—turn with me so that I may worship Yahweh your God" (v. 30). At one level Saul's request makes perfect sense; if Samuel's conduct gives high visibility to Saul's rejection, there could be dire consequences within Israel: unrest, confusion, disorder. At the same time, Saul's words seem to expose his own priority, as if he had said: "There is sin, but there is also politics; it would be suicidal for me to have an open rift with Samuel; hence it is vital to keep up appearances." The problem is not that Saul's concern is unfounded but that it is so dominant: what really matters is retaining the esteem of men. The support of men is more crucial than reconciliation with God.[14] "What he is most anxious about is that he should not appear dishonored before the people. It is his own reputation that concerns him."[15] If Saul's repentance is superficial we must not be too quick to pick up the first stone, for we ourselves have stood among those who love the praise of men more than the praise of God (John 12:43).[16]

Fensham, ed. W. Claassen, JSOT Supplement Series 48 (Sheffield: JSOI, 1988), 105–16.

13. Hans Wilhelm Hertzberg, *I & II Samuel,* The Old Testament Library (Philadelphia: Westminster, 1964), 128.

14. See my comments in note 10.

15. W. G. Blaikie, *The First Book of Samuel,* The Expositor's Bible (Cincinnati: Jennings and Graham, n.d.), 249.

16. Some readers may wonder why Samuel consented (v. 31) to Saul's last request. Gordon (*I & II Samuel,* 146) has put it tersely: "Samuel—a man (v. 29)!—relents, even though Saul's preoccupation is now with saving face."

The Sadness of Isolation (15:34-35)

Then Samuel went to Ramah, and Saul went up to his home at Gibeah of Saul. Samuel never saw Saul again to the day of his death; but Samuel mourned for Saul, and Yahweh was sorry that he had made Saul king over Israel. [vv. 34-35]

As with 13:15, these verses tell more tragedy than geography. "The Lord's communion with Saul as king through the prophet Samuel was broken."[17] No more direction for Saul from Yahweh's word; no more counsel, no more commands, no more encouragement. Without Yahweh's prophet, Saul is without Yahweh's word—an unbearable silence.

This isolation of Saul from Yahweh's prophet is nothing harsh, bitter, or cold. Quite the contrary; the text breathes both prophetic grief (v. 35b) and divine sorrow (v. 35c).[18] What can be more sad than to be cut off from God's word?

As Samuel plods home to Ramah, his departure spells the absence of Yahweh's word for Saul. But the danger is ours as well. The word of Yahweh can be taken from us whether it comes to us through the warm body of a prophet or the cold print of Scripture (Mark 4:24-25).

Yahweh has rejected the chosen (10:24). In 1 Samuel 16 he reveals a new choice—one for which he will never repent (Ps. 89:28-37).

Study Questions

1. Do you agree that if God pronounces judgement, we as believers must not quarrel with him but agree with him?

2. 'To obey is better than sacrifice.' This is true, but how superlatively good is that ultimate Sacrifice which is itself perfect obedience (Heb. 10:9-14)?

---

17. S. G. DeGraaf, *Promise and Deliverance*, 4 vols. (St. Catharines: Paideia, 1978), 2:102–3.

18. Regarding Samuel's mourning for Saul, Fokkelman observes that mourning usually follows death but here precedes it: "We realize that Saul as king is already dead; no stronger expression of the termination of his monarchy can be imagined" (*The Crossing Fates*, 110).

3. If Yahweh is grieved over lack of obedience, how great must that grief be when in Christ he has shown us even more fully how worthy he is of an obedience which is loving and complete'!

4. We worship a God 'who has both firmness and feeling'. Do you think these qualities should also be united in us, his servants?

5. If grasping the hem of somebody's garment is a gesture of supplication, does this help us to understand Luke 8:43 48?

15

Looking on the Heart
(1 Samuel 16)

No one knows why the town councilmen all looked white as sheets when they met Samuel at the city limits (v. 4). Perhaps such visits were not unheard of (cf. 7:16), but this one was certainly unexpected. Had Samuel gotten wind of some injustice, some wickedness going on in their community? Was this a disciplinary visit? Or maybe all the stuttering and hand-sweating was political. Folks down that way had listened to the news. They knew of the big falling-out between Samuel and Saul. If they receive Samuel, will Saul clamp them in his vise? Relief! A heifer had never looked so good. Samuel had come to sacrifice to Yahweh. So that was it.

Or was it? There is still something hidden here. None of the locals dreamed that in Bethlehem Yahweh was selecting the royalty who would rule his kingdom in this world. And even Samuel had his limits. He knew that Yahweh had "seen" (v. 1) for himself a king among Jesse's sons. But Samuel lacked the whole scoop. Yahweh had only said: "*I* will inform you what you are to do, and you shall anoint for me the one I indicate to you" (v. 3). How much a heifer can hide![1]

---

1. For a lively retelling of Samuel's arrival, see John Hercus, *Out of the Miry Clay* (Downer's Grove, Ill.: InterVarsity, 1968), 2–3. On the ethics of concealment in verse 2, see John Murray, *Principles of Conduct* (Grand Rapids: Eerdmans, 1957), 139–41; and Walter C. Kaiser, Jr., *Toward Old Testament Ethics* (Grand Rapids: Zondervan, 1983), 224–27.

The key word (or key root) in the chapter provides its theme. Yahweh's words introduce this theme in verse 1: "I have seen among his sons a king for myself." That is quite literal. The verb is *rā'āh*, which in this case carries the sense of "provide" (as in Gen. 22:8, 14). This root occurs nine times in this chapter, not readily visible in English translation. It appears as a verb meaning "provide" (vv. 1, 17) or "see, look at" (vv. 6, 7 [three times], 18) and as nouns meaning "appearance" (vv. 7, 12). The ideas of looking and providing in this root contrast with the "not chosen" (negative + *bāḥar*) in verses 8, 9, and 10. Hence the one Yahweh looks to and provides will be his chosen one. That is the theme of chapter 16—Yahweh's choice. Let us now develop the main lines of the teaching of this text.

The Hope in Yahweh's Choice (16:1)

It must have felt like a gray day in December, with rain falling and 41 degrees, especially for someone as perceptive as Samuel. Prospects seemed dark in the kingdom of Israel. Somehow Samuel couldn't view Saul's failure with professional detachment. Yahweh asked Samuel about his grief: "How long will you go on mourning for Saul?" (v. 1; the Hebrew participle indicates continuing activity).

Why was Samuel mourning? Over the failure of his own labors? After all, everything to which Samuel had devoted his life had seemingly collapsed. Was it merely lack of fulfillment in ministry? No; it was "for Saul." Samuel's sorrow was over Saul's rebellion and rejection, over a kingship that had begun with such promise. Doubtless Samuel had personal affection for Saul as well. But the mourning for Saul probably went beyond Yahweh's erstwhile king to Yahweh's people. Samuel may well have been mourning for Saul because he feared that Israel would disintegrate with Saul's sin and rejection. The experiment with kingship that had looked so promising had ended in Saul's polite rebellion against Yahweh and now, without leadership, God's people might self-destruct. Would Israel's enemies ravage her? Would civil strife break out within Israel?[2]

---

2. C. F. Keil, *Biblical Commentary on the Books of Samuel* (1875; reprint ed., Grand Rapids: Eerdmans, 1950), 167. See also my discussion in the preceding chapter on the "priority of obedience" and the section on Saul's repentance.

Yahweh's orders answer Samuel's grief and fears: "Fill your horn with oil and go; I want to send you to Jesse the Bethlehemite, for I have seen among his sons a king for me." That was Yahweh's answer: How long will you keep mourning for Saul? I have provided myself a king. I will not allow my people to become the mashed potatoes of history. I am going to provide new leadership. I have not let go of my people.

Yet was there not something proper in Samuel's grief? He was not upset over a lousy bowling score or because someone sideswiped his Chevy Beretta or because he had only a three-bedroom house. Rather he was distressed over the spiritual disaster of a promising instrument of God, over the welfare of God's people, over their condition and security. Do we ever mourn over such matters? Do we mourn or gossip over the sins of others? Do we ever sorrow over the unbelief in the churches and among the professional ministry? Do we ever grieve over the biblical and ethical ignorance among professing believers? Does anything ever move us, aside from our own comfort and security? There is something commendable, instructive, in Samuel's distress.

And there is something encouraging in Yahweh's instructions. Yahweh is able to provide a new beginning; he will provide for his people when all is coming undone. The true King never loses control of his kingdom; he is never nonplussed by the latest emergency in his realm. Hence Yahweh's choice spells hope.

The Wisdom in Yahweh's Choice (16:6-7)

Jesse's sons come trooping with the rest of their neighbors to the sacrifice, and, with only a look, Samuel has an immediate, intuitive hunch about whom Yahweh has in mind. As the text says:

> When they came, he saw Eliab, and he thought, "Surely his anointed one stands before Yahweh!" Then Yahweh said to Samuel, "Don't look at his appearance or at how tall he is, for I have rejected him; for it's not what man sees—for *man* looks at the outward appearance [lit., with respect to the eyes] but *Yahweh* looks on the heart. [vv. 6-7][3]

---

3. I have translated verse 7 following the Hebrew text as we have it. I know the arguments but am not yet convinced that the text needs correcting on the basis of

The text underscores the peril of our impressions. Yahweh had told Samuel that he had seen a king among Jesse's sons (v. 1). Samuel sees Eliab (v. 6) and fingers his horn of oil. Yahweh must immediately instruct Samuel not to look on what he can see; what man sees does not matter, for man sees to the eyes, while Yahweh sees to the heart (v. 7). Here in verses 1, 6, and 7, the writer rings the changes on the root *rā'āh*.

What a crucial moment this is! In 1 Samuel so much hangs on choices. Israel chose the ark in chapter 4—and disaster followed. Israel chose (in that they desired) a king in chapter 8—another disaster. But now the godly Samuel is on the scene; surely we can trust the faithful prophet of God with the fortunes of God's kingdom? No, the kingdom is safe only with Yahweh. Just as in chapter 3 Eli had to direct a young Samuel, so now God must correct a mature Samuel.

One can understand Samuel's thinking. Eliab was doubtless an impressive hunk of manhood. Around 6' 2" perhaps, about 225 pounds, met people well, all man but with social grace, excellent taste in after-shave lotion, and so on. Perhaps he'd starred as wide receiver for Bethlehem High School football. Probably made the All-Judean All-Star team. Samuel was not alone in his estimate of Eliab. Many thought "Future" was Eliab's middle name.

If we are mesmerized, Yahweh is not. He can see clearly. "It's not what man sees—for man looks at the outward appearance but Yahweh looks on the heart." Such is the principle of God's operation.[4] Thankfully so.

LXX, which includes "as God sees." However, most English versions follow LXX here; the MLB is an exception. A Dead Sea Scroll fragment (from 4QSamb) may support LXX (see Frank Moore Cross, "The Oldest Manuscripts from Qumran," in *Qumran and the History of the Biblical Text,* ed. Frank Moore Cross and Shemaryahu Talmon [Cambridge: Harvard University Press, 1975], 170. Cross's article was originally published in 1955).

4. Yahweh's choice or election in 1 Samuel 16 is an election not to salvation but to office, a choosing not for eternal life but for a function within God's kingdom. I am not saying that the Bible does not teach election to salvation; I am only saying that it is not taught here. The choosing and rejecting in this chapter have reference to the office of kingship. At the same time I think we must beware of inferring any extra baggage about some good-heartedness in David, a concern properly registered by Karl Gutbrod (*Das Buch vom König,* Die Botschaft des Alten Testaments, 4th ed. [Stuttgart: Calwer, 1975], 131), though I think he errs in taking eyes/heart as the vehicles rather than the objects of sight (i.e., God's heart sees rather than God looks on the heart). Strictly speaking, the statement in verse 7 explains the rejection of

Now we can see what would have happened had Samuel
been left to himself. We read verses 6 and 7a and our minds
immediately conjure up 9:2:

> ...Saul, a handsome young man. There was not a man among
> the people of Israel more handsome than he; from his shoulders
> and upward he was taller than any of the people. [RSV; see also
> 10:23-24]

Yet here Samuel looks at Eliab and is sure he sees Yahweh's
anointed. Only Yahweh's "I have rejected him" saves Israel
from ruin. In 16:6-7 we face another Saul situation; Eliab is
created in Saul's image, after his likeness. If Yahweh had not
chosen the king, Israel would have suffered Saul—Act II.[5]

Yet 16:7 reaches forward as well as backward. This text,
which I would call the key verse of 1 and 2 Samuel, sets itself not
only against the likes of Saul and Eliab but also, in later pages,
against everyone's ideal Mr. Israel, Absalom (2 Sam. 14:25-27).
This text also judges Adonijah (1 Kings 1:5-6), though he
appears outside the Samuel materials.

We must not conclude from verse 7 that God opposes fine
appearance, as if ugliness or repulsiveness constitutes the
sine qua non of God's call. The note in verse 12 about David's
robust good looks should knock that notion in the head.
Rather, external appearance neither qualifies nor disqualifies;
it simply does not matter. For Israel's good Yahweh looks on
the heart. That matters.

The text then contains a warning to prophets and others
among God's people; it provides a revelation of our need; it
shows us the discernment we lack. Only Yahweh's wisdom
is adequate for directing his kingdom. There is at least one
thing we can seek to do: beware of the impressiveness of
external appearances. We stumble here, for example, when
congregations or denominations select pastors (cf. John 7:24).

Eliab more than the choice of David. However, Yahweh is about to "find" the man
"after his own heart" (13:14), which does not mean a sinless heart (as subsequent
events will show) but at least means a submissive heart (in contrast to Saul).

　　5. The Saul-Eliab parallel has often been recognized; see, recently, Moshe
Garslel, *The First Book of Samuel: A Literary Study of Comparative Structures,
Analogies and Parallels* (Jerusalem: Rubin Mass, 1990), 113.

What we seem to want are the movers and shakers, the aggressive extroverts, the pushers who meet people well and sell the church in a community, who are smooth in the pulpit. Do we ever ask: How does he pray? Does he enjoy being with his wife? Can he weep?

But if this text reveals our need it also gives us reason for praise. Sometimes Yahweh must save us from our saviors, our self-chosen solutions to kingdom needs or personal dilemmas. And how often he has.

The Surprise in Yahweh's Choice (16:8-12)

Humor and embarrassment conspired to come as uninvited guests to the feast at Bethlehem. Yahweh had rejected Eliab. Jesse introduced Abinadab and Shammah for Samuel's inspection; in each case the verdict was the same: "Yahweh has not chosen this one" (vv. 8b, 9b). No need for Jesse to panic (yet) but some perspiration would be appropriate. But now Samuel has met seven sons and the decision has been the same each time: "Yahweh has not chosen these" (v. 10b). Puzzling, especially when one places Yahweh's revelation of verse 1 ("I have provided myself a king among his sons") beside his nonprovision of verse 10 ("Yahweh has not chosen these"). Samuel can only ask the logical question—Were these the full tally of Jesse's lads? "There still remains the youngest," Jesse confessed, "but, well, he's keeping the sheep" (v. 11). Who knows exactly what that meant aside from the matter of fact? Did Jesse expect Samuel to say, "Right, you can't leave sheep untended"? Or did he mean to imply, "That's where he is, but who knows how long it'll take to run him down? Could take quite a while; maybe..." But Samuel cut the matter down to the bone with his "Send and get him," especially when he added that there would be no sacrificial meal until the youngest son arrived. No shepherd, no food. He came, sheep smell and all. It's the stuff songs are made of (see Ps. 78:70). "This is the one," Yahweh said; Yahweh did as he had said (v. 12b compared with v. 3b).

Hence we have another of Yahweh's who-would-have-thought episodes. There was no need, so Jesse imagined, to invite the youngest; he could stay with the sheep. In fact, the

youngest son is so obscure that we aren't told his name until verse 13. Yet Yahweh insisted, "This is the one." Again we
see God's strange and refreshing way of trampling on human
standards. Again we see how Yahweh chooses the most unlikely people to do his will and how he frequently stands human logic on its head. Our God is not a slave to our conven-
tions.

Perhaps at no time did the living God disclose a more
flabbergasting choice than in the case of David's greater
Descendant. The vote was in. The folks at home said, "He's
just one of us" (Mark 6:3). Others complained, "He has too
much fun" (Matt. 11:18-19), and still others objected, "He's not
from the right place" (John 7:41-42). But the clincher for many
was: "Messiahs don't suffer" (Matt. 27:42-43). And what clout
did this opinion pack? None. "The stone which the builders
rejected has become the head of the corner" (Ps. 118:22; see
1 Pet. 2:4). What should we deduce from that? We should
realize Yahweh made his choice (Ps. 118:23a), and we should
relish it (Ps. 118:23b). There is a delight we should have over
Yahweh's unusual, unguessable ways. It honors him when we
revel in his surprises.

The Costliness of Yahweh's Choice (16:13)

At last Samuel could empty his horn of oil. "So he anointed
him in the midst of his brothers, and the Spirit of Yahweh
rushed upon David from that day onward." Yahweh both
chooses David for kingship and equips him for that work. He
appoints his servant to a task but at the same time gives him
what he needs to fulfill that task.[6]

---

6. On the significance of anointing, see Ralph W. Klein, *1 Samuel,* Word Biblical
Commentary (Waco: Word, 1983), 158–59. Klein (drawing on T. N. D. Mettinger) notes
that the "use of oil in diplomacy, business contracts, nuptial rites, and manumission of
slaves gives anointing a contractual or covenantal meaning. The person or persons
performing the anointing pledged themselves to the recipient and were obligated to
him." Hence, when someone was anointed at God's command, it meant that God
obligated himself to (for example) the king. "The secular anointing [e.g., 2 Sam. 5:3,
though it is hardly secular when it is "before Yahweh"] is the people's way of
pledging fidelity to the king; the sacral anointing expresses Yahweh's obligation to
the monarch or his election of him." Thus Samuel's anointing of David at Yahweh's
direction "places the whole following context under an umbrella of divine promise and
blessing." See also the succinct summary by J. A. Motyer, "Anointing, Anointed," *New
Bible Dictionary,* 2d ed. (Wheaton: Tyndale House, 1982), 50.

But the gift of Yahweh's Spirit is not merely gracious; it is severe. Yahweh equips David, but for conflict, one that will frequently make spine-tingling brawls with lions and bears (17:34-37) seem dull. No sooner does the Spirit touch David than he is catapulted into endless trouble—the envy, anger, and plots of Saul from chapter 18 on. David, the man with the Spirit, will be hunted and betrayed, trapped and escaping, hiding in caves, living in exile, driven to the edge—right to the end of 1 Samuel. We must see this larger view of verse 13 in the context of the whole: The Spirit comes, the trouble begins...

So it was for David's Son and David's Lord. What could be more encouraging than seeing the Spirit coming down as a dove to him? What could be more warming than that familiar voice: "You are my Son, the One I love; I am delighted with you" (see Mark 1:10-11)? And then what? The Spirit drives him out. The wilderness. Temptation. The enemy. Wild beasts (see Mark 1:12-13).

And the servants of David's Lord find the same pattern (Acts 14:22). No sooner are we brought into subjection to Jesus than we are swamped in trouble; there may seem no end to the pressures, no relief from the pounding we seem to be taking. But if we remember David and his Descendant we begin to understand that this conflict is not a sign of our sin but a mark of our sonship, that we are under not God's displeasure but his discipline. The wilderness is not the sign of the Spirit's absence but the scene of his presence. God treats us as sons, perhaps so we can later tell stories of angels who supported us (Mark 1:13) or of "Yahweh who redeemed my life from all distress" (2 Sam. 4:9).

The Irony in Yahweh's Choice (16:14-23)

One crosses a literary divide when one goes from verse 13 to verse 14. David and Saul could not stand in sharper contrast:

> The Spirit of Yahweh rushed upon David from that day onward.
> ... But the Spirit of Yahweh had turned away from Saul, and an evil spirit from Yahweh terrified him.[7]

---

7. "Terrify" or "terrorize" better connotes the flavor of the verb $b\bar{a}'at$ than the more usual "tormented" (as RSV, NIV) or "troubled" (KJV). We should not miss the watershed significance of verse 14 for Saul. As David M. Howard, Jr., has noted: "This was

These verses are, we might say, the hinge of the contrast. But the larger chunks of narrative in chapters 15-17 clearly underscore the stark contrast between Saul and David.

Rejection of Saul, 15
Choice of David, 16:1-13
Deterioration of Saul, 16:14-23
Rise of David, 17

However, our present attention is on 16:14-23, and a closer look at its structure will help us appreciate this passage:

Departure of Yahweh's Spirit, 14
  Proposal for therapy, 15-16
    Saul's authorization, 17
      David's nomination, 18
        Saul's call for David, 19
      David's arrival, 20-21a
    Saul's favor, 21b-22
  Experience of therapy, 23a
Departure of evil spirit, 23b

The center of this section is verse 19, Saul's order or request to Jesse for the services of David. This is the first reference to David by name in this section, as was verse 13 in the previous section. Again, David is the one who is "with the sheep" (as in v. 11). But the primary importance of this centerpoint consists

---

a tragic and momentous occasion for Saul: It is the only time in the O[ld] T[estament] that YHWH's (or God's) Spirit is said specifically to have left someone, and we see in 18:12 that Saul understood the import of this. He had forfeited the presence of YHWH himself" ("The Transfer of Power from Saul to David in 1 Sam 16:13-14," *Journal of the Evangelical Theological Society* 32 [1989]: 476). The terrorist tactics of the evil spirit were ongoing (but apparently intermittent) since the servants' words use the participle of $b\bar{a}^{\,\prime}at$, "keeps terrifying you" (v. 15). We should not, by the way, be surprised that the evil spirit is "from Yahweh." Where else would it come from but from him who is sovereign over all things? However, being an "evil spirit" may not mean morally evil as we sometimes suppose. The adjective ($r\bar{a}^{\,\prime}\bar{a}h$; N.B., not the same as the verb *to see*) can refer to what gives pain, misery, distress, or calamity. Howard is on the right track: "Concerning the nature of this spirit, it must be seen as more than a mere mental disturbance in Saul's case. It certainly introduced the effects of mental disturbance but, coming immediately after the departure of Yahweh's Spirit, it must be seen as an active, external power. Some see a demon here, although it may have been more in the nature of a spirit of calamity or distress" ("Transfer of Power," 482). See also H. L. Ellison, *Scripture Union Bible Study Books: Joshua–2 Samuel* (Grand Rapids: Eerdmans, 1966), 59.

in its irony—the rejected king unknowingly seeks to obtain relief from the newly anointed king! The use of the verb *rā'āh* (to see, provide) in verses 17 and 18 merely intensifies the irony. For example, just as Yahweh says he has "provided for [him]self" a king among Jesse's sons (v. 1), so Saul requests his servants to "provide for [him]" an expert on the lyre (v. 17). Moreover, verses 21 and 22 confirm the wisdom of the one servant's nomination (v. 18) and of Saul's royal order (v. 19), for Saul is greatly taken with David, perhaps not least because David's music brings relief from his terror and derangement. No wonder the writer has placed 16:1-13 and 16:14-23 back to back. He is saying to us: "Look at that! Doesn't that beat all? David is not only Yahweh's choice but Saul's choice! Doubly chosen. What confirmation, eh? And it's the chosen king who keeps the rejected king from falling apart." The chosen king is not a threat but a means of grace to Saul. But the sadness remains: Saul has therapy but not the Spirit of God.

We might ponder David's ministry of consolation to Saul. We know it will not be long before Saul hates David and seeks his life. Yet the picture of 16:14-23 proves instructive for Christ's disciples. Should our call not follow a similar pattern? As Saul will hate David, and as he is rejected by God yet sustained by David's service, so the world hates Christ's people (John 15:18-21) yet, in its doomed state, is only benefited by them. They are the ones who are the salt of the earth (Matt. 5:13), that is, who keep society and culture from rotting into complete decay, who keep the world from being worse than it is. They are a divinely-granted restraint upon the earth's putrifaction; they keep the world from drowning in its own vomit, which, strangely enough, it craves.

Not that Christians have all the answers; but woe betide the world if God's people, for all their faults, are not in it. Spurgeon knew this. One day an agnostic confronted him, challenging his Christian beliefs. Spurgeon pointed out how unbelievers' organizations failed to provide any definite and ongoing program of help to the thousands of needy around them. By contrast he pointed to the various works that flowed from evangelical faith. Then he closed the conversation by paraphrasing Elijah's defiant challenge before the prophets of

Baal (1 Kings 18:24), "The God who answereth by Orphanages, LET HIM BE GOD!"[8] End of discussion.

Endnote

One cannot study 1 Samuel 16 without sensing he or she is in the presence of Jesus Christ. Verse 7 dominates the chapter with its emphatic "*Man* looks on the outward appearance, but *Yahweh* looks on the heart." What is this but an Old Testament rendition of John 2:25, "For *he himself* knew what was in man"? Who then is this before whom we stand? Or have we failed to see him because we put so much stock in appearances (Isa. 53:2-3)?

Study Questions

1. 'Saul's polite rebellion' – quite a phrase! What other surprising adjectives can sometimes be associated with 'rebellion'? Remember that God hates it, whatever form it takes.

2. 'Do we mourn or gossip over the sins of others?' – quite a question! Be prepared for God to ask you that kind of question.

3. 'The future King never loses control of his kingdom' – quite a statement! How does it apply in the context of the present world, your local church, your family, your personal life?

4. 'The outward appearance .... the heart' – quite a contrast! Do we always seek the latter when pastors or elders or deacons are selected?

5. 'The Spirit comes, the trouble begins' – quite a surprise – or is it? If you are facing trouble in connection with your work for Christ, does this mean you are not in his place for you?

---

8. Arnold Dallimore, *Spurgeon* (Chicago: Moody, 1984), 130.

16

Glory to God in the Highest
and on Earth—Thud!
(1 Samuel 17)

A few years ago John Lawing's "What if" cartoons appeared regularly in *Christianity Today*. One of these was a take-off on David and Goliath. It showed a scrawny David with sling dangling to the ground turning up the volume of his feeble voice while Goliath with his "Mother" tattoo on his massive arm stoops down to hear him. And David pipes, "I said, 'We forgive you.'" We can enjoy the humor and at the same time rejoice that Israel did not forgive Goliath! That, our narrative avers, would have been a mistake.

Of course, that is the crucial question: What is the standpoint of the narrative? We can make major errors by not stressing the proper accent of a biblical narrative. If we don't listen to this text, then we'll end up bringing in all the junk about being courageous in the face of "your Goliaths," whether the bully down the street (for primary Sunday-school kids) or—everyone's preoccupation—one's poor self-image. We must protect ourselves from such deafness to the text. One such protection is to note where a narrative talks about Yahweh—that is liable to be where the accent falls. Sometimes there is also a key word or term that provides the main theme. The latter is the case in 1 Samuel 17, for some form of the root *ḥārap* (to reproach, defy, mock, deride) appears six times (vv. 10, 25, 26 [twice], 36, 45). The use of this term in connection with the brute from Gath helps us to view him properly. Goliath is not merely the big goon from Philistia; Goliath's blabbering dishonors Israel's God. That is the orientation. We will develop the teaching under the theme of (David's) faith; but we will not lose sight of this primary direction.[1]

Some Preliminary Matters

Before the exposition we should locate ourselves and be properly introduced to the cast. We are twelve to fourteen miles west of Bethlehem in the Valley of Elah; Socoh and Azekah were strong points on the south side of the valley, the latter a little over two miles northwest of Socoh (see vv. 1-3).[2]

The dramatis personae receive substantial introductions:

---

1. There is a major debate about the text of 1 Samuel 17 (–18). The Septuagint (the Greek translation of the Old Testament, ca. 200 B.C.) does not have verses 12-31, 41, 50, 55-58 as in most English versions, which follow the traditional Hebrew text (called the Masoretic Text). (LXX also omits 18:1-5.) If one reads the story as LXX has it one finds a flowing, consistent account, free from the tensions and apparent inconsistencies of MT. That is why I suspect LXX here; it is too neat. Nor is it free from its own difficulties; see Robert P. Gordon, *I & II Samuel: A Commentary* (Grand Rapids: Zondervan, 1986), 64–66. Some of the problems in MT are: 16:14-23 shows David installed at Saul's court, while chapter 17 has him back in Bethlehem; chapter 17 (vv. 12-15) reintroduces Jesse and David when we've already met them in chapter 16; if Saul had enjoyed David's musical therapy in 16:23, why does he not seem to know David in 17:55-58? Of course, 17:15 indicates David's appearances at court were intermittent and thus explains his absence at Goliath time. But in critical debate 17:15 hasn't a prayer. If 17:15 were not there, someone would scream that there is a contradiction between 16:14-23 and chapter 17. However, when it is there, many dub it an "obvious harmonization," placed there by an editor who wanted to smooth over the discrepancies in the accounts. So it's a no-win situation. Nevertheless, it is only natural for David to be reintroduced in 17:12-15. After all the press given to Goliath (vv. 4-10) surely David merits equal time. And MT specifies Jesse as "this/that Ephrathite" (v. 12), that is, the one who had already been mentioned (16:1, 18-19). As for verses 55-58, note that Saul's question is about *whose son* David is (three times). It is not that Saul doesn't know David's name but he wants certitude about his roots, since his father's house was to be made free (from taxation?) in Israel (v. 25). But don't 16:19, 22 show that Saul knew who David's father was? Not necessarily; such communication even at Saul's rustic court would be drafted by a bureaucrat, not directly by Saul. My own preference for MT in chapter 17 is no symptom of conservative paranoia; Robert Polzin argues for it (and especially the place of vv. 55-58) on literary grounds (*Samuel and the Deuteronomist* [San Francisco: Harper and Row, 1989], 161–76). On the problem of 2 Samuel 21:19 (Elhanan kills Goliath), see R. K. Harrison, *Introduction to the Old Testament* (Grand Rapids: Eerdmans, 1969), 704.

2. For a description see George Adam Smith, *The Historical Geography of the Holy Land,* 22d ed. (London: Hodder and Stoughton, n.d.), 226–28.

Geographical setting, 1-3
　Appearance of Goliath, 4-7
　　Goliath's words, 8-10
　　　Fear, 11
　　Arrival of David, 12-22
　　Goliath's words, 23
　　　Fear, 24-25
　David's words—theology, 26-27
　Eliab's complaint—contempt, 28-30

I should like to pick up the exposition at verse 26; however, I want to make two observations about these extended introductions given Goliath and David.

First, Goliath makes quite an impression. The writer makes sure we are awed with his line-upon-line description of Goliath's size, his protective armor, his offensive weaponry and the weight thereof (vv. 4-7). It's not hard to see an object 9' 6" high. That he wore about 126 pounds of armor and wielded a spear with a 15–16-pound iron head is, without doubt, a weighty consideration.[3] Then we must listen to three verses of his hairy-chested braggadocio (vv. 8-10) as Goliath bellows for a challenger to engage him in single combat.[4] No one has any trouble hearing him. Saul and Israel are both impressed and depressed (v. 11).

It seems that we have heard something about impressions, something that applies to giants as well as to kings? J. P. Fokkelman nicely reminds us:

> The reader just coming from Ch. 16, however, realizes that the impressive appearance provokes a thought rather on the lines of "Take no notice of his appearance or his tall stature!" [16:7] A prophetic criticism of this kind would not only have heartened the men of Israel but even given them a radically new view of the Philistine champion.[5]

---

3. Ralph W. Klein, *1 Samuel*, Word Biblical Commentary (Waco: Word, 1983), 175-76.

4. Cf. Roland de Vaux, *The Bible and the Ancient Near East* (Garden City, N.Y.: Doubleday, 1971), 122–35, and Claus Schedl, *History of the Old Testament*, 5 vols. (Staten Island, N.Y.: Alba House, 1972), 3:104–7.

5. J. P. Fokkelman, *Narrative Art and Poetry in the Books of Samuel*, vol. 2, *The Crossing Fates (1 Sam. 13–31 & II Sam. 1)* (Assen/Maastricht: Van Gorcum, 1986), 148.

Fokkelman may be too optimistic about Israel's potential response. But there is no excuse for us readers. We have 16:7. And Goliath is simply fodder for another application of that text. Here again is external appearance. We must see that 16:7 applies both to our finest choices and to our most formidable enemies.

A second preliminary observation: one cannot help seeing a stroke of providence in the lengthy introduction of David (vv. 12-23).[6] One comes to verse 12 with genuine relief. The biblical writer is anything but bungling; indeed, he is kind. A reader (assuming he or she really gets wrapped up in the text) carries away a lot of tension from verses 4-11. There I see this armored superman from Philistia (vv. 4-7), hear his superwords (vv. 8-10), and watch Saul and Israel frantically searching for the panic button (v. 11). Then I read, "Now David was a son of a man, this Ephrathite, from Bethlehem-judah ..." (v. 12). What a literary relief! A little family history never sounded so good.

And yet one realizes upon reflection that he is getting more than a momentary break from Goliath. The "now Davids" continue (vv. 14, 15), and the whole section follows David step by step until he is at the front lines and hears the brute from Gath. Had Jesse only known how much would rest on the parched grain, bread, and cheese David was lugging to the Valley of Elah. Had he only known how critical David's mission would be! But it's all so low-key and natural: "Now David, son of a man, this Ephrathite...." So it continues all the way: "And he went as Jesse had commanded him..." (v. 20). "Everything seemed to be casual, yet those things which seemed most casual were really links in a providential chain leading to the gravest issues."[7] Then Goliath talked one time too many—and David heard (v. 23). You know the rest.

---

6. It is interesting to note the detailed pattern of verses 12-23—short sections about David interspersed with one-liners about *the* Philistine or the Philistines:
David—explanation, 12-15
Philistine, 16
David—mission, 17-18
Philistines, 19
David—arrival, 20-22
Philistine, 23a
(David heard, 23b)
7. W. G. Blaikie, *The First Book of Samuel,* The Expositor's Bible (Cincinnati: Jennings and Graham, n.d.), 279.

Casual. Natural. But don't forget to worship before you proceed. Phillips Brooks was right: How silently, how silently the wondrous gift is given!

In chapters 13–14 Jonathan seemed to be the only believer in Israel (cf. 14:6). In chapter 17 David fills that role. Hence I will structure the exposition around the theme of David's faith without, however, ignoring the honor of Yahweh as the driving concern of the chapter.

The Voice of Faith (17:26)

"What will be done for the man who strikes down this Philistine?" David apparently wanted to know what would be in it for him should he take the risk (cf. v. 25). But this was not his whole question.

> Then David said to the men standing near him, "What will be done for the man who strikes down this Philistine and shall turn away derision from Israel? For who is this uncircumcised Philistine that he should deride the ranks of the living God?"

"David injects the first theological note into the narrative." [8]

Nevertheless, let us place literature before theology for a moment. This is the first time David talks—in the Bible, that is. I don't mean, of course, that in the events of chapter 16 and 17 (so far) David had never spoken to anyone. But as you read this material you now observe that as the writer has told the story he has never, to this point, represented David as saying anything. David has been a literary mute.[9]

Now there are some people (readers can recall examples at their leisure) who pretty much talk nonstop. They even comment on what does not need commentary and react to what requires no reaction. One's only defense from such a barrage is to tune them out. On the other hand, sometimes one has a friend or an associate who is rather quiet and pensive,

---

8. D. F. Payne, "1 and 2 Samuel," *The New Bible Commentary: Revised* (Grand Rapids: Eerdmans, 1970), 296.

9. This point surprised me when I happened on to it. I have since discovered that Polzin (*Samuel and the Deuteronomist*, 168) has alluded to it. The reader may want to compare Noah's silence in the flood narrative. What do you make of the fact that Noah never talks from Genesis 6:9 to 9:19?

one not particularly bashful but who simply doesn't thrive on hearing himself. When this friend speaks in some discussion or on some issue we are likely to perk up. He doesn't often speak, so when he does, we assume his words will be weighty and important—at least for him.

That is why David's words in verse 26b are as heavy as Goliath. David has never spoken before in our story. Now the silence is broken. David brings a whole new world view. To this point the narrative has been "godless" (much like our own stewing over some insoluble dilemma), but now David injects the godly question into the episode. Doesn't having a living God make a difference in all this? This fellow has mocked "the ranks of the living God." If God is so identified with Israel, do you think he is indifferent toward such slurs on his reputation? Do you expect a living God to allow an uncircumcised Philistine to trample his name in military and theological mud? Israel thought the Philistine invulnerable; for David he was only uncircumcised. A living God gives a whole new view of things.

David's question is not a magic charm for solving every problem; but surely it instructs us. It shows us how crucial it is that we hold the right starting point, that we raise the right question at the very first. All the believer's life and all the church's life requires theocentric thinking. The tragedy is that were someone to hear our thoughts and words in our dangers and troubles they would never guess that we had a *living* God.

The Vitality of Faith (17:34-37)

Eager as he is to eavesdrop on Saul's interview with David (vv. 31-39),[10] the reader meets at least one obstacle. We have to hear Eliab vent his spleen on David in typical older-brother style (v. 28):

> Why have you come down? And with whom have you left those few sheep in the wilderness? *I* know your insolence and the evil of your heart—you've come down to see the battle.

---

10. Cf. Fokkelman, *The Crossing Fates*, 161.

David gives a normal youngest-brother response: "What have I done now?" (v. 29a). Sounds like exasperation over a few years of carping. The last of David's words are a bit difficult, but something like "Can't I even talk?" (cf. NIV) may catch the sense.

One must not breeze by Eliab. Eliab tends to be a mirror. In 16:6 he was a mirror of the handsome Saul of 9:2. Here, however, Eliab mirrors someone else. His tongue drips contempt as he alludes to David's "few sheep in the wilderness" and when he omnisciently declares the evil of David's heart. Eliab is Goliath. He is Goliath before Goliath. Goliath will express contempt for David (vv. 42-44), but Eliab has already expressed it.

In fact, one might say David has to fight three Goliaths in this chapter, for in Eliab he faces the contempt of Goliath and in Saul he meets the mind of Goliath (i.e., it's only the experienced [v. 33] and equipped [vv. 38-39] warrior who carries the odds of winning). All that before he faces the carcass of Goliath himself (vv. 41-50).

Now comes the conversation between Saul and David; our attention fastens on David's words in verses 34-37a, for, it seems, they are the intended focus of the whole section (vv. 31-40). The following structure, which shows how David's speech is the hinge of the paragraph, supports this contention.

> Report to Saul, 31
>   David's willingness, 32
>   Saul's objection, 33
>   David's answer, 34-37a
>   Saul's consent and provision, 37b-38
>   David's "weakness," 39-40a
> Approach to Philistine, 40b

David's answer (vv. 34-37a) tells his secret, what it is that so enlivens faith that it dares to stare the premier citizen of Gath in the eye.

"Your servant has been shepherding sheep for his father" (v. 34). David explains what sheep have to do with Philistines. A shepherd lives with constant threat to his life and flock. (Perhaps David would suggest we read Genesis 31:38-40 *before* Psalm 23.) It was not unusual for a lion or a bear to make off with one of David's sheep. In such cases he went after it, struck down the marauder, and forced it to release its prey. If it turned on him, he collared it and struck it until he killed it. David uses the verb *nākāh* (to strike, strike down) three times in verses 35-36. As if to make the point with Saul: Don't say I've no experience of war; striking down enemies is part of my job—it's just that they are ferocious mammals rather than arrogant giants. And this Philistine has consigned himself to the lion-and-bear heap, "for he has mocked the ranks of the living God" (v. 36). Then comes the bottom line:

> *Yahweh* who delivered me from the paw of the lion and bear—*he* will deliver me from the hand of this Philistine. [v. 37; emphasis in Hebrew]

There is the interpretation of David's experience. He does not ascribe his escapes to luck or skill or audacity; *Yahweh* delivered me. Looking back in faith enables him to look forward in faith: "He will deliver me from the hand of this Philistine." What Yahweh has done in the wilderness of Judah he will do in the Valley of Elah.

This is instructive for the people of God. Faith is sustained in the present and for the present as it remembers Yahweh's provision in the past. The rich history of God's past goodnesses nurtures faith in its current dilemma. It is here that memory (Yahweh delivered me then and there) and logic (If he handled that, is he not adequate for this?) can be handmaids of faith. It is so crucial to remember God's past deliverances. If you've trouble doing so, invest in a diary. In God's economy no experience is wasted.

You must keep verse 37 ("*He* will deliver me") before you. If you don't, you will misconstrue verses 34-36. David will be delivered not because he has true grit but because he knows the true God. Circumstances vary, but Yahweh is the same whether among the sheep or in front of the Philistines.

The Victory of Faith (17:41-54)
At last we come to the combat itself, except that there is not much of it. Let us chart this section in order to discover what the text emphasizes:

The Philistine, 41-44
David's speech, 45-47
The contest, 48-49
Aftermath (losing your head and your army), 50-54

I want to make several comments about this arrangement. First, observe how the writer allows Goliath to dominate the scene in verses 41-44. Five times he specifically mentions the Philistine. "The Philistine" went, looked, said, cursed, and said again. Five times the writer specifies the subject with each verb—the Philistine this, the Philistine that, as if the text itself trembles under Goliath's tread! Goliath, of course, was used to dominating occasions and so the writer allows him his custom here. After all, Goliath would want it that way.

Secondly, notice how much press is given to David's speech (vv. 45-47) as compared with the combat itself (vv. 48-49). In the Hebrew text David's speech takes some sixty-three words while the combat report needs only thirty-six. After all the anticipation the knock-out blow comes so quickly; one might say in the first round. We should not, however, underestimate David's sling-and-stone routine. Such stones would range from two to three inches in diameter and, when flung by an accomplished warrior, could reach speeds of 100 to 150 miles per hour,[11] all of which could make for a stunning victory.

Third, David's speech is the third of his (major) speeches in the chapter (v. 26, vv. 34-37a, vv. 45-47), all of which are theologically loaded. It is as if the writer makes David his expositor, and, if one listens to David, he will understand the meaning of the event:

You are coming to me with a sword, a spear, and a javelin, but I am coming to you in the name of Yahweh of hosts, the God of the ranks of Israel, whom you have mocked. This very day Yahweh will close you up in my hand, and I shall strike you down and take your head off you and give the corpse of Philistia's army this very day to the birds of the sky and the beasts of the earth—that all the earth may know that there is a God in Israel; and that all this assembly may know that it's not with sword or spear that

---

11. J. K. Hoffmeier, "Weapons of War," *ISBE*, rev. ed., 4:1040.

Yahweh saves; for the battle is Yahweh's, and he shall give you [plural] into our hand.

Here we note the obvious: David can match Goliath for spicy speech; he can carry on about corpses and carrion as well as the big fellow (vv. 44, 46). There is no reason why the Philistines should have all the juicy lines. More important, David avers that all the earth will know from the box score in tomorrow's papers that there is a God, a real God, in Israel (v. 46). Yahweh of hosts, the God Goliath ridiculed, will show what puny powers Goliath serves (note that Goliath had cursed David "by his gods," v. 43). However, David especially stresses that Yahweh saves not by the instruments of human power but through the weakness of his servants. Goliath comes with sword, spear, and javelin (v. 45), but before the day is over everyone in the Valley of Elah is going to know that Yahweh does not save by sword or by spear (v. 47). The aftermath section (vv. 50-54) underscores this very point: David overcame the Philistine with the "sling and stone"; there was "no sword in David's hand" (v. 50). That's why he had to borrow Goliath's—without permission—to finish off the giant (v. 51). Yahweh gave victory but he gave victory through what the world regards as weakness.

This theme of "weakness" has been building throughout the chapter. All the important people regard David as weak. If we might colloquialize, Eliab tells him, "You're a pain" (v. 28), Saul warns, "You're green" (v. 33), and Goliath sneers, "You're puny" (v. 42). But he is the one Yahweh uses to deliver. Nor does David have the right equipment: he refuses to be a little Goliath and lays aside Saul's armor and sword (vv. 38-39); he insults Goliath with his staff (cf. v. 43); but he demonstrates that Yahweh brings deliverance without the symbols of man's strength (vv. 47, 50). We hear this throughout the Bible (see, e.g., Pss. 20:7; 33:16-19; 147:10-11; 2 Cor. 12:7-10). What matters is not whether you have the best weapons but whether you have the real God. In fact, your "inadequacy" may be precisely your qualification for serving God; for his strength shines most brightly behind the foreground of your weakness.

This holds true not only in Israelite-Philistine conflicts but also in the life of the individual believer. Under the reign of paganism, a Christian woman, even though she was pregnant, was condemned to die for her profession of faith. The day before her execution, she went into labor, naturally crying out in her pangs. The jailor took the opportunity to ridicule her: "If you make a noise to-day, how will you endure a violent death to-morrow?" She replied, "To-day I suffer what is ordinary, and have only ordinary assistance; to-morrow I am to suffer what is more than ordinary, and shall hope for more than ordinary assistance."[12] There was no bravado, no idolatry about having strong faith. She simply knew her weakness and precisely in that weakness she expected "more than ordinary assistance."

The Vision of Faith

I want to pick up on comments made at the beginning of this chapter about the primary theme of 1 Samuel 17. There I argued that the repeated use of some form or derivative of *hārap* (to deride, mock, defy, taunt) provides the focus of the chapter.

Those forms of *hārap* appear six times. Goliath himself says that he mocks or defies the ranks of Israel (v. 10) and Israel's troops acknowledge that he has done just that (v. 25). Only David seems concerned to turn away this mockery and derision of Israel (v. 26a), for he recognizes that mockery of Israel is mockery of Israel's God (v. 26b). David asserts this point with both Saul (v. 36) and Goliath (v. 45).

Hence the driving concern of this chapter is the honor of Yahweh's name, his reputation, his glory. David is driven by a passion for the honor of God. Does this make any difference in how one interprets the chapter? Yes! It should keep us from going around talking about the cleverness of David or the bravery of David. The focus of the chapter is not on David's courage but on Yahweh's adequacy in David's weakness. David himself has told us this (vv. 37, 45, 47). An interpretation that refuses to see this steals the glory from God which in this Scripture he has designed to receive for himself. Hermeneutics can be hazardous. The chapter will allow us to

---

12. John Whitecross, *The Shorter Catechism Illustrated from Christian Biography and History* (reprint ed., London: Banner of Truth, 1968), 169.

focus on David in one respect, to follow him in one particular, namely, to share the vision of his faith, a faith that kept its eyes fixed on the honor of Yahweh. Hence in this chapter David essentially says to Israel and to us: "Yahweh's reputation is at stake; that matters to me; that matters enough to risk my life for it."

Can we say that? Is that our vision, our point of view? What situations are there in our own day, in our own various worlds, where we can clearly see God's honor is at stake? Can we say that that matters to us more than our advantage or reputation or security?

These questions may not often be answered in great, breath-taking scenarios where Philistines and Israelites by the hundreds look on. More often it will be in the pastor's study when he tells a couple he will not perform their marriage ceremony because in doing so he would be uniting a professing Christian with, from all he can discern, an unbeliever. It may anger the couple; it may anger the family; the family may leave the church. My reputation or Yahweh's honor? Or it will be with your associate at work who uses God's name and that of his Son as though they were punctuation marks. And you take him or her aside, confront the person about the matter, explaining that offending you does not matter but offending God will. Will that person think you worse than weird? Might you not face ridicule for your efforts? And yet, whose honor matters?

In 1 Samuel 17 the promised king defeats the enemy of his people. He had to do it, for the enemy derided Yahweh. Yahweh's honor, his glory, must be upheld; if Yahweh is to have his glory his enemy must be silenced. Without the thud there would be no glory. It is the same in the reign of David's greater Son; some refuse to "kiss the Son" (Ps. 2:12) and so there must be a "rod of iron" (Ps. 2:9).

STUDY QUESTIONS

1. 1 Samuel 16 is a very reassuring chapter, coming as it does before Chapter 17. Isaiah 52:13-53:12 is an amazing prophecy of Christ. Can you see that Isaiah 52:13 fulfils a similar function in relation to that passage?

2. A person's words should be weighed, not counted, and the same applies to the books in a Christian's library. How heavy are your words and books?

3. 'Theocentric thinking' – it should be normal for Christians but often proves to be rare. Is it the normal way you think?

4. 'In God's economy no experience is wasted.' Think that through in terms of your own life. It will enable you to find causes of thankfulness in the unpleasant as well as the pleasant times.

5. 1 Samuel 17 emphasises David's weakness. Study the way Paul deals with the theme of weakness in 2 Corinthians 10-13.

17

The Shadow of the Almighty
(1 Samuel 18–19)

Country music changes things. At least it did in Israel; at least it did for Saul (and because it changed things for Saul it willy-nilly changed them for David). When war season was over (18:6) and the troops were returning from the Philistine campaign, the Israelite women came out to welcome them home from Operation Elah. They danced, sang, and celebrated. The text includes a snatch of their victory song:

> Saul has slain his thousands
> and David his ten thousands. [18:7]

They were not trying to be political; they hardly intended a dig at Saul. But Saul is the older brother at the prodigal's party (Luke 15:25-32). Saul's ear went far beyond beat and melody; he heard far more than soprano and alto. He analyzed lyrics and decided the girls might better use their talents on a dirge for a funeral in Bethlehem (18:8-9). While Saul awaits his opportunity, we should back up and begin to set out the teaching of these chapters.

Yahweh's Servant Is So Provocative (18:1-9)
Goliath's fall shook more than the ground. Everyone, it seems, now took notice of David. At the first of these chapters our writer relates a dual reaction to David, one that will pervade the rest of 1 Samuel; he places Jonathan's esteem (18:1-5) side by side with Saul's envy (18:6-9).

Jonathan was apparently taken with David immediately. "Jonathan loved him like his very self" (v. 1 NJB). Because of this they made a covenant. Jonathan, so verse 3 indicates, took the initiative: "So Jonathan—along with David—cut a covenant because he loved him as himself." If we press the verb, the bond was inaugurated by severing an animal and by both parties passing between the pieces as if to say, "If I am unfaithful to my word in this covenant, may I end up in pieces as this animal."[1]

But there was more. Jonathan also stripped himself of his robe and gave it to David, as well as his war coat or armor, his sword, bow, and belt (v. 4). All this was both significant and surprising; significant because the clothes signify the person and his position—hence Jonathan renounces his position as crown prince and transfers, so far as his own will goes, the right of succession to David.[2] No one in the Near East would do that. (It's like telling your real estate agent, "Let's set the price fifteen thousand dollars lower; I'm not concerned to get as much as I possibly can for my house." And his or her reaction is. . . ?) You did not transfer your crown rights to an upcomer, you eliminated him! But Jonathan does not ape the boring expectations of his culture. S. G. DeGraaf is on the right track when he says, "This deed on his part was an act of faith. Only faith makes us willing to be the lesser. Faith causes us to surrender the rights we pretend to have over against the Christ, who is truly Israel's king."[3]

1. See *TWOT*, 1:456–57.
2. See Stan Rummel, "Clothes Maketh the Man—An Insight from Ancient Ugarit," *Biblical Archaeology Review* 2 (June 1976): 6–8; P. Kyle McCarter, Jr., *I Samuel,* The Anchor Bible (Garden City, N.Y.: Doubleday, 1980), 305; and J. P. Fokkelman, *Narrative Art and Poetry in the Books of Samuel,* vol. 2, *The Crossing Fates (1 Sam. 13–31 & II Sam. 1)* (Assen/Maastricht: Van Gorcum, 1986), 198. Rummel refers to an Akkadian document discovered at Ugarit in which Utrisharruma, a thirteenth-century king of Ugarit, makes a divorce settlement with his queen. The couple's son, the crown prince, may go with his mother if he wants, but in that case he will abdicate his right to the throne. He must indicate this decision by leaving his *clothes* on the throne. Compare also Numbers 20:22-28 and I Kings 19:19-21. In the last scene of chapter 19 Saul, rendered harmless by the power of God's Spirit, strips off (*pāšaṭ*, 19:24; same verb as in 18:4 of Jonathan) his clothes, which may signify that even Saul, against his will, acknowledges that he has forfeited the kingship (cf. Robert P. Gordon, *I & II Samuel: A Commentary* [Grand Rapids: Zondervan, 1986], 165).
3. S. G. DeGraaf, *Promise and Deliverance,* 4 vols. (St. Catharines: Paideia, 1978), 2:116.

Saul will have none of this. Not after he hears the ladies' accolades for David (vv. 8-9). David draws such different reactions: faithful love from Jonathan, murderous envy from Saul. David's Descendant had the same knack for bringing division (John 7:43; 9:16; 10:19). "I have come to set a man against his father" (Matt. 10:35); Jonathan would have understood *him* perfectly.

Yahweh's Favor Is So Clear (18:10-30)

One cannot miss the repetitions in chapter 18. There are four references to David's success (vv. 5, 14, 15, 30), three assertions that Yahweh is "with" David (vv. 12, 14, 28), and six uses of some form of the verb *to love* (Hebrew, *'āhab*) with David as the object (vv. 1, 3, 16, 20, 22, 28). Everyone seems to love David. Jonathan loves David; Michal loves David; all Israel and Judah love David. Not Saul, however; he fears and stands in awe of David; the text says so—three times (vv. 12, 15, 29).

It may be easier to catch this emphasis on David's success and Yahweh's favor visually. If we take in all of chapter 18, we can summarize it this way:

Saul's son and his clothes, 1-4
    David's success, 5
Saul's displeasure and his spear, 6-11
    David's success, 12-16
Saul's daughter and her price, 17-27
    David's success, 28-30

In any case, at the end of the chapter the point has been drummed into us: David is successful because Yahweh is with him, and everyone (almost) loves David.

But there is another emphasis in the chapter, not as easily seen. We can see it but David probably couldn't at the time. The reader sees both Yahweh's favor and Saul's malice; he sees that David is the object of both Yahweh's goodness and Saul's envy. Saul's scheme to eliminate David remains a secret in chapter 18; it doesn't come out in a cabinet meeting until 19:1. And David seems unaware of his danger.

Naturally, some readers will wonder about that last statement. How could David swivel twice from Saul's flying spear and not think he was in danger (18:10-11)? David was playing his lyre because Saul was having one of his "spells" (v. 10; cf. 16:23). That may well have been how Saul's attendants talked about him at such times: "The king's really bad today, David." They may well have thought of Saul's condition as something not quite under his control (cf. 16:15). In any case, Saul's moodiness was well known, and David would have no particular reason to interpret Saul's spear throws as murderous in design. More likely they were construed as outbursts of Saul's recurring madness. Dangerous but not malicious.

Even less would David have cause to suspect Saul's offers of his daughters in marriage. Saul's intent was clear (vv. 17b, 21, 25) but secret: If David fought the Philistines long enough both the law of averages and some Philistine would be sure to catch up with him. Saul would be saved the messy part. For whatever reason Saul reneged on his offer of Merab, his older daughter (vv. 17-19; cf. 17:25). But Saul was delighted when he heard that Michal, his younger daughter, loved David (v. 20). Michal would be useful. With a little indirect communication through his lackeys (who also would have no reason to know his real intentions) Saul made it clear that if David was strapped to come up with the proper bride price he needn't fret. All the king wanted for a marriage present was a little vengeance on his enemies. Let David knock off a hundred Philistines, bring their foreskins to Saul, and he'd call it square (vv. 22-25). Meanwhile, Saul would trust in his law of averages. David took Saul's offer but thought one woman worth two hundred Philistines, supplied the double tally of gruesome tokens, and walked off with Michal (vv. 26-27).[4]

Here is where Yahweh's favor appears most brightly yet most quietly—in his protection of David in danger of which David was unaware. Chapter 18 contains two keynotes side

---

4. Some people are repulsed by such ancient "barbarism." But barbarism is as much modern—more so—than ancient, something a little history of warfare and of persecution will make clear. At least these Philistines were dead before they were mutilated; much warfare is not so "merciful." Such practices were not uncommon in the Near East. Egyptians might count severed hands of their enemies (cf. Judg. 8:6, Heb.); Assyrians might tally heads. Egyptians sometimes cut off and counted the male organs of the sea peoples they killed in battle. See Claus Schedl, *History of the Old Testament*, 5 vols. (Staten Island, N.Y.: Alba House, 1972), 3:118. Philistine males did not practice circumcision as did Israelites and others (e.g., Moabites, Ammonites); hence Saul could ask for a hundred foreskins of Philistine dead.

by side: Yahweh's favor and Saul's malice; but the former is stronger than the latter. Was this written only for David's sake? Might it mean to suggest that this quiet protection of Yahweh is the heritage of others among his servants? Might it imply that much of Yahweh's protection is completely unknown to you? Maybe you should sit down again with Mary and ponder these things in your heart (Luke 2:19).

Yahweh's Protection Is So Consistent (19)

It happened at a top-secret staff meeting (19:1). Saul laid his design on the table: his men were to kill David. So begins a chapter in which Saul engages in a whole chain of deliberate plans to wipe out David and in which David experiences a whole chain of deliverances (of deliberate plan?) in highly unusual circumstances.[5] The chapter consists of four deliverance episodes (vv. 1-7, 8-10, 11-17, 18-24). We should survey these; then I want to highlight certain marks of Yahweh's protection appearing in them.

No sooner had Saul disclosed his plan than Jonathan, Saul's son, intervened on David's behalf. After putting David on alert (vv. 2-3), Jonathan conferred with Saul, pressing rational, moral, and theological considerations upon him: David has not wronged you; he risked his life for Israel when he killed Goliath; Yahweh saved us and you were so glad; "why will you sin against innocent blood by putting David to death for nothing?" (vv. 4-5). With a mercurial about-face Saul went on oath guaranteeing David's safety (v. 6). Jonathan informed David and brought him back to court. The whole difficulty had been worked out (v. 7). Amazing how many dilemmas can be resolved if we simply face them and talk them out. Or so it seemed.

But there was more war, more Davidic success—and more Saulide madness. The evil spirit from Yahweh was plaguing Saul (we must not forget he is a man under Yahweh's judgment). On this occasion David provided his customary music for Saul, and Saul's "spear was in his hand" (v. 9). Saul's

---

5. Karl Gutbrod, *Das Buch vom König*, Die Botschaft des Alten Testaments, 4th ed. (Stuttgart: Calwer, 1975), 161.

spear always seemed to be in his hand. Again he attempted to nail David to the wall but succeeded only in nailing the wall. David evaded the throw and fled home. There is a sad irony about verses 8-10. In verse 8 David "struck down" (Hebrew, *nākāh*) the Philistines so that they fled (Hebrew, *nûs*); in verse 10 Saul tries to "strike down" David so that he is forced to "flee" (same verbs as in v. 8). Hence David, the victor over the Philistines, is treated like a Philistine.

Yet home was no refuge, for Saul had posted his henchmen to watch the door and to dispose of David in the morning (v. 11a). One can imagine an animated, whispered conversation between Michal and David in their little kitchen. Michal had perhaps seen Saul's hit men in their positions, for she was a keen observer (cf. 2 Sam. 6:16, 20-23). She knew how desperate David's plight was: "If you are not going to escape with your life tonight—tomorrow you are going to be killed" (v. 11b). No one knows if David's and Michal's house was built into the town wall like Rahab's (Josh. 2:15); but in some way Michal let David down through a window and he escaped.[6]

Then Michal set the stage to buy David a little time. The details of verse 13 are a bit elusive, however. What did Michal do with the teraphim, the images of household or family deities (cf. Gen. 31:19, 30-35)? Did she stash them in the bed to give bulk to the sick "David" (i.e., they really were, appropriately, used as dummies) or place them beside the bed as "protectors of the ill"? And what was Michal doing with such relics anyway? But the overall picture is clear: something like a quilt rumpled up at the head, perhaps some used gods to give form to the "body," and a bedspread pulled up. In our day, Michal would have plugged in the vaporizer and answered the door with a thermometer in her hand. It was a masterful delay tactic (vv. 14-16), though it earned her the wrath of her father (v. 17a). But Michal was up to that; she deceived him with another deception, so much as to say, "Dad, do you realize what a brute that man can be? What choice did I have?" (v. 17b).

---

6. The verb *escape* (Niphal of *mālaṭ*) occurs five times in chapter 19 (vv. 10, 11, 12, 17, 18).

Meanwhile David flees to Samuel in nearby Ramah and unburdens his soul to the old prophet (v. 18).[7] But what could Samuel do? Saul has informers everywhere (v. 19) and soon has his police on the way to apprehend David (v. 20). But a funny thing happened to Saul's men when they saw Samuel's prophetic group prophesying: "the Spirit of God came over the messengers of Saul and they too prophesied" (v. 20b).[8] Saul sent a second and then a third group but the result was the same: "they too," "they too" prophesied (v. 21). The point is clear. David's back is to the wall; Saul will not grant him sanctuary even in Samuel's company. So God sends forth his Spirit in raw, irresistible power on Saul's police forces and compels them into helplessness.

Saul, however, was too dense to get the point. He probably muttered something about "if you want something done right you have to do it yourself." Off Saul went to Ramah. Now the repeated "they too" is replaced by "he too" (four times, vv. 22, 23, 24). But the Spirit of God is no respecter of persons and saw no reason to exempt Saul from his brute force simply because Saul was king; and so David's Defender assaulted Saul while he was on his way, before he ever arrived at Prophecy Point (v. 23). Since he was already in the Spirit's vise, the worship service suffered no unnecessary disturbance when Saul joined in (v. 24). His helpless condition persisted for some time (v. 24b).[9]

The message of chapter 19 should be clear: Yahweh repeatedly protected his servant. I want to look more closely at that protection now that we have sketched all four samples of it. Since we've hardly left Naioth-Ramah (vv. 18-24) we'll linger there first.

---

7. It is hard to know whether "Naioth" in verses 18, 19, 22, 23 (twice; also 20:1) is a place name (RSV, NIV) or a plural noun, "huts" or "camps" (NJB and Ralph W. Klein, *1 Samuel,* Word Biblical Commentary [Waco: Word, 1983], 198).

8. The Hebrew text reflects the surprise in this by placing "upon/over the messengers of Saul" in emphatic position. What exactly were Samuel and Co. doing when they were "prophesying"? I am not sure. Was it in any way analogous to the musical "prophecy" of 1 Chronicles 25:1-3? See J. Barton Payne, "1, 2 Chronicles," *The Expositor's Bible Commentary,* 12 vols. (Grand Rapids: Zondervan, 1988), 4:424. On our passage in 1 Samuel 19, see E. J. Young, *My Servants the Prophets* (Grand Rapids: Eerdmans, 1952), 88–92.

9. For the curious or the concerned, "naked" (v. 24) does not necessarily connote "in the buff." See the commentaries by Driver and Keil.

Observe, first of all, how *instructive* Yahweh's protection is. It is instructive for us, the readers. As we work our way through chapter 19 we observe God protecting David by means of Jonathan (vv. 1-7) and Michal (vv. 11-17). When, therefore, we read that David "came to Samuel at Ramah" (v. 18), we expect that now, in some way, Samuel will be a means of deliverance for David. The text surprises us. Samuel can do nothing; rather, it is the sheer power of Yahweh's Spirit that keeps David in safety. Providing the "way of escape" is supremely the work of Yahweh. True, he may use human instruments (a Jonathan or a Michal) to provide such protection, but sometimes he bypasses them (e.g., Samuel) in order to make clear that "salvation is from the LORD" (Jon. 2:9 NASB). The means of deliverance must never eclipse the source of deliverance, and sometimes the Deliverer makes that point abundantly obvious.

Yahweh's regimen of protection should have proven instructive for David as well. At the end of chapter 19 the danger is still live for David; nevertheless even in this distress and in this momentary relief David should have been able to look back and see assuring evidence of Yahweh's care and intention to preserve him. Much—in fact, almost everything— seemed discombobulated, yet in it all there was this clear evidence that David has not been forsaken, has not been abandoned. Sometimes the clearest evidence that God has not deserted you is not that you are successfully past your trial but that you are still on your feet in the middle of it.

Poverty pressed in on the people of the northeast Highlands of Scotland in the mid-nineteenth century. It was then that a certain John Murray was praying for guidance by a riverside. Many of the folks were emigrating to America, and he was wondering if he should do so. While absorbed in his prayer he heard a thud on the grass beside him—a salmon had leaped clean out of the water! He took this as an answer that the Lord could provide for him in Scotland.[10]

Not that we should go constantly looking for signs, yet we should note them when God provides them. Signs do *signify*, whether a salmon on the grass or a friend's intercession (vv. 1-7),

---

10. Iain H. Murray, *The Life of John Murray* (Edinburgh: Banner of Truth, 1982), 10n.

a spear in the wall and not in the heart (vv. 8-10), a wife and a window (vv. 11-17), a helpless enemy (vv. 18-24).

Finally, David's protection should have proven instructive to Saul, especially after he experienced the frustrating impotence inflicted by the Spirit of God in verses 18-24. He should have seen the hopelessness of his murderous schemes. In all of chapter 19, but particularly in verse 18-24, we have Psalm 2 in miniature. Here is one of the kings of the earth plotting against Yahweh and his anointed, and Yahweh is saying to him, as he does to others, "Wise up! Accept instruction!" (Ps. 2:10). You can bash yourself against omnipotence but the success rate is nil. Heaven laughs at such stupidity (Ps. 2:4). If Saul did not gain wisdom, we should—and hope as well. There is a whole eschatology (scheme of last things) in 1 Samuel 19:18-24 and it should steel the faith of all who love the appearing and the kingdom of the David to come (see Ezek. 34:23-24).

As we take in the sweep of the whole chapter note, secondly, how *diverse* Yahweh's protection is. Once it comes by Jonathan's talking Saul toward reconciliation (vv. 1-7). Again, it comes in a suspense-filled, nail-biting episode of out-the-window-and-run-for-your-life (vv. 11-17). Once more, it comes more directly as God bares his own right arm (vv. 18-24). Shaddai's shadow is there but in a refreshing variety of ways and instruments. The means and methods of deliverance reflect the imagination of the Deliverer.

It is in this diversity of God's protection that one sees, thirdly, how *ironic* his protection is. There is irony bordering on humor here, because Saul's enemy is preserved by Saul's family. Who counters Saul's plot to eliminate David? Saul's son, Jonathan, (vv. 1-7). Who masterminds and covers up David's escape from Saul's agents? Saul's daughter, Michal (vv. 11-17). It is not knee-slapping humor but a low-key humor, the slightly amusing kind that brings a quiet smile once we see it. Saul probably expected Jonathan and Michal to stand with him; instead his own son and daughter shield David from Saul.

Does not the text put a claim upon us at this point? Don't we owe a response once we see the diversity and irony in Yahweh's protection? Don't Yahweh's interesting, imaginative ways call for praise? When the apostle caught a glimpse of this sort of thing he threw up his hands in adoring frustration: "O the depth of God's riches, wisdom, and knowledge! How unsearchable his decisions, how untrackable his ways!" (Rom. 11:33).

Before leaving these chapters the Christian should ask a question: How much of David's experience can I write over into my life? Can I simply say that what God has done for David, he'll do for me? I cannot do that for myself. David will hold a special office over Yahweh's people; he will be the recipient of covenant kingship (2 Sam. 7); he has been set apart already for that kingship. My life holds a far more modest place in God's kingdom plan and the scheme for my life is almost totally hidden from me. I have no clear and specific promise or appointment as David did for the kingship. Nevertheless, when all qualifications are stated, it seems I can still claim "Davidic protection" in principle, that is, I can be confident that God will keep me until whatever he has ordained for me to be or to do is accomplished. Some would perhaps crave more; but that is no small comfort. I do not need to share David's experiences; it is enough to know David's God. As long as the Angel of Yahweh keeps pitching his camp around those who fear him and delivering them (Ps. 34:7) I should be content. No, I may not (I hope) shinny out of a window at night to run from my killers and write Psalm 59 because of it, but if David's God is my God I can still enjoy his quiet, diverse, instructive protection.

Study Questions

1. Do you see in Jonathan any anticipation of him who 'made himself of no reputation' (Phil. 2:7 AV.)?

2. Like David you have probably been protected from dangers of which you have been unaware. Think about this and tell God how thankful you are.

3. How resourceful the Lord was in protecting David, using so many means! Pray that he will enable you always to look to him rather than to particular means he uses.

4. It has been said that Christians are immortal until their work is done. Does that give you assurance when you face unavoidable danger in your work for Christ?

18

How Do You Spell Security?
(1 Samuel 20)

The answer is simple: C-O-V-E-N-A-N-T. That is what this chapter is about: covenant, and the security it gives. Though the chapter depicts David's and Jonathan's friendship it does not mean to dredge up sentimentality over friendships. Their friendship has been formalized in a covenant (18:1-5), and that covenant, reaffirmed and extended, is the focus of this chapter. The word itself occurs only once (v. 8), but the provisions and oaths of verses 12-17, the allusion to Yahweh as covenant guardian in verse 23, Saul's knowledge of Jonathan's commitment to David in verses 30-31, and Jonathan's parting words in verse 42 should banish doubt that covenant carries the thematic freight of the chapter.

Some scholars find difficulties with the chapter in its present form and position. After Saul's various attempts on David's life in chapter 19, "it is hardly likely that David would still need to determine if Saul's intentions toward him were hostile" as in 20:1.[1] But that was not David's question; he knew Saul was hostile! Rather, he asked Jonathan what he'd done wrong. He didn't know *why* Saul kept after him. Had David wronged Saul in some way? Had he failed in some duty? Knowing a killer's motives doesn't increase safety but may reduce the apparent irrationality of it all. In fact, it seems David may

---

1. Ralph W. Klein, *1 Samuel*, Word Biblical Commentary (Waco: Word, 1983), 205.

have been more concerned to make Saul's intentions clear to an incredibly naive Jonathan (vv. 2-3).

Again, after the events of chapter 19 it seems inconsistent for David to assume that he "would be an expected or welcome guest at the king's new moon celebration" (see vv. 5-7, 25-34).[2] But he knew he wouldn't be welcome; that's why he didn't go. Yet, in accord with court procedure, Saul had every right to expect him (as Saul seemed to assume, v. 26). David apparently thought that his absence would become another element in Saul's asinine case against him. Certainly, it would have been stupid for David to attend. But Saul hadn't actually given David a pink slip; hence his absence could have been dubbed negligence.

Some scholars also insist that verses 40-42 (David and Jonathan parting) cannot be original since the whole signal system (vv. 18-23) assumes that such a personal meeting would be impossible.[3] But that assumes too much. Certainly David and Jonathan couldn't bank on a personal meeting. That's why they needed the signal system. That provision did not exclude a personal parting should the coast be clear; they simply couldn't depend on a face-to-face departure. What if Saul had snoopers tracking Jonathan? I loathe burdening readers with debate over alleged inconsistencies (and normally I don't), but these kinds of objections arise so frequently in commentaries and studies that occasionally they need to be questioned. Some of us assume that the situations of biblical characters and/or texts can be as complex and complicated as ours, which means that what an onlooker thinks is inconsistent may only be normal.

Since chapter 20 is a lengthy narrative, an outline will condense the details and give us a mental map of the textual territory.[4] The chapter contains four scenes:

---

2. Ibid.
3. Ibid., 206. I do, however, agree with Klein regarding one of the functions of chapter 20: it underscores that David "did not flee because of disloyalty or because of a desire for gain" (p. 210). Much of the material in 1 Samuel 15–2 Samuel 8 seems designed to provide a defense of David. More on this later (e.g., with 1 Sam. 24). On the "Davidic apology" in 1–2 Samuel, see H. Wolf, "Samuel, 1 and 2," *ZPEB*, 5:259–61.
4. Chapter 20 also sports some textual/grammatical twisters (e.g., vv. 14-16, 19). Comparing several English versions on these verses will alert the reader to the problems.

Scene	Summary
Before Jonathan, 1-11a	Debating the danger, 1-4
	Proposing a test, 5-7
	Appealing to a covenant, 8-9
	Transition, 10-11a
In the field, 11b-23	Covenant promises, 12-17
	Necessary signals, 18-22
	Covenant guardian, 23
At the table, 24-34	Absence and silence, 24-26
	Question and excuse, 27-29
	Anger and clarity, 30-34
In the field, 35-42	Signal—total secrecy, 35-40
	Parting—covenant peace, 41-42

Now I want to sketch the teaching of the chapter in the form of several propositions about the covenant theme.

The Covenant Provides Recourse in Uncertainty (20:1-9)

The day and night of Saul's prophetic marathon (19:24b) gave David time to escape somewhere; he arrives, apparently in Gibeah, at Jonathan's home. David knows what Saul is trying to do. Your father, he tells Jonathan, "keeps seeking my life" (v. 1b). But why is he doing so? Is there some wrong David committed, some guilt on his part of which he is unaware? What is at the bottom of this?[5] If David could discover the problem perhaps he could address it. If nothing else, knowing what had so infuriated Saul would help David understand such irrational behavior.

Jonathan remains unconvinced that there is any real danger for David. Jonathan is, after all, his father's confidant, and

---

5. Probably many of Saul's retinue kept chalking up his strange and wild behavior to his "condition." David himself had probably done this at first (e.g., in the wake of 18:10-11). But after the repeated attempts of 19:8-10, 11-17, and 18-24, David could hardly pass off Saul's schemes as due to his condition. Madness or no madness, there was too much concentrated intentionality in Saul's homicidal attempts for David to explain them away. Some scholars may hold that David was playing word games in 20:1—surely David knew Saul was envious of David as claimant to the throne; after all, David had been anointed (16:1-13). But that anointing had not been public, nor had David made any play for the throne. He had faithfully and successfully served Saul. Saul kept his thinking to himself (18:8). His real designs remained secret (18:17, 21, 25). Even when Saul proposed David's liquidation to his inner circle (19:1), he did not indicate, according to the narrative, why he wanted David out of the way. In the story Saul doesn't disclose his reason to others until 20:30-31 (he divines David is the threat to his [rejected] dynasty). Hence there is no internal inconsistency in David's perplexity in 20:1.

Saul has not disclosed any new scheme for eliminating David
(v. 2; cf. 19:6). David knows it doesn't take a master's degree
to figure that out. Who would expect Saul to keep Jonathan
posted, pro-David as he clearly is (v. 3a)? Saul lost the Spirit
of Yahweh but not his political sense. David knows the true
score; on oath he asserts there is "only a step between me and
death" (v. 3b). Jonathan consents to assist David however he
can, and David proposes a test situation that may reveal Saul's
mind especially in reference to the David-Jonathan association
(vv. 5-7). So David's place among the brass will be empty at
the monthly dinner.

At this point David both appeals to Jonathan and explains
why he has now turned to him:

> And you shall act with *hesed* toward your servant, for into a
> covenant of Yahweh you have brought your servant with you;
> but if there is guilt in me, *you* put me to death.... [v. 8]

Why would David dare turn to Saul's son when under Saul's
attack? Only because Jonathan had concluded a "covenant
of Yahweh" with David, that is, a covenant in which Yahweh
was witness to and guardian of its promises. He refers to the
covenant of 18:3-4. The covenant involves firm promises and
solemn commitments. That is why in his uncertainty and
in his pillar-to-post flight David turned to Jonathan. There
was a covenant, a bastion of certainty, a safe haven, in both a
dangerous and a helter-skelter time.

David then expects Jonathan to act with *hesed* toward him
because of their covenant (v. 8), even though David is the
"lesser" and needy partner in that covenant (three times in
vv. 7-8 David refers to himself as "your servant"). Covenant
and *hesed* are corollaries. Better, covenant and *hesed* may be
corollaries and are so in this passage.

English versions vary in translating *hesed*. In this text
(with *hesed* + verb) the Revised Standard Version and
the New American Standard Bible render "deal kindly,"
while the New Jerusalem Bible uses "show faithful love."
The term occurs nearly 250 times in the Old Testament.
Traditionally and frequently it is "mercy" in the King James
Version, "steadfast love" in the Revised Standard Version,

"lovingkindness" in the New American Standard Bible, and sometimes simply "love" in the New International Version. It carries ideas of love, compassion, affection, but often with the additional connotation of loyalty, reliability, faithfulness (hence RSV's "steadfast love"). ḥesed often has that flavor: it is not merely love, but loyal love; not merely kindness, but dependable kindness; not merely affection, but affection that has committed itself. In our passage then David appeals to Jonathan to treat him with "devoted love." He has reason to believe Jonathan will do so because Jonathan has so promised in a "covenant of Yahweh." Hence the covenant gives him reason to look for and depend upon ḥesed, devoted love. It is crucial, however, to remember that Jonathan's covenant itself was the expression of love, initiated by love (18:1, 3). The order is: love gives itself in covenant and gladly promises devoted love in that covenant; the covenant partner then rests in the security of that promise and may appeal to it,[6] as David does here.

The text is not merely describing a relation of David and Jonathan; rather, the text is extending its comfort to any Israelite who will receive it. Its message is: In confusion and trouble, you take yourself to the one person who has made a covenant with you. In David's disintegrating world there was yet one space of sanity, one refuge still intact—Jonathan. There was covenant; there David could expect ḥesed. There was kindness in a raw world.

We should not be surprised then when we catch believers in the Bible in the act of doing what David did in 1 Samuel 20: running to the one dependable refuge that remains, to the One who has bound himself to them by covenant and from whom they can expect ḥesed-like treatment (see, e.g., Neh. 1:5; Pss. 13:5; 17:7; 25:6-7). But that ḥesed ultimately flows not from a formal covenant promise but from the very nature of the covenant God, Yahweh, who is "rich in ḥesed

---

6. On ḥesed see, briefly, TWOT, 1:305–7; Merrill F. Unger and William White, Jr., eds., Nelson's Expository Dictionary of the Old Testament (Nashville: Nelson, 1980), 232–34. For a thorough study and needed correctives in light of past studies, see Francis I. Andersen, "Yahweh, the Kind and Sensitive God," in God Who Is Rich in Mercy: Essays Presented to Dr. D. B. Knox, ed. P. T. O'Brien and David G. Peterson (Homebush West NSW, Australia: Lancer, 1986), 41–88.

and fidelity" (Exod. 34:6).[7] You will never perish when you fall into the abyss of God's lovingkindness. Ultimately, that is our only recourse. And, of course, the One "rich in *ḥesed* and fidelity" has come near to his beleaguered people; for if we translate the Hebrew of Exodus 34:6 into Greek and then into traditional English we are facing him who is "full of grace and truth" (John 1:14). You seek *ḥesed* and simply find yourself in the arms of Jesus Christ. Don't forget what David has taught you: in confusion and trouble, you take yourself to the one who has made a covenant with you. He is the only recourse in uncertainty.

The Covenant Proves a Vehicle for Uncommon Faithfulness (20:12-17)

Verses 12-17 do not have to be in the text. In fact one can go immediately from the end of verse 11 to the beginning of verse 18 with no loss in the flow of the story. If verses 12-17 were not there one would not miss them. That's why some critics dub these verses secondary, that is, they were inserted into the account later. There is, however, another obvious way of viewing the matter. If the verses interrupt or delay the flow of the story the writer (or an editor) must have placed them here because they were of special importance. They carry more weight than does knowing what happened next.

If verses 12-17 are very significant they are also very difficult, verses 14-16 particularly so. Yet the text is sufficiently clear to show us that the friends' covenant almost works miracles. Let me explain.

First, in verses 12-13 Jonathan goes on oath to formalize his commitment to warn David should he find that Saul intends to destroy David. In his own words,

Yahweh, God of Israel! When I search out my father about tomorrow this time [or] the third day, and should it be good news

---

7. It is important to remember that in the context of Exodus 34 Israel had absolutely no claim on Yahweh's *ḥesed* because they had broken the covenant in the bull-calf worship (Exod. 32). If Israel receives *ḥesed*, it will only be because it flows from Yahweh's heart—because of what/who *he* is, "rich in *ḥesed* and fidelity." Hence *ḥesed* really passes over into grace (Heb., *ḥēn*), which is, as my father used to say, something for nothing—when we don't deserve anything.

for David, will I not then send to you and make you aware of it? May Yahweh deal harshly—all the more so—with Jonathan if it is my father's intention to bring disaster on you.... I shall make you aware of it, send you away, and you shall go in peace. And may Yahweh be with you as he has been with my father.

Jonathan is formally committing himself always to act as he did in 19:2-3. But that is why this covenant is so unusual. One simply didn't do what Jonathan does! You didn't hand over your place to your rival and promise to protect him, especially when your place was that of crown prince. If Jonathan were "normal," he would dispose of David. In fact, that is what angers Saul so (vv. 30-31)—Jonathan's covenant commitment to David flies smack in the face of all political sense. Jonathan really did "seek first" another kingdom; it didn't make sense. One of the strange things covenant accomplishes.

Even more unusual is the commitment Jonathan urges upon David in verses 14-16. Time will come when Jonathan, not David, will be in the fugitive role, the needy one. Though the text is difficult the overall sense is clear:

And will you not—if I am still alive, will you not treat me with the devoted love of Yahweh that I not die? And you must not cut off your devoted love from my house forever, not even when Yahweh cuts off each one of David's enemies from the face of the ground. So Jonathan cut [a covenant] with the house of David. [vv. 14-16a][8]

David gave his oath to these provisions (v. 17). When he came to power he would preserve both Jonathan's life and that of his descendants (see 2 Sam. 9). But according to the wisdom of the age such promises would be regarded as the height or depth of folly. When a new regime or dynasty came to power, the name of the game was purge. You needn't go wandering into the ancient Near East to confirm this. You can stay within the pages of biblical history and watch Baasha (1 Kings 15:27-30)

---

8. On the text see S. R. Driver, *Notes on the Hebrew Text and the Topography of the Books of Samuel*, 2d ed. (1913; reprint ed., Winona Lake, Ind.: Alpha, 1984), 164–66; and J. P. Fokkelman, *Narrative Art and Poetry in the Books of Samuel*, vol. 2, *The Crossing Fates (I Sam. 13–31 & II Sam. 1)* (Assen/Maastricht: Van Gorcum, 1986), 314–15.

or Zimri (1 Kings 16:8-13) or Jehu (2 Kings 10:1-11) to find out what happens to the remnants of a previous regime. The new king always needed to solidify his position. It was conventional political policy: solidification by liquidation. Everybody knew it; everybody believed it; everybody practiced it.

Well, almost. David wouldn't. He would preserve the crown prince's family because he gave his promise by covenant to do so. Culture and politics preached otherwise. But covenant conquered culture. Both Jonathan and David made commitments to each other that trample on customary human standards. Covenant has become the vehicle for uncommon faithfulness.

I know: God's people today are not living on the edge of a dynastic transition directly involving them. No matter. You still see this uncommon fidelity in the Christian life of God's people though perhaps in a less dramatic form. I have seen it in my own family: in my mother's care of my father in his last years as his health but particularly his mind began to slip. Nine months after my father died my mother died, perhaps because she felt she could. She had accomplished her mission: taking care of her husband. Not sensational or glamorous—just covenantal. It had something to do with "in sickness and in health"—something about a covenant.

The Covenant May Demand Costly Commitment (20:24-34)
Now we readers gather (at a distance) to watch the table scene (vv. 24-34). It is mostly a typical monthly occasion—Saul is there in his seat by the wall (v. 25), Abner is there, Jonathan is there. David's place is empty. That's different. But Saul is silent. He surmises David may be ritually unclean (see Lev. 7:20-21) and therefore unfit to partake. Clearly Saul expected (or thought he had a right to expect) David's presence at table even after the episode of 19:18-24. However, when David was absent the second day, the fireworks began.

The whole section (vv. 24-34) begins with David's place empty and ends with Jonathan's place empty. After the setting has been given and Saul's silence at David's initial absence explained, the conversation begins; it develops in a sort of structural counterpoint:

Saul's question, 27b
   Jonathan's "revelation," 28-29
   Saul's anger, 30-31
Jonathan's question, 32
   Saul's "revelation," 33
   Jonathan's anger, 34

Saul asked of the whereabouts of the "son of Jesse." As David had requested, Jonathan passed on David's excuse to Saul (vv. 28-29).[9] That was all the catalyst Saul needed (vv. 30-31):

> You son of a perverse and rebellious woman! Don't I know that you are choosing the son of Jesse to your own shame and the shame of your mother's nakedness? For as long as the son of Jesse remains alive on the earth you and your kingdom will never be secured. And now, send and bring him to me, for he is a son of death!

The rulers of this age understand neither the wisdom nor the power of God. Saul is no exception. Jonathan's "stupidity" made Saul beside himself with rage. Jonathan put Yahweh's servant (David), Yahweh's word (the rejection of Saul's line and the promise of kingship to David), and Yahweh's kingdom first, even though he was officially and normally the one in line for the throne. One could say Jonathan "emptied himself" (Phil. 2:7); he was willing to suffer the "loss of all things" and to count them rubbish (Phil. 3:8). If I might continue the anachronism, Matthew 6:33 was not a cliche for Jonathan. Which is precisely why Saul could not fathom Jonathan, why he thought him so dim-witted and dense, why with blue veins bulging in his neck and red flush rising in his face he shouted at Jonathan the only four words that mattered: "You and your kingdom!"

---

9. Two comments: (1) Some readers may be disturbed to see that the Bible records Jonathan's apparent "storying" for David. That is all the text is doing: reporting what Jonathan did. It does not recommend what he did. The Bible, as so often in such cases, ignores the rub the modern reader may feel. It is important, however, to distinguish between what the Bible reports and what it recommends. It tells you that Jonathan prevaricated for David; it does not say, "Go, and do thou likewise." The Bible is telling a story, not teaching ethics here. (2) Robert Polzin (*Samuel and the Deuteronomist* [San Francisco: Harper and Row, 1989], 189) believes that Saul would view David's alleged return to Bethlehem as insubordination in light of Saul's prohibition in 18:2. I cannot agree with Polzin. There is no reason to take the prohibition of 18:2 as absolute. Why couldn't David have asked for time off once in a while?

But "you and your kingdom" did not move Jonathan. He was bound and committed by covenant to David. He would remain faithful to the covenant even if it cost him the good-will of his father. Jonathan would have understood Jesus: "If anyone comes to me and does not hate his father and mother, his wife and children, his brothers and sisters—yes, even his own life—he cannot be my disciple" (Luke 14:26 NIV).

If Jonathan is a scribe discipled about the kingdom of heaven, what does he teach us? This: That true life does not consist in securing "you and your kingdom" but in reflecting Yahweh's faithfulness in covenant relationships. There is something liberating about that! Jonathan had acknowledged that the kingdom was Yahweh's and therefore David's, so his life did not need to be centered in his ambition (what can I get) but in God's providence (what Yahweh has given). Even as a believer and not as a crown prince my reigning passion is not to make my way, my living, or my mark; not to gain my place or to get ahead. That may be costly; but it is certainly liberating. Life does not consist in achieving your goals but in fulfilling your promises. That (previous) sentence is only cold print. But watch it; it's dynamite. Handle with care.

The Covenant Provides Peace in the Middle of Confusion (20:35-42)

The little lad who went with Jonathan that morning (v. 35) to chase arrows may have been of more help than he could know. If Saul's henchmen had Jonathan under surveillance, they might have relaxed their vigilance when they saw that Jonathan did not go out alone. In any case, when Jonathan hollered, "Isn't the arrow beyond you?" (v. 37) David had his answer (v. 22). Otherwise it was all so typical, as Jonathan prodded, "Quick! Hurry up—don't stand around!" (v. 38). Not even the lad had a clue about things (v. 39). He had likely had this chore numerous times before.

David's gratitude and mutual affection and grief mark the parting scene (v. 41). Jonathan has the last word: "Go in peace, because we two have sworn an oath in Yahweh's name, saying, 'May Yahweh be between me and you, and between my seed and your seed forever'" (v. 42).

Given the circumstances Jonathan's words could seem almost laughable. "Go in peace." But we know he's serious.

Go in peace while Saul stalks your life? Jonathan, however, is not claiming that all is peaceful or that David will not meet danger on every hand. Jonathan is saying that David can go in peace because there is peace between the two of them. There is peace "because we two have sworn an oath." Their covenant bond has established peace between them. It is as if Jonathan urges, "go in peace, because there is peace in this one item; in this one relation of ours there is safety. There is an anchor here; there is this one relation that holds fast when all else may be flux and confusion. There is this one area where peace is established and reigns."

Is that not an accurate sketch of biblical peace? Biblical peace is not often a general tranquillity but rather a rightness at the center in the midst of much turmoil. Paul implied that Christians "enjoy peace" with God (Rom. 5:1) and at the same time endure "afflictions" (Rom. 5:3). Jesus told his disciples, "*In me* you may have peace; *in the world* you have affliction" (John 16:33; emphasis in Greek). The Christian then does not have peace because things are peaceful. He has peace because a greater one than Jonathan has pledged his friendship to him. If you doubt that, you have not been listening at the Lord's Supper: "This cup is the new covenant sealed in my blood." It is the covenant bond of that unforsaking Friend that speaks peace in our disappointments, dangers, and even disasters.

The last line of our chapter is poignant: "Then he [David] rose up and went away; but Jonathan went into the town" (v. 42b). Who knows what will happen to either? But at least covenant had secured one relation among all others. Obviously, "security" is an eight-letter word. And when spelled out it looks like this: covenant.

Study Questions

1. Sometimes we may think of our relationship to God as an amazing Divine/human friendship, but how far does a covenant relationship go beyond that?

2. If you are a Christian you are a member of the new covenant people of God. Ponder the cost of this to Christ in the light of Mark 14:24.

3. Jonathan and David's commitment to each other cut right across the normal outlook of the time. Consider the extent to which it challenges the modern world also.

4. 'Life does not consist in achieving your goals but in fulfilling your promises.' Do you agree that at the highest level – commitment to Christ – our promises and our goals may coincide? 'O Jesus, I have promised to serve Thee to the end.'

5. In his grace, God offers us peace with himself through Christ. How can we communicate this wonderful aspect of the gospel to others?

19

Desperation
(1 Samuel 21:1–22:5)

Jerusalem was slowly being strangled. Arab attacks on the supply road to the west had intensified; the plan was to starve out the Jewish population of the city. It was February 1948. Jewish leadership came under increasing pressure to evacuate Jewish women and children while it could still be done in relative safety. But Dov Joseph, a Canadian lawyer in charge of Jerusalem's survival plan, refused to budge. Not without anguish. Evacuation to the coast seemed the rational way. But Joseph wouldn't give; "he reasoned the fighting spirit of Jerusalem's men would be raised if they knew that their homes and families lay helpless just behind them."[1] Those men knew what would happen to their families if the city were overrun. Dov Joseph believed that desperation could have its benefits.

I wouldn't dispute that. Yet if one is in a desperate condition for long, one begins to get desperate about getting through desperation. It becomes wearing, especially if, like David, one is on his own. David now has the unassuring assurance that Saul, if it's up to Saul, *will* have his head. There can be no Jonathans, Michals, or Samuels now. Where to go? What to do? The words of 21:10a sum up the next few chapters: "David rose up and fled on that day from before Saul." What

---

1. Larry Collins and Dominique Lapierre, *O Jerusalem!* (New York: Pocket, 1972), 148.

benefits can there possibly be in such nip-and-tuck, skin-of-the-teeth times? This stretch of narrative (21:1-22:5) seems to have a quiet answer to that question. The text seems to say that even in their most desperate moments Yahweh does not let go of his servants, least of all David, his king-elect. And there is some evidence for this contention.

Desperation and Provision (21:1-9)

David came to Nob, apparently the primary sanctuary site at the time, one or two miles north of Jerusalem.[2] Ahimelech the priest smells something wrong. Otherwise, why "tremble" to meet David (v. 1)? Why was David alone, and so on? Though some readers may judge differently, I think David's story rather flimsy. He is, he tells Ahimelech, on a highly sensitive government assignment, his papers are top secret—that is the reason for traveling alone; though, to be sure, he does have a cadre of men waiting to meet him later (v. 2). Perhaps David convinces us here, but he makes us skeptics when he tells Ahimelech that the king's mission was so urgent he left even without his sword or weapons (v. 8). He sounds like a plumber asking to borrow a customer's pipe wrenches or an insurance salesman without requisite forms. David needs food (v. 3) and weapons (v. 8) but his cover story is less than satisfying.

There are enough difficulties with this interchange. But it gets worse. The reader winces in fear at verse 7. The literary camera turns to show the briefest clip of the narrowed eyes and curled lip of Doeg the Edomite, Saul's lackey. Only a momentary glance but it sends a shudder up the reader's spine (all the more so if you've cheated and read ahead!).

Why did David take this tack with Ahimelech? We can only guess. Perhaps he was trying to save Ahimelech from being implicated in aiding an enemy of the crown. If David did not tell Ahimelech he was fleeing from Saul then Ahimelech could rightly claim that he knew nothing of David's renegade status at the time he helped him (cf. 22:14-15). David's story may have been his attempt to protect Ahimelech.

---

2. See Isaiah 10:32 in context; A. van Selms, "Nob," *ISBE*, rev. ed., 3:545–46.

In any case, the text neither condemns nor justifies David for his conduct. (The Bible would prove a boring tome if in every suspense-filled narrative it turned aside to provide moral-ethical evaluations.) We can understand David's difficulty—dare we say panic? He seems at his wits' end and certainly at life's edge. That does not justify his jeopardizing Ahimelech, however. The text is not recommending David's conduct, only reporting it; it may describe what he did but does not care to discuss it.[3]

We do better to ask a different question: What does *God* seem to be doing here? We note that in the confusion and danger and fear David received daily bread. Is it too much to say the text depicts something simple, namely, that Yahweh sustained him? It was no small item but a clear need (vv. 4-6). And the bread he received was nothing less than the "bread of the presence," which ordinarily only the priests were to eat (see Lev. 24:5-9). Every Sabbath twelve loaves of this bread were piled on the table on the north side of the holy place in the tabernacle. They were, among other things, a quiet witness that Yahweh sustains his people and supplies their needs (cf. Exod. 16).[4] In 1 Samuel 21 Ahimelech's holy bread becomes David's daily bread.[5]

Some scrupulous reader may object and complain that David in all his finagling and deception does not deserve this provision. So what else is new? Who would have daily bread if it rested on our deserts? We'd all be skeletons. We can

---

3. Cf. Hans Wilhelm Hertzberg, *I & II Samuel,* The Old Testament Library (Philadelphia: Westminster, 1964), 179.

4. See O. T. Allis, "Leviticus," in *The New Bible Commentary: Revised* (Grand Rapids: Eerdmans, 1970), 163–64; and G. L. Carr and Nola J. Opperwall, "Presence, Bread of the," *ISBE,* rev. ed., 3:955–56.

5. I am not convinced by J. P. Fokkelman's contention that David deliberately went to Nob because he knew Goliath's sword was there (this part may be so) and because he wanted to receive holy bread as food befitting a king (following Ackroyd). Fokkelman argues that there was sufficient population in Nob for David to have obtained ordinary bread upon request (*Narrative Art and Poetry in the Books of Samuel,* vol. 2, *The Crossing Fates (I Sam. 13–31 & II Sam. 1)* [Assen/Maastricht: Van Gorcum, 1986], 352). David, however, may not have trusted every Tom, Dick, and Harry at Nob or any other burgh. Even at this early turn of affairs, how better could folks ingratiate themselves to the crown than by exposing David? Moreover, if we can believe Doeg (admittedly, a risky venture; 22:9-10) and Ahimelech (22:15), David also wanted to receive divine guidance through Ahimelech.

only second Jacob's position (Gen. 32:10). When everything is scraped down to the bone, I receive my daily bread not because I am godly but because Yahweh is gracious.

There may well be a word in David's provision for the contemporary Christian. One may be under a heavy load, boxed in and pressed down under various vocational, emotional, spiritual, or circumstantial pressures. But am I still eating every day? At least once? Doesn't God's small provision in my big problems tell me something? Doesn't it assure me that God has not yet cast me off?

Desperation and Praise (21:10-15)

One can scarcely believe it. Whatever possessed David to flee to Achish the king of Gath (v. 10b)? Would a steer walk, knowingly, into a meat grinder? Yet here is David showing up in Goliath's home town (with Goliath's sword!), apparently hoping to find sanctuary. I suppose David was thinking Achish would welcome the defection of Saul's prize lieutenant; but Achish's servants and advisers saw it differently (v. 11), which was no surprise. There were more than one or two reasons David would be *persona non grata* in Gath. What, for example, would the widows of Philistine veterans think? And David even in his hurry had probably weighed such reasons. The fact that he still took the risk indicates how desperate he was. When Achish is my best hope I'm in real trouble.

Achish's advisers could not be accused of cultural provincialism. At least they had listened to Israelite music and vividly remembered the lyrics of one song (v. 11; see 18:7). Here, they tell Achish, is the legendary David, the one who has slain "his ten thousands" — most of whom, dear king, have been Philistines.[6] David had reason to be very afraid

---

6. Actually, Achish's counselors call David "the king of the land" (v. 11). Fokkelman (*The Crossing Fates,* 365–66) notes that they do not call David "king of Israel," which would have been literally untrue. He suggests Achish's men used somewhat ambiguous terminology to make Achish uneasy. The biblical writer likely had another purpose in view; he portrays even the Philistines as witnesses to David's future. When they call David the "king of the land" they are merely confirming Yahweh's word. The Philistines have become prophets who speak far better than they know; they speak the truth but cannot foresee the real depth of that truth (see Karl Gutbrod, *Das Buch vom König,* Die Botschaft des Alten Testaments, 4th ed. [Stuttgart: Calwer, 1975], 181). This happens B.C.—before Caiaphas, another of the "Philistines" Yahweh used to speak his truth (see John 11:49-52).

(v. 12): his hopes had flopped. He was under arrest, confined and taken into custody; at least that is what the words *in their hands* (v. 13a) imply.

David turns to acting and proves convincing. He dabbles nonsense graffiti on the doors to the town gate (more maintenance for Gath's Parks and Recreation Department) and let his spit run down his beard. A little exposure to the constant scratching and soaking convinces Achish he's got another crazy around him, as if, in his view, he doesn't already have his quota of such folks (vv. 14-15). Apparently confinement ceased and David was permitted to go slobbering on his way.

We must not merely call this episode David's Folly and sigh about how lucky he was to get out. I suggest our response be governed by David's own response. According to the headings of Psalms 34 and 56, those psalms arose in the wake of this fiasco in Gath.[7] You may look at 1 Samuel 21:10-15 and wonder, "Can anything good come out of Gath?" Here is David—foolish, desperate, confused. Ah, but it's the stuff psalms are made of. So David does not say, "I am lucky," but, "God is for me"; he sees men not as frightful but as flesh. His deliverance from all his fears and all his troubles (Ps. 34:4, 6) is the pledge that Yahweh will follow suit for other believers (vv. 15-22) and the basis for his continuing praise (vv. 1-3). Along with desperation there is nevertheless praise. I do not mean that we should act foolishly in order that praise may come but only that we should never forget God's mercies given us even in our foolishness.

Desperation and Providence (22:1-4)

David escaped to a cave near Adullam, a town in the low hills (Shephelah) of west Judah about twelve miles east of Gath. His brothers and family were probably fearful of Saul's vindictiveness, so they came to Adullam and joined David there (v. 1).

They were not the only ones who came! A motley kaleidoscope of social riff-raff, malcontents, folks in debt and/

---

7. On Davidic episodes in psalm headings, see Derek Kidner, *Psalms 1–72*, Tyndale Old Testament Commentaries (London: InterVarsity, 1973), 43–46.

or distress, began filtering to David (v. 2).[8] At this time four hundred of them looked to David as their captain. Ruling all Israel might not be much more difficult than controlling and molding such a rag-tag body.

However, our primary interest centers on the arrangements David made for his parents (vv. 3-4). They were certainly up in years (cf. 17:12) and the thrill and chill of running from Saul was not what they needed. Hence David went to the king of Moab (east of the Dead Sea) and asked that his parents be given sanctuary until David might discover "what God will do for me" (v. 3b). David must have felt much relief to have obtained this refuge for his parents. In contrast to Saul and Achish, here is one king who gives him aid.

There may have been a reason why the king of Moab proved so helpful. One can hardly keep from remembering that Ruth the Moabitess was David's great-grandmother (Ruth 4:18-22). Naturally, we cannot be sure how heavily this fact weighed with the king of Moab, but we may assume it must have counted for something. Having a tad of Moabite blood in his veins certainly wouldn't hurt David's case.

Our text does not dogmatize on this connection, but it does suggest to the reflective Bible reader that David's Moabite ancestress may have aided his request for asylum for his parents. Doesn't this put a new light on the events recorded in the Book of Ruth? Does it not shed some light on Naomi's trial? On her husband's and her sons' deaths? On her facing almost certain poverty and destitution? On her one daughter-in-law's insistent faithfulness? On all the quiet twists of circumstance by which Ruth came to Boaz's attention? And so on. All that formed the perfect backdrop so that David could nicely and cogently appeal to the king of Moab now. Old Naomi could never have had a clue that her suffering would bear much fruit for one of her descendants over a century later.

In 1938 Roman Turski, a Polish flyer, was returning home from France. His plane developed engine trouble, and he had

---

8. We needn't assume all the men and/or their families were in the same cave. But neither should we imagine a cave as a cramped hole in the side of a hill. There are caves in the area today that easily rival or exceed large hotel lobbies for space. A game of full-court basketball would be no problem in some of them.

to land for repairs in Nazified Vienna. Next morning, as Turski stepped out of his hotel to buy souvenirs before resuming his flight, a fellow came running through the door and slammed into him. Before Turski could inflict verbal vengeance he saw the man was white with fear. When he said, "Gestapo! Gestapo!" Turski rushed him through the lobby, up to his own room, and arranged the man's slender body under the covers at the foot of his bed. Turski made himself look like he'd just gotten up. And after the visiting Gestapo had checked his passport and shouted questions, they left without searching the room. The pilot showed his grateful visitor his flight map; they communicated by gestures. No, Turski couldn't take him to Warsaw—he had to land for fuel in Cracow and, drawing prison bars on the margin of the map, he indicated his new friend would be arrested at any airport. He would land in some meadow just over the Polish border and his passenger would be on his own. They did and he was. When Turski landed at Cracow the police were there to search his plane; they'd been told he'd assisted a man to escape from Vienna. They found nothing, so had to release him. He asked why the man had been wanted. He was a Jew!

Turski served as a fighter pilot in the Polish Air Force. After Poland's defeat he and others crossed to Rumania, where they were caught and sent to concentration camps. Turski managed to escape and join the French Air Force; after France's fall he went to England and fought in the Battle of Britain. On one of his missions he rammed a German plane and was hit by a scrap of its tail. Partially blinded with blood, he was unconscious when he crash-landed his Spitfire in England. His skull had been fractured and the chief surgeon at the hospital thought it useless to operate.

But he awoke and saw a narrow face looking down on him. The fellow in the white smock spoke: "Remember me? You saved my life in Vienna." Turski remembered and learned the rest of the story.

The fugitive passenger had eventually arrived in Warsaw. Before the war he escaped to Scotland. He heard that a Polish squadron had distinguished itself in the Battle of Britain; he thought Turski might be in it; he wrote to inquire; he was. He knew

Turski's name because it had been written on the margin of his map. The day before he had read of a Polish hero shooting down five enemy planes and crash-landing near a certain hospital. The piece had indicated the flyer's condition seemed hopeless. He asked the RAF in Edinburgh to fly him to the hospital named. Turski asked him, "Why?" His answer: "I thought that at last I could do something to show my gratitude. You see, I am a brain surgeon—I operated on you this morning."[9]

Who could have guessed that by shielding a fugitive one was saving his savior! One would think that would not have anything to do with anything. The twists of Turski's story, however, were confined within the scope of several years. In David's case all the unusual arrangements had been made over a century before. Yahweh plans his kindnesses long beforehand. He directed circumstances long in advance in order to bring a ray of relief in David's present distress. It was not something David set in place; it was a gift. Yahweh "arranged" it long before. Nor is it something he does only for chosen kings. A great number of his saints have stories to tell about desperation and providence.

Desperation and Prophecy (22:5)

> Now the prophet Gad said to David, "You must not stay in the stronghold; go—you must go to the land of Judah." So David went and came to the forest of Hereth.[10]

Where did Gad come from? Was he one of Samuel's prophetic group? In any case, what difference does a passing reference to an unknown prophet make?

The answer to that question is easy: An enormous difference. This verse shows that Yahweh gives David direction and special guidance through a prophet. Why is that so significant? Because Saul did not (16:14; 18:12) and would not (28:6) enjoy such a privilege. Saul was a man on his own, shut up to his

---

9. Roman Turski, "The Evaders," *Secrets and Spies: Behind-the-Scenes Stories of World War II* (Pleasantville, N.Y.: Reader's Digest Association, 1964), 149–51.

10. It is hard to say where the stronghold of 22:5 was. Perhaps Adullam (22:1) or somewhere in Moab (vv. 3-4); possibly En-gedi, west of the Dead Sea (cf. 24:1, 22). We don't know and it doesn't much matter.

own wits, a man without direction from God. He had no light in his misery. But the gleams of God's guidance shine on David through the counsel of the prophet Gad.

Desperation is no fun, but desperation *and* silence are unbearable. Being in the slimy pit (Ps. 40:2) is not quite so bad if one can hear his Shepherd's voice and know he is near. David heard that voice directly through the prophet Gad. God's troubled people still hear that voice through the "prophetic word made more sure" (2 Pet. 1:19-21) in Scripture and rejoice that through the endurance and the encouragement the Scriptures give they have hope (Rom. 15:4).

Yahweh does uphold his desperate people but not necessarily to the sound of trumpets. He does so rather quietly. The tokens of his help are hardly obvious: five loaves of bread; the back side of the Gath city-limit sign as one leaves town; a Moabite ancestress; a prophet giving orders. Not the usual arsenal of strength.

Don't despise this desperate, lonely king-to-be. I hope you know another just like him (Matt. 8:20).[11]

Study Questions

1. Think about your life before you became a Christian. How many kinds of provision can you identify which God made for you even though you were a rebel against him?

2. List the convictions about God which David demonstrates in Psalm 34 and consider the relevance of each to his situation in Gath.

3. David was concerned for his elderly parents and translated that concern into practical action. Is there a lesson in this for you?

4. 'A great number of his saints have stories to tell about desperation and providence.' You too, or perhaps your family or Christian friends?

---

11. Cf. S. G. DeGraaf, *Promise and Deliverance*, 4 vols. (St. Catharines: Paideia, 1978), 2:125–26.

20

Even Now Many Antichrists Have Come
(1 Samuel 22:6-23)

In the mid-1970s Gerald R. Ford served as President of the United States. Jerry Ford was known as Mr. Nice Guy. If we accept that characterization of Mr. Ford, we would likely say that we have met other Jerry Fords. Similarly, yet by contrast, the next president had a beer-guzzling, rabble-rousing brother. Billy Carter occasionally swiped the spotlight from his presidential brother. And many of us can likely say we've met other Billy Carters. Gerald Ford and Billy Carter are individual persons; yet in one sense they stand for more than themselves—they are types of other folks we know. There is Jerry Ford, but, we might say, there are also other Jerry Fords.

The apostle's teaching about the Antichrist seems to make this distinction. In 1 John 2:18 he warns his readers, "As you have heard that the antichrist is coming, even now many antichrists have come" (NIV). There is Antichrist with a capital A who will be coming (cf. the little horn of Dan. 7, the man of lawlessness of 2 Thess. 2, and the beast out of the sea of Rev. 13), the final antichrist before Christ's second coming (see 2 Thess. 2:1-12), but, so John insists, many antichrists have already come. There is Antichrist and there are antichrists. In the course of history there are antichrist figures who prefigure the full embodiment of evil to come. The apostle John smelled these antichrists in their false teaching (e.g., 1 John 2:22-23).

But another premier characteristic of the antichrist figure is that he opposes, enters into conflict with, and seeks to crush God's people (Dan. 7:21-22; Rev. 13:7-8). That is where King Saul comes in. In 1 Samuel 22 the veil slips away and Saul is seen for the antichrist figure he really is as he has Yahweh's priests summarily butchered. Even now, in 1 Samuel 22, many antichrists have come.

We should pick up the story. Saul is conducting a royal pity party under the tamarisk in Gibeah. He addresses his inner circle of Benjaminite henchmen, asking them if they think the "son of Jesse" will pass out government jobs and perks to them as he, Saul, has done. He is speaking to all his select circle, for three times he refers to "all of you" (vv. 7-8). And they have, he alleges, all entered a conspiracy of silence, callously withholding from him intelligence about his own son's subversive support for the "son of Jesse" (v. 8).

Doeg the Edomite knows when to talk. He is supervisor of the herdsmen (21:7), and he discloses (in contrast to the silent Benjaminites) to the king what he saw while detained at Nob. Now we understand 21:7. The son of Jesse (it is important to refer to people the way Saul refers to them) came to Nob, Doeg asserts, and Ahimelech asked direction for him from Yahweh, and also fed and armed him (22:9-10). Goliath's sword—you remember, O king.

Reality now seems as big as Saul's suspicions. Saul summons Ahimelech and "all his father's house."[1] All of them come to the king (v. 11). Saul applies his conspiracy theory to the aid Ahimelech gave the "son of Jesse" (vv. 12-13) and Ahimelech musters what appears to be a capable defense given the circumstances (vv. 14-15). Ahimelech raises questions: Doesn't David have high rank and fine reputation at court? Isn't he the king's son-in-law? Was my seeking Yahweh's direction for

---

1. Note that Saul does not call Ahimelech by name (until he sentences him in v. 16!) but addresses him as "son of Ahitub" (v. 12), just as he usually alludes to David as the "son of Jesse" (vv. 7, 8, 13; cf. v. 17). This seems akin to calling someone by the last name in a North American setting. It works but is usually a bit distant. Calling Jackson for help will likely bring it; but saying "Allan" gives a softer touch. Saul, however, is on a last-name basis with just about everyone. One can't help but notice a sense of distance in the way he addresses people, a distance created by his madness and his alienation from God.

him some new twist? Haven't I done that regularly? Where then are you getting all this "conspiracy" thinking? I have no clues in the whole matter (vv. 14-15). (Ahimelech may have had some misgivings, 21:1, but he had apparently no clear knowledge.) Saul has heard enough: the edge of the sword for the priests of Yahweh (vv. 16-18).

Force yourself to look at the scene: terror and bloodbath at Gibeah (v. 18), butchery and annihilation in Priestville (v. 19). And the witness of the text is that you have both need for realism and reason for confidence as you face the work of antichrists. Now to the teaching of the text.

God's Enemies Prove the Truthfulness of His Word

> Then the king said to Doeg, "You turn—and lay into the priests." So Doeg the Edomite turned and he himself laid into the priests and put to death that day eighty-five men wearing the linen ephod. [v. 18]

Ghastly, brutal, and unjust—yet one cannot read of Doeg's slaughter without recalling the prophecy of 2:30-36 (especially vv. 31-33). Doeg's butchery fulfills the word of God against the house of Eli.[2] That word had been spoken perhaps forty, maybe fifty years before; now in the carnage at Gibeah and Nob it had come to pass. Don't berate the word of God; God is not the author of this evil. Place the blame where it belongs—on this renegade Edomite[3] and the antichrist who commands him. They dared to destroy the "priests of Yahweh" (vv. 17 [twice], 21). It is a horrid wickedness for which Saul and Doeg are fully responsible; it is a clear fulfillment of the word

---

2. Cf. Claus Schedl, *History of the Old Testament*, 5 vols. (Staten Island, N.Y.: Alba House, 1972), 3:131, and Ralph W. Klein, *1 Samuel*, Word Biblical Commentary (Waco: Word, 1983), 222. See our discussion of 2:27-36, including the footnotes. If 2:33 refers to "one man" who will not be "cut off," the fulfillment comes in Abiathar's escape (22:20). If we follow the Qumran fragments and LXX at 2:33, then the majority of Eli's house is to die "by the *sword* of men"—note the two references to the "edge of the sword" in 22:19 (Doeg's work at Nob). Note also the reference to the "house of your father" in the prophecy against Eli (2:31) in connection with the threefold "all the house of his/my/your father" here in chapter 22 (vv. 11, 15, 16).

3. "Three times his gentilic, *the Edomite*, is given (vv. 9, 18, 22), doubtless to emphasize that it was not an Israelite who was responsible for the foul deeds that follow" (Robert P. Gordon, *I & II Samuel: A Commentary* [Grand Rapids: Zondorvan, 1986], 174)

Yahweh had spoken. Put it together and one truth becomes clear: Even in opposing God's kingdom God's enemies only bring to pass God's word.

When I was a toddler one of my brothers had made a wooden duck for me. This duck consisted of two ends or sides cut out of one-fourth or three-eighths-inch wood in the shape of a large duck; in between these ends was a seat where a toddler could sit, hold on to a wooden bar, and rock in the duck. The whole thing was probably 2 x 2 x 2-1/2 feet. When I was about six I shared an attic bedroom with another of my brothers who, at the time, was a smart high-school freshman. One evening I came up to bed and saw a sizable mound under the covers of my bed! Immediately I divined it was Jim "hiding" in my bed. I decided whatever the consequences to teach him a lesson. I can still recall savoring the hostility before the blow. I pulled back my fist and punched the mound with all my might, met something terribly solid, instantly decided I had hit Jim's head—until he popped up, laughing, from behind his bed. A flip of the covers revealed I had punched the wooden duck he had placed there. With all my nastiness and viciousness I had carried out his design.

I recognize such illustrations have severe limitations. They are illustrations, not analogies; God is not like a manipulating prankster brother, and so on. But I would only highlight the one principle: one can vigorously attack the "enemy" and all the time simply be executing the enemy's will. So with Saul, with Doeg. Even in their wicked slaughter of Yahweh's priests they nevertheless fulfilled his word. God's enemies prove the truthfulness of his word. In their hostility against him they carry out his will.

This truth is clear even if mysterious; it is plain though not simple.[4] It is what the early Christians both preached (Acts 2:23—Peter packs it all into one verse!) and prayed (Acts 4:27-28). It is what puts steel into Christian endurance.

---

4. Karl Gutbrod underscores the irony and mystery in verses 18-19: "The judgment of God, which already since chapter 2 hovers over this house [of Eli], is carried out by the man who himself stands under God's judgment and who snares himself more deeply into it with this deed." He notes the "unnerving insight into the mysterious, intricate ways of divine judgment" given in this text (*Das Buch vom König, Die Botschaft des Alten Testaments*, 4th ed. [Stuttgart: Calwer, 1975], 187).

If we know that as men oppose God and his people they will only fulfill his word, it doesn't take away sorrow or grief or suffering; but it gives secret certainty of victory. First Samuel 22 is as clear as any text on this. There is no way Yahweh's enemies can gain the edge. He has them completely outclassed. If they knew what they were doing, they would kick themselves. If Yahweh's word of judgment is so sure, certainly his word of consolation is just as solid.

God's People Experience the Hatred of His Enemy (22:16-19)

Antichrist's characteristic passion is to crush and destroy God's people (cf. Dan. 7:21-22, 25; Rev. 13:7-8). And Saul proves himself a scale-model antichrist here: he vents his fury on the priests of Yahweh (vv. 17, 21), Yahweh's designated servants and representatives of his people. He annihilates a village of Israel as though it were one of Yahweh's enemies (see 15:2-3). Hans Wilhelm Hertzberg states it well in discussing verse 17:

> This is open war against the servants of the Lord, and therefore against the Lord himself, and the refusal of the servants, who are by no means sensitive men, to lay a hand on the Lord's anointed [priests] is intended as a deliberate contrast.[5]

True, Saul does not destroy all Israel—"only" eighty-five priests and their families. Saul does not wipe out all cities of Israel but only one town. But antichrists are not measured by statistics. The text is clear enough: here is Saul, Destroyer of Israel.

Saul joins an infamous company. He stands among the ranks of antichrist Pharaoh, who instituted the government's postnatal care policy for Hebrew babies (Exod. 1:22). He becomes colleague to antichrists Balak and Balaam who by curse (Num. 22:1-6) and by counsel (Num. 31:16 and Num. 25) respectively plotted the destruction of Abraham's seed. He stands with antichristess Jezebel who tried to purge the prophets of Yahweh (1 Kings 18:4) and with antichristess Athaliah who wiped out well-nigh the whole Davidic seed

---

5. Hans Wilhelm Hertzberg, *I & II Samuel*, The Old Testament Library (Philadelphia: Westminster, 1964), 188.

(2 Kings 11:1). Saul may seem a far cry from antichrist Haman (Esther 3:5-6, 13) and from antichrist Antiochus Epiphanes (Dan. 8:9-14, 23-25; cf. 1 Macc. 1),[6] but the difference is one of degree rather than of kind. Saul becomes one of a legion of antichrists who have always vented their spleen on the Lord's servants. Whether we think of the edicts of Diocletian, the dragoons imposed on the Huguenots under Louis XIV, Charles II and the "killing time" in Scotland, or the atrocities of Idi Amin in Uganda—all these are but fragments lifted from the larger, continuous, and ongoing antichrist tradition. We should not be surprised (1 Pet. 4:12); but neither should we forget. Even now many antichrists have come.

There is one fact, however, that gives God's people some consolation: antichrists tend to be fragile. In a word, weak. At least that is the case in 1 Samuel 22. True, Saul can have priests butchered by mere royal order (provided he orders the right stoolie). But that is just his problem: "Saul has nothing left but raw power."[7] Saul is increasingly isolating himself, divesting himself of whatever true support he could have had. He has pushed away his own son (20:30-42), exterminated Yahweh's priests, and repulsed his closest servants (22:17).[8] Saul has had all but is in the process of losing everything. Now he can only say, "Doeg is for me" (contrast Ps. 56:9). When only Doeg is for me, I am in trouble. Make no mistake, the picture of Saul is tragic and sad. Nevertheless to see the weakness of his power is consoling to God's people. It provides an encouraging supplement to the apostle's statement: Even now many antichrists have come—and gone.

God's Remnant Reveals the Invincibility of His Church (22:20-23)
Saul may have nothing left but raw power but a look around Nob convinces us that raw power is pretty powerful. But not

---

6. On Antiochus Epiphanes, see F. F. Bruce, *Israel and the Nations* (Grand Rapids: Eerdmans, 1963), 143–46.

7. Walter Brueggemann, *First and Second Samuel*, Interpretation (Louisville: Westminster/John Knox, 1990), 161. Brueggemann goes on to add: "He has no religious support, no legitimacy, no charisma. We are watching the performance of power from which the spirit has departed. Such power can only cause death."

8. See Gutbrod, *Das Buch vom König*, 187.

completely so. One of Ahimelech's sons, Abiathar, escapes, flees to David, spills the tragic news, and finds sanctuary with him. David treats Yahweh's priests much differently than Saul does. The whole section seems designed to depict this contrast. Note the pattern of the major scenes:

```
Saul and servants, 6-8
    (Saul's complaint)
    Doeg's disclosure, 9-10
        Saul and Ahimelech, 11-16
            Summons, 11
            Accusation, 12-13
            Defense, 14-15
            Sentence, 16
Saul and servants, 17
    (Saul's order)
    Doeg's deed, 18-19
        David and Abiathar, 20-23
            Flight, 20
            Information, 21
            Confession, 22
            Protection, 23
```

The "Saul and Ahimelech" and "David and Abiathar" sections stand in direct opposition to one another, especially the final words of Saul and David respectively: "You shall surely die" (v. 16) versus "You will be safe with me" (v. 23 NJB). David is the protector and preserver of the priests.[9]

We must not downplay Abiathar's escape. We would be wrong to think it insignificant. Joseph Stalin prohibited the movie version of *The Grapes of Wrath* from being shown in the Soviet Union. The intent of the filmmakers was to depict the downside of American life. What problem could Stalin possibly have with showing the Soviet people a dreary picture of life in the States? Ah, but the movie showed that in the United States the poor had trucks and could go wherever they wanted. That was, in a word, too "political."[10] We may think

---

9. J. P. Fokkelman, *Narrative Art and Poetry in the Books of Samuel*, vol. 2, *The Crossing Fates (I Sam. 13–31 & II Sam. 1)* (Assen/Maastricht: Van Gorcum, 1986), 412, has worked out a far more sophisticated structure of 22:6-23 that sees Ahimelech's defense (vv. 14-15) as the centerpoint. My proposed structure is developed around the scenes in the chapter.

10. Lloyd Billingsley, *The Seductive Image: A Christian Critique of the World of Film* (Westchester, Ill.: Crossway, 1989), 148.

nothing of poor folks in the thirties having a beat-up truck, but it was too significant for Stalin. So too Abiathar's escape and preservation are more important than we may surmise. Abiathar's escape and safety are important for they are a sign of how Yahweh always preserves his people in the midst of destruction. Abiathar is another exhibit of evidence for a pattern Yahweh seems to follow. Are Israel's infant sons ordered to Davy Jones' locker by Pharoah's decree? God will preserve one of them, one who will make quite a difference (Exod. 2:1-10). Does it seem that Baal has conquered and is lord and master of Israel? Yahweh will see that there will be seven thousand whose knees never bend to him (1 Kings 19:18). Does Athaliah's murder of the royal seed threaten to falsify the Davidic covenant? One of God's dear ladies will see that baby Joash does not fall to Athaliah's dripping sword (2 Kings 11:2-3). Will a new pharaoh named Herod cut down Bethlehem's toddlers in his fury? One of those toddlers will escape (Matt. 2:13-15). Herod had no idea that it was difficult to reverse redemption once God had ordained it.

Abiathar then stands as a witness to the way Yahweh insistently preserves a remnant of his people. The priests of Yahweh may be destroyed, but not completely destroyed. The people of God may often be put down but never put out. Abiathar's escape does not mean that all God's servants are immune from the world's butchery but that the world's butchery can never wipe out all of God's servants. The Lord does not promise that we will never die for the kingdom of God but that the kingdom of God will never die. (If that is what we are seeking anyway, Matthew 6:33, that will be comforting news.) I like the way the Westminster Confession of Faith underscores this point in its chapter (25) on the church. The confession rehearses a number of semidisclaimers: this catholic (i.e., universal) church has been sometimes more, sometimes less visible, and particular churches in this church are more or less pure, and public worship is performed more or less purely in them. Even "the purest churches under heaven are subject both to mixture and error" and some have gone so far into error that they have become nonchurches, that is, synagogues of Satan. Then comes the bottom line: "Nevertheless, there shall be always a church on earth to worship God according to his will." And Abiathar is witness.

STUDY QUESTIONS

1. Can you identify 'antichrist' figures in modern history? Note, of course, that 'antichrist' is not spelled with a capital letter in this question.

2. The truth of God's sovereignty even over the evil designs of his enemies was both preached and prayed by the early church. What such situations can you identify, on a world scale or a local scale, today?

3. Look at Question 1 again. How many of these figures have now gone and how did God's sovereign overruling in history figure in their demise?

4. Because of his royal power, Saul could kill the priests. Reflect on the fact that those in authority should have moral qualities as well as power, and pray for local, national and international leaders, as the Bible exhorts us to do (in 1 Tim. 2:1,2).

5. Consider how many of God's promises apparently hung on the preservation of the life of Joash as recorded in 2 Kings 11:2-3.

21

The God Who Provides
(1 Samuel 23)

Anyone coming fresh from 1 Samuel 21 and 22 into chapter 23 can easily note some fascinating contrasts. At Nob Saul is the destroyer of Israel (22:16-19), but here, at Keilah, David becomes the savior of Israel (23:1-5).[1] Saul complains that no one discloses urgent matters to him (22:7-8), but God discloses via Abiathar all that David needs to know (23:6-13). Saul's companion is Doeg, the Edomite killer (22:9-10, 18-19), who covers Saul's hands with blood; David's support is Jonathan, the royal son, who strengthens his hand in God (23:16-18). Previously, the Philistines were a dangerous threat to David (21:10-15); now they are his welcome saviors (23:25-28).

David, however, can hardly afford to ponder literary contrasts. He is a wandering outlaw on the run from Saul, his life always at risk (v. 14b). David needs assurance that Yahweh provides for his servants in their desolate, trying times. Apparently, he received that—if Psalm 54 is any indication (see the "Ziphite" heading of the psalm). In the face of human treachery, David bears his witness: "Surely God is my help; the Lord is the one who sustains me" (Ps. 54:4 NIV).[2] What

---

1. See Moshe Garsiel, *The First Book of Samuel: A Literary Study of Comparative Structures, Analogies and Parallels* (Jerusalem: Rubin Mass, 1990), 122, and J. P. Fokkelman, *Narrative Art and Poetry in the Books of Samuel*, vol. 2, *The Crossing Fates (1 Sam. 13–31 & II Sam. 1)* (Assen/Maastricht: Van Gorcum, 1986), 422.

2. The structural center of the psalm; see Willem A. VanGemeren, "Psalms," *The Expositor's Bible Commentary*, 12 vols. (Grand Rapids: Zondervan, 1991), 5:389.

resources then does God make available to his servant in his continuing trial?

Divine Access (23:1-13)

There was trouble at Keilah—the Philistines were raiding the threshing floors and making off with the grain (v. 1), which was both frustrating (Keilah's farmers do all the work, the Philistines get the goodies) and life-threatening (no grain, no bread). Keilah was a fortified town in the Shephelah of Judah, located a bit over eight miles northwest of Hebron and about three miles south of Adullam.

Someone told David about the trouble. (Someone is always telling David—or Saul—something [vv. 1, 7, 13, 25]; both must have had effective intelligence networks.) We don't know where David was at the time. He was spotted in the forest of Hereth (22:5)—wherever that is.[3] David is most willing to counter the Philistine menace and asks direction from Yahweh (v. 2).[4] David received assurance from Yahweh that he would have success against the Philistines (v. 2b). But David's men were not so sure—trying to jockey out of Saul's path in Judah is one thing but is it really sane to attempt a direct hit on the Philistines (v. 3)? David asks direction from Yahweh again. No, there was no mistake (v. 4). So David and his men go, attack, drive off the Philistines' cattle, decisively defeat them, and "save" Keilah (v. 5) just as Yahweh had said (v. 2b).[5]

Verse 6 constitutes a for-your-information note, explaining how it was that David could "ask" direction from Yahweh (vv. 2, 4) and get such clear guidance. When Abiathar fled to join David, "the ephod came down in his hand."[6] Far from being a throwaway line, verse 6 is the hinge of the whole

---

3. There is no certainty about the location; see William Sanford LaSor, "Hereth, Forest of," *ISBE*, rev. ed., 2:687.

4. In his willingness to protect Keilah "David appears here as the man who takes up the task of the king of Israel although he does not occupy his throne" (Hans Wilhelm Hertzberg, *I & II Samuel*, The Old Testament Library [Philadelphia: Westminster, 1964], 190).

5. The Philistines' cattle may have been their beasts of burden brought along to transport the plundered grain; so Hertzberg, *I & II Samuel*, 191.

6. On the ephod and its attachments, see Exodus 28; 1 Samuel 14:36-42. For explanation see my *Such a Great Salvation: Expositions of the Book of Judges* (Christian Focus, 2000), 113–14.

section, highlighting both how Keilah was saved (vv. 1-5)[7] and how David and his men were saved (vv. 7-13). Yahweh's guidance through Abiathar's ephod directed David both to go to and to get out of Keilah. The structure of verses 1-13 shows that verse 6 is indeed the centerpoint of the passage:[8]

> Report about Philistines' attack, 1
> Guidance from Yahweh, 2-4
> (two inquiries about going to Keilah)
> David saves Keilah, 5
> Abiathar and ephod, 6
> Saul to attack Keilah, 7-8
> Guidance from Yahweh, 9-12
> (two inquiries about leaving Keilah)
> Report about David's escape, 13

Everything then hinges on Abiathar and the ephod. By such guidance David has success in both his attack and his escape. Saul thought he traced the smile of providence because David could be cornered in a fortified town (vv. 7-8). But David had recourse to Abiathar (v. 9). Verses 10-12 probably give us as close a look at ephod-guidance as we'll ever get. In a moving plea David asked Yahweh two specific questions (v. 11a) and received two affirmative answers (vv. 11b-12).

---

7. Robert Polzin (*Samuel and the Deuteronomist* [San Francisco: Harper and Row, 1989], 201) thinks Abiathar and the ephod figured only in the guidance of verses 9-12 but not in that of verses 2 and 4. He thinks the formula in verses 2 and 4, to "ask [$\check{sa}$'al] from Yahweh," more likely points to direction received by a prophet's word. This is not the case. First Samuel 14:37 shows in context that $\check{sa}$'al is being used of asking for divine guidance via the priest, and 30:7-8 depict David using Abiathar's ephod to ask ($\check{sa}$'al) direction from Yahweh. The real rub with verse 6 is that, taken strictly, it implies that Abiathar did not join David until David was already on location at Keilah; so how could Abiathar and the ephod have been at David's disposal beforehand? The Septuagint solves it with bug-free geography: "When Abiathar son of Ahimelech fled to David, he went down with David to Keilah having an ephod in his hand." That dissolves the problem, and McCarter prefers LXX here (see P. Kyle McCarter, Jr., *I Samuel,* The Anchor Bible [Garden City, N.Y.: Doubleday, 1980], 369). But I see no major problem with the Hebrew text; we needn't milk the topography for all it's worth. "To Keilah" could be equivalent to "in the Keilah situation." Compare C. F. Keil, *Biblical Commentary on the Books of Samuel* (1875; reprint ed., Grand Rapids: Eerdmans, 1950), 229, and R. Payne Smith, *I Samuel,* The Pulpit Commentary (London: Funk and Wagnalls, n.d.), 432.

8. Hardly in an "awkward position," nor a "gloss" as Ralph W. Klein holds (*1 Samuel,* Word Biblical Commentary [Waco: Word, 1983], 229). Fokkelman (*The Crossing Fates,* 421) recognizes the central position of 23:6 but does not seem to map it out structurally.

David didn't need to ask any more questions; he knew what to do (v. 13).

One can scarcely overestimate the privilege David enjoys in verses 1-13. Again, David's advantage stands opposed to Saul's deficiency (see our comments on 22:5, guidance through the prophet Gad). In contrast to Saul (16:14; 18:12; see too 28:6, 15), David has access to Yahweh and Yahweh's guidance through the appointed priest (whom, ironically, Saul had driven into David's arms, 1 Sam. 22).

A contemporary believer may say, "I see that, and it's all very nice, but I don't receive the kind of precise, direct guidance that David did." Neither do I. Because I don't need it. I'm not the chosen king. It does my ego no damage to concede that David's function in salvation history is far more crucial than mine. The fortunes of the kingdom of Yahweh in this world rest far more on David's preservation than on mine. What was essential for Yahweh's elect king to have he received. For me, it is not so essential. But in principle there is no difference between this elect king and myself. In what context was Yahweh's guidance given? Was it not in access to God through the appointed priest? And is that not the privilege I enjoy? Through a much greater one than Abiathar? What, after all, does Hebrews 4:14-16 mean? "Since we have a great high priest," we come to the throne of grace and find grace "for help at just the right time." Knowing whether Saul will come down to Keilah can't be any better than that.

Divine Encouragement (23:14-18)

This brief chunk of text consists of a general summary (vv. 14-15) and a particular episode (vv. 16-18). The general summary gives us David's location, the wilderness of Ziph. The site of Ziph was about four miles southeast of Hebron. David then is very deep in the territory of Judah, losing himself in the wilderness area to the east of Ziph.[9] But, more importantly, this summary tells of David's preservation (v. 14b). In all the topography and geography David, though he may escape Saul, never escapes the shelter of the Most

---

9. For a description, see George Adam Smith, *The Historical Geography of the Holy Land*, 22d ed. (London: Hodder and Stoughton, n.d.), 312–14.

High. "Saul sought him constantly, but God did not give him into his hand." That text wraps its arms around all of David's "outlaw" experience.[10]

But if Saul did not find David, Jonathan could! "Then Jonathan, Saul's son, arose and went to David at Horesh, and strengthened his hand in God" (v. 16). What an oasis Jonathan must have made in the wilderness of Ziph with such encouragement! The text does not say how Jonathan knew where to find David; it doesn't dwell on the risks Jonathan ran; it only says that "he put David's hand as it were into God's hand."[11]

Yet how did Jonathan so encourage David? By what he said in verse 17: "Don't be afraid, for the hand of Saul my father will never find you, but *you* will reign over Israel, and *I* will be second to you; moreover, Saul my father knows this."[12] Jonathan simply reaffirms God's promise to David, a promise nowhere directly stated to David in 1 Samuel but which everyone seems to know about (see 24:4; 25:28-31; 2 Sam. 3:9-10, 17-18). Of course Jonathan's presence itself would have been a great comfort and refreshment for David. Yet our personal presence does not have the *abiding* encouragement that God's sure word does. We best encourage not by being cuddly with people but by reminding them of the promises of God. Encouragement from God for the people of God comes from the word of God. I am not depreciating the helpfulness of the personal touch or care, but in an age that wallows in "caring" and "sensitivity" on every hand believers need to know that solid encouragement comes not from emotional closeness but from God's speech.

The reader will not appreciate Jonathan's encouragement fully until he or she places it within the context and/or general

---

10. David "knows that Saul is constantly on his tracks. Hence the remark at the beginning, that God did not give David into Saul's hand, is an important one. It gives a title to the whole section. Saul may pursue and David may be pursued, but it is firmly fixed in the divine plan that David will remain safe. No man can alter anything in this long-arranged course of events" (Hertzberg, *I & II Samuel*, 193).

11. W. G. Blaikie, *The First Book of Samuel*, The Expositor's Bible (Cincinnati: Jennings and Graham, n.d.), 360.

12. Fokkelman (*The Crossing Fates*, 440) understands the covenant of verse 18a to be not so much a reconfirmation of the covenant of chapter 20 but a ratification of the work distribution spelled out in verse 17 David king, Jonathan his vizier.

structure of the chapter. It is a simple matter but easily overlooked:

The slipperiness of Keilah, 7-13
The encouragement through Jonathan, 14-18
The treachery of the Ziphites, 19-24

One can understand the dilemma Keilah's town council faced (vv. 8, 10). No doubt they'd heard how Nob (1 Sam. 22) had fared under Saul's ire. Their willingness to hand David their savior over to Saul (vv. 11, 12) is hardly commendable but certainly typical. Keilah's spinelessness was not impulsive; she might even have regretted her inconstancy. All the same David could not count on Keilah any more than he could count on Ziph. If the Ziphites were treacherous, the men of Keilah were, in American slang, flaky. If David cannot lean on the gratitude of those he has helped (Keilah) or on people within his own tribal territory of Judah (Ziph), where is fidelity to be found? Ironically, in the son of Saul his enemy. After disappointment with Keilah and before betrayal from Ziph, "Jonathan, Saul's son, arose and went to David in Horesh" (v. 16a).

How well then Yahweh times the encouragement of his servants. Some questions we can't answer are yet worth asking. Without Jonathan's ministry to David would the Ziphite betrayal (vv. 19-24) have been more than David could bear? Would treachery (Ziph) on the heels of disillusionment (Keilah) have proven too much? How large verse 16b looms! How necessary to have the faithful one standing amid the infidelities of life.

Perhaps believers cannot help seeing here in Jonathan's mission the shadow of a greater than Jonathan. Andrew Bonar referred in his diary for May 26, 1860, to a visit in the neighborhood of a previous parish he had served:

> Spent an hour in my old retreat in the wood of Dunsinnane, the place which I used to call the 'Wood of Ziph,' where God has often strengthened my hands, my divine Jonathan meeting me there.[13]

---

13. Marjory Bonar, ed., *Andrew A. Bonar: Diary and Life* (Edinburgh: Banner of Truth, 1960), 203.

Jonathan Edwards longed for the same "divine Jonathan" when on his deathbed he asked, "Now where is Jesus of Nazareth, my true and never-failing Friend?"[14] It was this friendship of the Lord that Paul cherished when others left him:

> At my first defense, no one came to my support, but everyone deserted me. . . . But the Lord stood at my side and gave me strength ... [2 Tim. 4:16-17 NIV]

The scene at Horesh closes on a solemn note. Neither David nor Jonathan could know at the time how solemn it was. "So David stayed on in Horesh, but Jonathan went to his house" (v. 18b). It was the last time they ever saw each other. Hence there is a heaviness in those words, "But Jonathan went to his house." He went home but he had accomplished his mission. "He strengthened his hand *in God.*" Jonathan is not the presence David needs.

Divine Providence (23:19-28)
Lastly, Yahweh grants displays of his providence to his hard-pressed servant in the face of a nearly fatal betrayal.

Some of the folks around Ziph, probably wanting to ingratiate themselves with Saul, go up to Gibeah and disclose David's location: "Is not David hiding himself among us in the strongholds in Horesh, at the Hill of Hachilah to the south of the Desolation [or: Jeshimon]?" (v. 19). Let Saul come and they will be only too glad to hand David over (v. 20). Saul's response, taking three verses, begins with benediction and self-pity (v. 21), worries over the caution, precision, and accuracy needed (vv. 22-23a), and ends with a burst of premature braggadocio (v. 23b).

Things develop rapidly when condensed into two verses: the Ziphites return for the finishing touch (v. 24a); David and Co. are now in the wilderness around Maon (v. 24b), a site a little over four miles south of Ziph (hence about eight miles south of Hebron); Saul comes to hunt David (v. 25a); David remains in the wilderness of Maon but goes down (seemingly

---

14. Iain H. Murray, *Jonathan Edwards: A New Biography* (Edinburgh: Banner of Truth, 1987), 441.

eastward) to an area called "the Rock" (v. 25b); Saul is now in full pursuit (v. 25c), and soon it looks as though the Rock will become the grave.

Readers are in for a real nail-biter; the tension becomes nearly unbearable in verse 26. Saul and David are on opposite sides of the same hill (v. 26a); then the graphic Hebrew participles in verse 26b depict in slow but unrelenting motion how Saul is tightening the noose:

> Now David and his men were hurrying to get away from Saul, and Saul and his men were closing in on David and his men to seize them.

Sympathetic Bible readers close their eyes at this point. They refuse to watch the capture, humiliation, and, likely, death. Wait—what is that shouting? That frantic calling for the king? "But a messenger came to Saul: 'Quick! Come on! for the Philistines have made a raid upon the land'" (v. 27). "So Saul turned back from pursuing after David..." (v. 28a). You see it, don't you? "Saul and his men were closing in on David... but a messenger came....'"

Of course you can read this with blind, unbelieving eyes, babbling about how David can thank his lucky stars he eluded Saul, or you can read it with the clear vision of faith, exulting in the endless variety of ways in which Yahweh delivers his servants, laughing at the humor of it all (David, not for the last time, accepting the Philistines as his personal savior), marveling at Yahweh's timing, and rejoicing that even Philistines can be pressed into the Lord's service. "The Rock of Divisions" (v. 28b) indeed! A suitable name for an unforgettable place.

This episode reminds me of a prayer of Alexander Peden, a Scottish covenanter. Once Peden and some others were being pursued by horse and foot soldiers. Peden and his friends gained some distance from their pursuers and stopped for a needed breather and desperate prayer. Peden prayed: "Lord, this is the hour and the power of Thine enemies; they may not be idle. But hast Thou no other work for them than to send after us? Send them after them to whom Thou wilt give strength to flee, for our strength is gone. Twine them about the hill, O Lord...." The Lord answered with a cloud of mist between them and their persecutors.[15] "Hast Thou no other work for them than to send after us?" In David's case God had other work Saul could do, so a messenger came.

Yahweh's deliverance, however, is not only of the just-the-right-time variety—there is also a delightful irony about it. Let us get at this point with a thematic layout of the whole chapter, which will both summarize the emphases of the text and allow us to explain the irony mentioned:

Unexpected saviors, 1-5
   Human faithlessness, 6-13
      Divine faithfulness, 14
      Human faithfulness, 15-18
   Human treachery, 19-24a
Unexpected saviors, 24b-28

Sections 1 and 6 correspond to one another. David and his men fill the role of unexpected saviors in that one would normally think such a work of deliverance (i.e., for Keilah) would be the task of the king. But Saul did not deliver Keilah. David did. Naturally, in section 6 the Philistines are the unexpected saviors; it is a who-would-have-ever-guessed? episode. The irony comes with the reversal of roles. In verses 1-5 the Philistines are the enemy, but in verses 27-28 they have become the savior. That is so frequently a mark of Yahweh's providence, that strange twist, sometimes with a touch of humor.

Verses 19-28 then teach us what providence means—the strange ways God works to keep his people on their feet. Is this providence for David only? Don't some of us have some stories to tell about God's strange saviors and startling timing? Is it only in Bible pages that Yahweh's providence works?

"Surely God is my help; the Lord is the one who sustains me." No, Saul is not gone for good; David's distress is not over; final relief has not arrived. But 1 Samuel 23 does show what resources Yahweh gives his servants in the middle of their trials so that they can withstand the pressure of them.

---

15. John Whitecross, *The Shorter Catechism Illustrated from Christian Biography and History* (reprint ed., London: Banner of Truth, 1968), 20.

True, the darkness is still there, but perhaps part of it is the *shadow* of the Almighty (Ps. 91:1).

Study Questions

1. Christians often do not feel too much at home in the Epistle to the Hebrews because it uses so much the language of priesthood and ceremony – but what are the vital spiritual consequences for us of the fact that Christ is our great high Priest, a truth which finds its major exposition in Hebrews?

2. How much do you owe to encouragers, people like Jonathan and Barnabas? Identify some of them and thank God for them.

3. Why not memorise some of the great promises of Scripture, not only for your own comfort but to encourage others when you find they need this?

4. 'How well then Yahweh times the encouragement of his servants.' Can you think of examples from your own experience of God's wonderful timing?

5. Do you think we are sensitive enough to the ironies of Scripture? How full the accounts of the passion and death of our Lord are of this feature!

22

This Is the Day! Or Is It?
(1 Samuel 24)

Like the mozzarella cheese on your pizza, chapters 24, 25, and 26 all hang together. They recount different situations but share a common theme, as the following summary shows.

Text	Characterization	Theme
1 Samuel 24	The robe episode	The "control" of
1 Samuel 25	The feast episode	David, who waits for
1 Samuel 26	The spear episode	Yahweh's promise

Readers have long known that David is the man after Yahweh's own heart (13:14), and chapters 24–26 show that the man after Yahweh's own heart does not seize the kingship Yahweh promised but waits for it to be given to him.

Here our focus is 1 Samuel 24. With scarcely time for breath, readers are dragged eastward from Maon to En-gedi (23:29–24:2), an oasis on the western shore of the Dead Sea, favored with a perennial spring located several hundred feet up a large cliff. Some of the older writers give a picturesque and memorable description of the area, the sheepfolds in front of the caves, and the caverns.[1]

---

1. See, e.g., W. M. Thomson, *The Land and the Book*, 2 vols. (New York: Harper and Brothers, 1873), 2:419–21; George Adam Smith, *The Historical Geography of the Holy Land*, 22d ed. (London: Hodder and Stoughton, n.d.), 269–72; and A. F. Kirkpatrick, *The First Book of Samuel*, The Cambridge Bible for Schools and Colleges (Cambridge: Cambridge University Press, 1896), 195. En-gedi = "spring of the kid/goat." See, more recently, Theodor H. Gaster, *Myth, Legend, and Custom in the Old Testament*, 2 vols. (New York: Harper Torchbooks, 1975), 2:457–58.

Our writer is abrupt with us. He does what no Israelite would normally do—he shuns the Philistines. Saul had gone off to fight them (23:28), but our writer gives us no hint as to how Saul or the Philistines fared.[2] In the written account so quickly is Saul at David's throat again that even David may wonder if he had enjoyed a breather! Saul is never without a scouting report (24:1); hence he comes after David near En-gedi with three thousand of his top-flight troops (v. 2). Needing a rest room (lit., to cover his feet), and perhaps a rest, Saul enters a cave (v. 3a). Then the writer springs his surprise: "But David and his men were staying in the inner recesses of the cave" (v. 3b). He sets the scene in three quick verses, and, in light of verse 3b, whatever happens can't fail to be exciting.[3]

A Test for Yahweh's Servant (24:4-7)

While Saul relaxes, David and his men carry on a spirited debate about the will of God for David's life. It is almost as if David's men began singing a snip of that chorus, "This is the day, this is the day that the Lord hath made...." Who could not see what God had brought about? "Look! Here's the day Yahweh spoke to you about: 'See! I am giving your enemy into your hand and you shall do to him as you please' " (v. 4). It doesn't matter whether David's men are quoting a previous oracle of Yahweh or simply interpreting the present occasion.[4] They can tell a stroke of providence when they see one, and no one needs to go to Bible college to understand what Yahweh is up to in this situation.

David's action follows—he cuts off part of the edge of Saul's robe (v. 4b). In 15:27-28 the tearing of a robe, probably Samuel's, signified the forfeiture of the kingdom for Saul. Hence David "staked his claim to the kingdom that day in the cave when he removed a piece from Saul's robe."[5] David's act may have been a symbolic declaration of revolt. Only such

---

2. Cf. J. P. Fokkelman, *Narrative Art and Poetry in the Books of Samuel*, vol. 2, *The Crossing Fates (I Sam. 13-31 & II Sam. 1)* (Assen/Maastricht: Van Gorcum, 1986), 451.

3. Note that the majority of the story is told via speeches and conversation.

4. Cf. S. R. Driver, *Notes on the Hebrew Text and the Topography of the Books of Samuel*, 2d ed. (1913; reprint ed., Winona Lake, Ind.: Alpha, 1984), 192–93.

5. Robert P. Gordon, "David's Rise and Saul's Demise: Narrative Analogy in 1 Samuel 24-26," *Tyndale Bulletin* 31 (1980): 55–56.

heavy symbolism explains David's remorse: "David's heart struck him" (v. 5). Even his symbolic action had gone too far.

David's action and especially his remorse explain his principle: "May Yahweh keep me from doing this thing to my lord, to Yahweh's anointed—to stretch out my hand against him, for he is Yahweh's anointed" (v. 6). As Yahweh's anointed, Saul's person was sacrosanct and must not be violated.

> Why did men consider the anointed to be inviolate, to be kept from attack, and to be preserved from degradation? The answer lies in the fact that once anointed, the individual was set apart or consecrated to God. A specific bond was established in relation to God, in separation from men and women in general, and from the common aspects of life in particular.
>
> ...Hence to touch, defile, and attack the anointed one was to approach the Lord himself and to seek to defile, harm, and remove the Lord from his rightful place.[6]

But try to tell that to David's men. Apparently David had to get quite forceful with them. One would never know it from our Bible versions, most of which allege in verse 7 that David "persuaded," "rebuked," or "restrained" his men with words. But the Hebrew text reads, "So David *tore apart* his men with the words," suggesting that David had to resort to violent and threatening language to cool their blood. Many commentators (and seemingly some ancient versions) think the word is too strong, but I do not see why. It is the writer's very point: David had to "tear them up" or "cut them down" with his words in order to prevent the spilling of Saul's blood.[7] Meanwhile, Saul gets up and goes his way (v. 7b), oblivious to the fact that his premier enemy had just saved his skin.

Let us punch the rewind button and go back to the cave. There sits helpless Saul. David squats down on his haunches watching him. Words flow through David's mind. "See! I am giving your enemy into your hand." Was this providence or

---

6. Gerard Van Groningen, *Messianic Revelation in the Old Testament* (Grand Rapids: Baker, 1990), 25. See his whole discussion, pp. 23–28. See also Roland de Vaux, "The King of Israel, Vassal of Yahweh," *The Bible and the Ancient Near East* (Garden City, N.Y.: Doubleday, 1971), 152–66.

7. On the verb šāsaʿ in verse 7 (v. 8 in Heb.), see Driver, *Notes on the Hebrew Text*, 193–94. Of English versions, NEB comes closest to the sense with "David reproved his men severely."

temptation? And how does one discern the difference? It was a searching test for Yahweh's servant. Only the principle of the sanctity of Yahweh's anointed (v. 6) answers the dilemma. That was not so clear, seemingly, to David's men (v. 7). For David, however, it was one thing to have the promise of the kingdom (20:13-16; 23:16-17); how the kingdom should come to him was another matter. Yahweh's will must be achieved in Yahweh's way; the end that God has ordained must be reached by the means that God approves. David's men do not see this; they "claim to have God in their pocket and to know how he relates to the specific situation."[8] It is so obvious, so clear!

David's Son faced the same test. The devil showed him "all the kingdoms of the world and their splendor, and said to him, 'All these things I will give to you...' " (Matt. 4:8b-9a). What the devil offered him was the will of God for Jesus' life. Jesus doubtless knew that God had promised him all these kingdoms and their splendor (Ps. 2:8-9). But God's will must come to pass in God's way—not via obeisance to the devil but through the humiliation of the cross.

This kind of test is not confined to David and Jesus; it comes again and again to most all Yahweh's servants. It is the temptation of the short cut. How even in our thoughts we often hanker to take it. We sometimes long to find a "key" or a major "breakthrough" or a decisive "insight" that will place our Christian living on some kind of higher plane where we are most always above hindrance, frustration, and despair. Don't some Christians claim they have found this secret? How we yearn for a short cut around the arduous, wearing, time-consuming labor of sanctification (Heb. 12:1-13). What *discernment* we need! No wonder the apostle left us his prayer: "That your love may abound more and more in knowledge and *depth of insight,* so that you may be able to *discern what is best....*" (Phil. 1:9-10a NIV; emphasis added).

An Appeal to Yahweh's Justice (24:8-15)
"My lord, the king!" That shout surely brought goosebumps to Saul's psyche, especially after he turned round and saw

---

8. Fokkelman, *The Crossing Fates,* 454.

David with his face to the ground doing homage (v. 8). David gives no time for Saul to reply but launches into an extended speech in which he argues the case for his innocence (vv. 9-11) and enters his plea for Yahweh's justice (vv. 12-15).

David rehearses for Saul what readers already know: the fact of providence ("Your eyes see how Yahweh gave you into my hand today in the cave," v. 10a), the voice of opportunism ("some said to kill you," v. 10b), the principle of restraint ("I will not put forth my hand against my master, for he is Yahweh's anointed," v. 10c), and the proof of it all (v. 11). Did the bottom drop out of Saul's stomach when David held up that chunk of his robe? "Look, yes look, at the edge of your robe in my hand" (v. 11a). David could have been far more cutting than this! How can Saul seek to bushwhack David when there is obviously no harm, revolt, or wrong in David toward Saul (v. 11b)?

Yet David does not seek his security in any change of heart in Saul or in any fresh promise from Saul. Rather, he casts his case upon Yahweh: "May Yahweh judge between me and you" (v. 12a). David is confident that Yahweh will bring vengeance upon Saul for him (v. 12b). Yet David doubly assures Saul, "But I shall never lay a hand on you" (vv. 12, 13 NJB [verses cited according to usual English versification]). Such wickedness will not come from David (v. 13)—this seems to be the point of alluding to the old proverb. David may, however, intend the proverb (= "from wicked men comes forth wickedness") in a two-pronged way, that is, as a vindication of himself (he has no murderous designs on Saul) and as a condemnation of Saul (who is wickedly seeking David's life; what sort of person then must Saul be?). Yet Saul is both wicked and stupid, for the king of Israel is trying to track down a dead dog, a single flea (so the Hebrew; v. 14). The import is that David not only will not but cannot harm Saul. David then comes back to his original point. He has committed his cause to Yahweh (v. 15): "May Yahweh be the judge and decide between me and you; may he examine and defend my cause and give judgment for me by rescuing me from your clutches!" (NJB).[9]

---

9. Actually, the first part of verse 15 is not a wish but a statement, but only NEB and TEV recognize this.

Here then is the secret that explains David's waiting—he has confidence in Yahweh's justice, or better, in Yahweh who will bring justice for him. There will be vengeance (v. 12) but Yahweh will bring it. David will take no vigilante action himself. The case is in Yahweh's hands; he will prosecute it and decide it in David's favor. Therefore, David will await rather than grasp Yahweh's gift. David obeyed Romans 12:19 before Paul wrote it (though Paul derived it from Deut. 32:35-36 and Lev. 19:18).[10]

One qualification. Leaving judgment in God's hands and committing vengeance to God's calendar is no pale, sedate, anemic affair. Check some of our biblical prayers (e.g., Pss. 54:5; 58:6-9; 139:19-24): "In your faithfulness destroy them"; "Break the teeth in their mouths, O God"; "If only you would slay the wicked, O God!" (all NIV). Some folks seem to reel in shock before such "harsh" and "vindictive" prayers. They never get past the words themselves but are held captive by their own western sentimentality. Certainly, these are passionate, volatile, high-temperature prayers. And obedient prayers. What is the pray-er doing except what Scripture commands him to do, namely, committing vengeance to God? The psalmist does not retaliate but asks Yahweh to bring judgment, to set things right. Why criticize him for putting feeling into his obedient prayers? If Yahweh's crushed and afflicted people cannot place their case in his hands and expect him to bring just vengeance in their behalf, what hope can they have? Only a God who rights the wrongs inflicted on his people can be their well-proved help in troubles. Who can blame them if their cries are wrapped in emotion? We commit vengeance to *Yahweh*, but we commit *vengeance* to Yahweh.

In 1661 the "Drunken Parliament" of Charles II sentenced James Guthrie, the covenanter, to be hanged at the cross of Edinburgh, his head to be struck off and publicly displayed,

---

10. Consider John Murray's perceptive comment on Romans 12:19 (also apropos the situation in 1 Sam. 24): "Here we have what belongs to the essence of piety. The essence of ungodliness is that we presume to take the place of God, to take everything into our own hands. It is faith to commit ourselves to God, to cast all our care upon him and to vest all our interests in him. In reference to the matter in hand, the wrongdoing of which we are the victims, the way of faith is to recognize that God is judge and to leave the execution of vengeance and retribution to him" (*The Epistle to the Romans,* The New International Commentary on the New Testament, 2 vols. [Grand Rapids: Eerdmans, 1965], 2:141–42).

his estate to be confiscated, his children declared incapable, in all future days, of holding any office, possessions, lands, or goods in the kingdom. After the deed Guthrie's headless corpse was placed in a coffin and brought into the Old Kirk aisle, where a number of highly respectable ladies prepared his body for proper burial. One gentleman present noticed that some of the ladies dipped their napkins in the blood of the martyr and accused them of performing a "piece of popish superstition." One lady spoke up in defense: "We intend not to abuse it to superstition or idolatry, but to hold that bloody napkin up to Heaven, with our address that the Lord would remember the innocent blood that is spilt."[11] That is appealing to Yahweh's justice. That is the secret behind waiting for his kingdom and righteousness.

An Assurance of Yahweh's Faithfulness (24:16-22)

After Saul recovers himself (v. 16), he answers David. Saul's speech (vv. 17-21) can be broken down very simply:

What Saul acknowledges, 17-19
What Saul knows, 20
What Saul wants, 21

In the first section (vv. 17-19) Saul uses the term *tôbāh* (good, goodness) four times (vv. 17, 18, 19 [twice]), though one cannot easily see this in English translations.[12] Saul admits that David, the "cave man," has shown him indisputable goodness. Then Saul declares what Jonathan had already said Saul knew (23:17)—that David would certainly be king (v. 20). Hence Saul wants David to go on oath that when he comes to power he will not liquidate Saul's household (v. 21), a protection David had already sworn to Jonathan and his house (20:14-17). And David gives his word (v. 22a).

What does David receive from all this? Only another assurance that Yahweh's promise of the kingdom to him will

---

11. Thomas M'Crie, *The Story of the Scottish Church from the Reformation to the Disruption* (1875; reprint ed., Glasgow: Free Presbyterian, n.d.), 259–61.

12. E.g., in RSV: "You have repaid me *good*," v. 17; "how you have dealt *well* with me," v. 18; "will he let him go away *safe*?" lit., on a good road, v. 19a; "the Lord reward you with *good*," v. 19b. See Fokkelman, *The Crossing Fates,* 469.

surely come to pass (v. 20). He only hears once more that
Yahweh's word is dependable. (Sometimes Yahweh's servants
need something that simple.) But how can the words of
David's enemy carry divine assurance to David? Doesn't the
character of the speaker negate the quality of the message?
Not necessarily. Sometimes the firmest assurances can come
from the enemy. At the beginning of the American Civil War
one confided to a friend:

> There is one West Pointer, I think in Missouri, little known, and
> whom I hope the Northern people will not find out. I mean Sam
> Grant. I knew him well at the Academy and in Mexico. I should
> fear him more than any of their officers I have yet heard of. He is
> not a man of genius, but he is clear-headed, quick and daring.[13]

U. S. Grant may have had numerous detractors in the North
but General Richard Ewell of the Confederacy was fearfully
convinced of his competence.

That is David's situation here. He should be greatly heart-
ened that even his enemy confirms the certainty of Yahweh's
promise (v. 20). If Yahweh can speak sense through the
jaws of Balaam's ass (Num. 22), surely he can confirm truth
through the lips of a deranged king. And it should be doubly
assuring when even Saul recognizes David's coming kingship. Maybe it was a day the Lord had made—but for his own
purposes.

To be reassured is one thing; to be stupid is another. David
has no illusions. Saul may go home, but David wisely doesn't
trust him. He and his men get up to the stronghold (v. 22b).[14]

Study Questions

1. 'Providence or temptation' – this can be a dilemma still.
   List for yourself some principles of the godly life which will
   help us to decide in such situations.

---

13. Robert Leckie, *The Wars of America*, 2 vols. (New York: Harper and Row,
1968), 1:410.

14. References to the stronghold(s) frame this narrative. It begins with, "And David
went up from there and stayed in the strongholds of En-gedi" (23:29 = Heb. 24:1),
and closes with, "But David and his men went up to the stronghold" (24:22).

2. Think about godly discernment. Knowing the Word of God is certainly an important factor in it. Can you think of others?

3. You may have some situation in your own experience where you need confidence that the Lord is a God of justice. Are you prepared to wait confidently for this without taking matters into your own hands?

4. Do you think we tend to sanitise too much some of the strong language used in the Bible?

5. If you have been upset by the sad fall of some Christian who has been a blessing to you in the past, remember that the character of the speaker does not necessarily negate the quality of the message – although of course we should never use this fact to excuse ourselves.

23

Preventive Providence
(1 Samuel 25)

The Characters We Meet

It's always interesting to meet interesting characters. Our writer quickly introduces us to two, but not first by name, at least not for the man. His home is Maon and his work is in Carmel, sites in the deep south of Judah, roughly eight miles south of Hebron; he is prominent and wealthy (i.e., three thousand sheep, one thousand goats); currently, he is holding a profitable and festive (but especially profitable) sheep-shearing time in Carmel (v. 2). Only now are we introduced to Nabal by name. Walter Brueggemann is right:

> This way of introducing Nabal is precisely on target, because Nabal's possessions precede his own person. His life is determined by his property. Nabal lives to defend his property, and he dies in an orgy, enjoying his property. Only after being told of his riches are we told his name (v. 3a).[1]

This fact doesn't encourage our hopes, for Nabal means "fool." Perhaps there is some variety among fools, but Nabal is (in low-level American parlance) a thick-headed clod. Biblically, however, he is worse: Isaiah 32:6 shows that a *nābāl* does

---

1. Walter Brueggemann, *First and Second Samuel*, Interpretation (Louisville: Westminster/John Knox, 1990), 175. See also J. P. Fokkelman, *Narrative Art and Poetry in the Books of Samuel*, vol. 2, *The Crossing Fates (I Sam. 13-31 & II Sam. 1)* (Assen/Maastricht: Van Gorcum, 1986), 481, 489.

not merely lack manners—he is a spiritual, moral, and social disaster.

In the same breath that our writer mentions Nabal by name he also names his wife—Abigail. The couple is a study in contrasts. The writer himself puts it succinctly in verse 3b: Abigail has "good sense and good looks" but Nabal is "hard and nasty." Don't think our writer is being uncharitable toward Nabal. He's simply telling the truth. Nabal's servant (v. 17), his enemy (v. 21), and his wife (v. 25) all agree that the narrator has correctly assessed Nabal. Indeed, Nabal's own words (vv. 10-11) vindicate the writer's estimate.

Nabal's crabby response (vv. 10-11) came in answer to David's request (through his emissaries) for some provisions from Nabal's abundance. As David saw it, Nabal may have had far fewer sheep to shear had David's men not served as voluntary protectors of Nabal's flocks and men. Nor had David and Co. plundered Nabal's flocks themselves. Of course, Nabal had never asked for David's assistance, but it was only right to expect a wealthy man like Nabal to show generous appreciation for services rendered (vv. 7-8). Nabal, as noted, said, "No," but not so simply. He called David a no-count runaway slave and his men a bunch of nobodies who had no right to "*my* bread," "*my* water," and "*my* meat" (v. 11a; emphasis mine—and probably Nabal's).

There is only one way, as conventional wisdom has it, to deal with such obnoxious muleheads. In a word, "sword" (three times in v. 13):

> So David said to his men: "Everyone strap on his sword!" So every man strapped on his sword, and even David strapped on his sword. And four hundred men went up following David....

This problem can be handled quickly. And we are apt to think that Nabal now has a problem. But, of course, we are wrong. David has the problem. He has just now created it—and he does not yet know it.

The Story We Read
Let us leave David while we make one or two additional literary observations.

The chapter before us is a long narrative with little narrative, that is, with little explanation from the narrator himself. The story is dominated by and carried by direct speech: David (vv. 6-8), Nabal (vv. 10-11), David (v. 13), a servant of Nabal's (vv. 14-17), David (vv. 21-22), Abigail (vv. 24-31), and David (vv. 32-35, 39). There are four statements or speeches by David but, clearly, Abigail's speech (vv. 24-31) is the hinge and turning point of the story. There are several ways the story could be displayed structurally but the following proposal will furnish both an overview of the content and some sense of its literary art:

> Nabal and Abigail, 2-3
> > Tension: the stupidity of Nabal, 4-17
> > > David's request, 4-9
> > > Nabal's rejection, 10-11 (anti-David)
> > > David's response, 12-13
> > > Servant's witness, 14-17 (anti-Nabal)
> > Intervention: the wisdom of Abigail, 18-35
> > > Gathering the goods, 18-19
> > > > David's perspective—vengeance, 20-22
> > > > Abigail's plea and wisdom, 23-31
> > > > David's perspective—restraint, 32-34
> > > Accepting the goods, 35
> > Resolution: the work of Yahweh, 36-39
> > > Nabal's revelry, 36
> > > Abigail's news, 37
> > > Yahweh's stroke, 38
> > > David's gratitude, 39
> David and Abigail, 40-42

With this background in mind, let us go on to sketch the teaching of the chapter.

The Restraint of Yahweh's Providence

By "providence" I simply mean that frequently mysterious, always interesting way in which Yahweh *provides* for his servants in their various needs. The dominant note of this chapter is that Yahweh in his timely providence *restrains* his chosen king from his own impulsive folly and wrong. Four times the story confesses Yahweh's restraining action (vv. 26, 33, 34, 39),[2] once in Abigail's counsel, three times in

---

2. In all, three distinct Hebrew verbs are used, but the thematic idea is the same.

David's gratitude. David, in post-Abigail time, had the right hermeneutic: "Yahweh... sent you this very day to meet me" (v. 32).

Back to the story. Every reader of verse 13 knows what four hundred men with swords intend to do, but readers are not told explicitly until verses 21-22. David had probably spoken verses 21-22 at the time of verse 13 (rsv, e.g., is right in translating v. 21a, "Now David had said..."), but the writer reports them as Abigail is about to meet David in order to stress what high stakes are involved in Abigail's mission. If she fails, every male in Nabal's household will bite the dust.

Fortunately, stupid Nabal had a perceptive servant and a resourceful wife. The servant told Abigail how Nabal had vented his spleen on David's servants (v. 14), how good David and his men had been to Nabal's shepherds (vv. 15-16), how vicious they would surely be toward Nabal's household (v. 17a), and, finally, why he was telling all this to Nabal's wife rather than to Nabal: "he is such a brute that no one can say a word to him" (v. 17b njb). But Abigail could do smart things in a hurry. Bread, wine, sheep, grain, raisins, figs (v. 18)—and she was off. But she didn't tell Nabal (v. 19b), because she agreed with the servant's estimate of her husband (v. 17b plus v. 25).

After elaborate obeisance (vv. 23-24a), Abigail asks to assume the guilt (v. 24b) though she herself had known nothing of David's emissaries and their request (v. 25b). She first strikes the note of Yahweh's restraining providence in her opening argument of verse 26. It is a most solemn statement, introduced by an oath:

> And now, my lord, by Yahweh's life and by your own life, since Yahweh has held you back from coming with bloodshed and taking matters into your own hand—now may your enemies and those seeking to harm my lord be as Nabal.[3]

---

3. "Taking matters into your own hand" is my attempt to capture the sense of the Hebrew, which is literally, "Your own hand saving you." English versions commonly translate it with some idea of vengeance ("taking vengeance with your own hand," "avenging yourself"). See William McKane, *I & II Samuel*, Torch Bible Commentaries (London: SCM, 1963), 151. Note that Abigail calls David "my lord" fourteen times in verses 24-31 (count according to Hebrew text).

Apparently Abigail foresaw that Nabal, in some way, would reach his own appropriate end, but clearly she interpreted her intercepting David as Yahweh's deed. Yahweh had held David back from hasty bloodshed and vengeance. This is so important, because it meant that this situation would never prove "a staggering or a stumbling-block of heart" (v. 31, lit.) to David. That is, he would keep his stability by not being haunted by remorse of conscience because he had bloodied his hands out of personal pique.

David confesses that Yahweh through Abigail has kept him from tragic wrong (v. 34). Abigail's intervention kept David from walking in Saul's sandals, kept him from turning Nabal's Carmel into another Nob (see 22:11-19).[4] The rejected king may practice sheer butchery but that is not the way for the chosen king. Yet the chosen one wanted his gore and would have obtained it had Yahweh not sent him a savior in skirts. So...

> [t]hrough Abigail, the Lord saves David from a danger different from that in the cave with Saul, but none the less great. It consists ...in the possibility that David may take matters into his own hand and thus make himself master of his fate, instead of letting it be guided by the Lord.[5]

Abigail's mission is successful. We follow her home where she finds Nabal too drunk to hear sense. Next morning when Nabal had recovered from his royal debauchery (v. 36a), Abigail told him "these things" (v. 37a), apparently how he and his men had narrowly escaped extinction and how she had averted it. (Ironically, Abigail was Nabal's savior too.) Who knows? Was it because of a sudden, sobering fear over such a narrow escape from David's sword? Or was it because of a greedy apoplexy that begrudged Abigail's too-generous bribe? In any case, right there at the breakfast table, or wherever it was, "his heart died within him and he became stone" (v. 37b). But

---

4. On the potential David-Carmel/Saul-Nob parallel, see Karl Gutbrod, *Das Buch vom König*, Die Botschaft des Alten Testaments, 4th ed. (Stuttgart: Calwer, 1975), 208–9; and Fokkelman, *The Crossing Fates*, 516–17.

5. Hans Wilhelm Hertzberg, *I & II Samuel*, The Old Testament Library (Philadelphia: Westminster, 1964), 204.

the *coup de grace* was Yahweh's: "About ten days later Yahweh struck Nabal so that he died" (v. 38). The brevity of verse 38 is probably deliberate. As if to say to David, "Note the simplicity, note the magisterial ease with which Yahweh cares for this matter; how unnecessary all your blusterings."

The text then teaches us how Yahweh rescues his servants from their own stupidity, how he restrains them from executing their sinful purposes, how sometimes he graciously and firmly intercepts us on the road to folly. In the text, of course, Yahweh does this for his anointed king. But Yahweh is not bound up in the biblical text, his mercy is not confined to his special servants, his vigilance over his erring people is not restricted to 1020 B.C. (or whenever). What loving hands construct the roadblocks to our foolishness!

What mercy sends frustration to our purposes! What kindness builds hindrances in our path! It is important that, like David, we respond rightly to such episodes of Yahweh's restraining providence. We could hardly do better than to worship with David's own words: "Blessed be Yahweh who ...has held back his servant from evil" (v. 39).[6]

The Instruction of Yahweh's Providence

Chapter 25 must be seen in its larger context, alongside chapter 24. Anyone reading the narrative straight through should note the contrast. In chapter 24 David is the restrainer; he will not harm Saul himself or permit his men to do so. But in chapter 25 David must be restrained; he is bent on spilling Nabal's blood and that of his men because of Nabal's affront. He refuses to harm the anointed king but is most willing to liquidate a private Israelite. He sees clearly that he must not take personal vengeance against Yahweh's anointed (24:6) but does not make the same connection when it comes to Abigail's husband (25:13, 21-22). Abigail must instruct David here: to slaughter Nabal and his household would be shedding blood without cause (v. 31). In fact, Abigail's words in verses 30-31 suggest that David's vendetta would be both wrong and

---

6. Blaikie's comment is apt: "It is a mark of sincere and genuine godliness to be not less thankful for being kept from sinning than from being rescued from suffering" (W. G. Blaikie, *The First Book of Samuel,* The Expositor's Bible [Cincinnati: Jennings and Graham, n.d.], 386).

foolish, against both precept and policy. Yahweh, she assures him, will certainly bring David into the kingship (vv. 28, 30), but he must leave that matter in Yahweh's hands; he must not allow either a murderous Saul or an obnoxious Nabal to throw him off course. He must not mar God's work with his own folly. David must extend the restraint he showed to Saul to Nabal as well; such is the writer's point.[7]

In chapter 24, therefore, David saw clearly what he must, or rather, must not, do; in chapter 25 he does not see it at all. He does not make the connection between the situations with Saul and Nabal. He does not see the wideness of God's wisdom. Such failure is not unique to David among all the Lord's servants. Have we not been caught in the same net? Can we not recall times in which we saw God's way quite clearly in some dilemma but missed it completely in a fresh situation when the same principles applied? There was no "wisdom transfer."

A few years ago the "Daily Bread" devotional booklet told how a philosophy professor used to begin each term by asking students, "Do you believe we can show that there are absolute values such as justice?" The students, free-thinking as they were, all said no. "Everything is relative" was the consensus— no principle applies to all at all times in all places. Before the semester ended the professor allotted one class session for debating the issue. At the end he concluded: "Regardless of what you think, I want you to know that absolute values can be demonstrated. And if you don't accept what I say, I'll flunk you!" One angry student shot out of his chair and made for the door. As he went out he said, "That's not fair!"

Perhaps our friend, upon reflection, eventually saw what he had done. He had simply demonstrated absolute values. In classroom discussion he had apparently been eager to argue that there are no absolutes (justice) but when a new situation came along, namely, the question of his grade in the course, he suddenly assumed there were such absolutes (justice). "That's not *fair!*" He was not being consistent with his own principles or lack of them. Now I do not agree with his starting point,

---

7. On the parallels in chapters 24–26, see Robert P. Gordon, "David's Rise and Saul's Demise: Narrative Analogy in 1 Samuel 24-26," *Tyndale Bulletin* 31 (1980): 37–64.

but at least we could (I could say "should" but that would sound too absolute) expect him to display greater consistency in answering his professor. If, as he thought, all is relative, he should have said, "Well, sir, while I can acknowledge that to be your position and that your opinion may be valid for you, I hope you can appreciate the fact that most here do not share your opinion. If, however, you insist on imposing it, I suppose we will have to suffer the consequences since you are, for better or worse, in the position of power in this situation. However, since, as I believe, all is relative, my grade—which matter smacks of absolute values anyway—really makes no difference, and I can see no importance in it at all." But that was not his answer. He was blind when it came to thinking through a new situation in a consistent manner.

Our philosophy student needs more help than David. But the manner of their error is the same. Nor is this error unique to Yahweh's king-designate. We often have our blinders on. We see clearly how we must be obedient in some dilemma but change the time, the actors, the circumstances, the background, and we simply don't see the connection. We don't see how the wisdom of the former situation applies to the latter one. How multifaceted Christian wisdom must be. How often our gracious God must stoop down to show us our inconsistency. How we need the instruction of his providence.[8]

The Servants of Yahweh's Providence

Yahweh frequently orders his providential care through human instruments, and 1 Samuel 25 is a textbook rather than an exceptional case of this. There is no doubt that Abigail is the primary servant in arresting David from an impetuous disaster. David acknowledged as much: Yahweh had sent Abigail to meet him (v. 32) and she, thankfully, talked sense (v. 33). Throughout the story Abigail vindicates the narrator's judgment of her (v. 3): she is decisive and resourceful in action (vv. 18-19a), perceptive in circumstances (vv. 19b, 36b-37), courageous in danger (v. 20), engaging in demeanor

---

8. The need for consistent insight pervades Scripture; it is the burden of Hanani's critique of King Asa (2 Chron. 16:7-9), of Jesus' questioning his disciples (Mark 8:17-21), and of Paul's exasperation with Peter (Gal. 2:11-14).

(vv. 23-24), theological, rational, and convincing in argument (vv. 26-31a), and shrewd in suggestion (v. 31b). Clearly, Abigail is the Lord's stop sign, mercifully placed in David's path.

However, I would propose that there is another human instrument of Yahweh's providence in the story. His place is not so prominent yet his role is essential. One might say he is the quiet servant of Yahweh's providence. I refer to the unnamed servant of verses 14-17. I do not want to emphasize something the text does not stress, but, though the writer does not ring bells at verses 14-17, any reader looking back over the whole narrative can realize at once how crucial this servant's speech is. In retrospect everything depends on his having spoken to Abigail. Abigail's intervention depends on the servant's information. He is a minor character of major significance; his role is small but essential.

One sees a similar pattern in the story of 2 Kings 5:1-18. Here is Naaman, part of the brass of the Syrian military, formerly a leper, now perfectly well, thanks to the interesting and baffling grace of Yahweh through Elisha the prophet. But how did he ever meet up with Elisha in the first place? Oh, the Syrians just happened to make one of their raids on Israelite territory. And among all the captives taken there happened to be a "little maid," who just happened to end up serving Naaman's wife. She cared enough about her lady's husband to mention how she was sure the prophet in Samaria could cure the general of his leprosy (2 Kings 5:2-3). Everything in the story, in one sense, depended on that small girl and her perhaps casual remark while busy at her chores.

We must guard our responses to such narratives. We must not wax sentimental over the sweet little maid of 2 Kings 5 or lobby for more recognition for the nameless servant of 1 Samuel 25. We must rather marvel at and adore the God who in his kindness and wisdom leaves no detail untended in his work of delivering his people. He even has nephews precisely where they need to be at just the right time (see Acts 23:16-22)!

The Surplus in Yahweh's Providence
David receives more than the merciful restraint of God's providence in this episode, for in the process he hears fresh

assurance of Yahweh's promise (vv. 28-29). Abigail is both a rein upon David's folly and a goad to his faith. Abigail speaks as a quasi-prophetess, knowing about Yahweh's promise to David and affirming that David will certainly enjoy its fulfillment. There is no doubt: "Yahweh will certainly make for my lord a sure house" (v. 28a). And he will preserve David through all dangers: "Though a man has risen to pursue you and to seek your life, the life of my lord shall be bundled up in the bundle of life with Yahweh your God; but the life of your enemies he will sling away from the hollow of the sling" (v. 29).[9] Saul's traps will never touch one in Yahweh's custody. Hence Abigail confidently speaks of the time when Yahweh will have fulfilled what he had promised David (vv. 30, 31b).

Abigail joins those who know and attest that David will be king as Yahweh promised. She stands then with Jonathan (23:17) and Saul (24:20). And her confident word was likely needed. The reader can go back to chapter 18, comb the whole story again, and see how Yahweh repeatedly grants deliverance and escape (I can tally twelve situations in chaps. 18-23). But David had to run rather than read. In the midst of pressure one does not always calmly garner all the previous evidence for assurance. When your avowed killer uses your cave for his rest room (24:3) one tends to be impressed with the relentless presence of danger. Even an ongoing series of gracious escapes does not exorcise the wearing effect (see 27:1). My point is that David likely needed Abigail's word. This was the "plus" of providence here. Yahweh not only intercepted but encouraged David. And typically he did so with a word of promise. At least that is how he equipped the Servant of Isaiah 50:4: "how to sustain *with a word* him that is weary" (RSV; emphasis added).

Anyone who stands back and looks at 1 Samuel 25 as a whole should sense the necessity of God's providence. First Samuel is depicting how Yahweh is establishing his kingdom on earth and is showing us why that can only be Yahweh's work. The task can never be fully entrusted to human instru-

---

9. The first part of verse 29 is not general and potential as in most English translations ("If men rise up...") but definite and actual, as I have translated it (so too NIV). It is an indirect glance at Saul.

ments, for one will honor his sons above Yahweh (Eli) and another will not be ruled by Yahweh's word (Saul). The kingdom is not even safe in the hands of godly servants, for Samuel would have chosen another Saul as king (1 Sam. 16) and David, for his part, would have greased the kingdom path with Nabal's blood (ch. 25). There was only one Servant who could be trusted with the kingdom—he understood that kingdom glory came from enduring the hostility of Nabals against him (Heb. 12:3).

STUDY QUESTIONS

1. Suppose it was alleged that in this story David is simply carrying on a 'protection racket', what would you say in his defence?

2. Are you as much aware of the Lord restraining you as you are of times when he is prompting you to action?

3. Can you think of incidents in your own life when God's providential intervention has saved you from a wrong course of action? Do such interventions frequently figure in your thankful worship?

4. 'Absolute values' – is such a phrase, for a Christian, another way of affirming the consistency of God?

5. The servant had a small but essential role. Can that apply also to your prayers for others?

6. Can you see how the fact that the kingdom was not even safe in the hands of the Lord's godly servants prepares the way for Jesus Christ. 'There was no other good enough to pay the price of sin, he only could unlock the gate of heaven and let us in.'

24

The Spear Makes the Point
1 Samuel 26

Audacity is usually exciting, and successful audacity especially exciting. In the closing hours of the Battle of Perryville in the War between the States, Confederate General Leonidas Polk found himself in a nasty predicament. A body of troops had fired on his men. Polk was sure they were fellow Confederates and rode round to them, ordering the colonel in charge to cease firing at once. When Polk asked the colonel to identify himself he did so, indicating that he was a commander of an Indiana regiment. Polk had misidentified these troops, and now he was face to face with a Federal officer who demanded that Polk also identify himself. The twilight and the fact that Polk wore a dark cape probably kept him from being easily identified. Polk quickly decided on a bluff, riding right up to the Federal colonel, shaking his fist in his face, and exclaiming, "I'll soon show you who I am, sir. Cease firing, sir, at once." He turned his horse and trotted slowly down the Federal line shouting to the troops to lower their guns. He dare not give the gag away by making a run for it and so kept up his slow pace until he reached a thicket of trees and reasonable safety. When he arrived behind his own lines, he told his men, "I have reconnoitered those fellows pretty closely, and I find there is no mistake who they are; you may get up and go at them."[1]

---

1. Robert P. Broadwater, ed., *The Bronze and the Granite: Stories and Anecdotes of the Civil War Leaders* (Martinsburg, Penn.: Daisy Publishing, n.d.), 32.

In this chapter David is more audacious than Polk, for David's audacity is offensive and deliberate, not defensive and reactionary. The Ziphites had done it again (v. 1; see also 23:19-20) and Saul came stalking David again (vv. 2-3). But as David scouted the layout of Saul's camp (v. 5), he conceived a bold stroke: "Who will go down with me to Saul to the camp?" (v. 6). He asked this of Ahimelech the Hittite and of Abishai, Joab's brother. The latter volunteered. Likely Abishai thought they would form a two-man hit squad to wipe out Saul: they came, they saw, they plundered. But the only plunder David permitted was Saul's spear and water jug (vv. 11b-12a). The spear would make the point.

The overall structure of chapter 26 is clear:

Setting, 1-5
David and Abishai, 6-12
David and Abner, 13-16
David and Saul, 17-25

The last section may be given in more detail:

Saul's question, 17a
David's first answer, 17b-20
Saul's confession, 21
David's second answer, 22-24
Saul's assurance, 25a
Closure, 25b

A quick survey of the three major sections (vv. 6-12, 13-16, 17-25—vv. 1-5 are introductory) finds four speeches of David (vv. 9-11, 15-16, 17b-20, 22-24); these carry much of the theological freight of the chapter. Observe too that Saul's spear is mentioned at least once in each of these three main sections (sometimes along with his water jug). In all there are six references to Saul's spear (vv. 7, 8, 11, 12, 16, 22). It is the dominant symbol of the episode,[2] and, of course, it is essential that David have Saul's spear and canteen (e.g., v. 16) as irrefutable evidence that he really was in Saul's camp, over Saul's body, able to end Saul's life.[3]

---

2. Remember that I have previously characterized chapters 24–26 as the robe episode, the feast episode, and the spear episode, respectively.

So what point does the spear make? The keynote of chapter 26 is that the anointed king receives assurance that the kingdom will certainly be his. Receiving assurance, however, and feeling assured may be two different things. Certainly David's faith does not reach the end of its struggle in this chapter. I would like to develop the teaching of the chapter in terms of the faith of Yahweh's servant.

The Patience Faith Maintains (26:6-12)

David and his men have tracked Saul's movements as Saul and his crack troops arrived south of Hebron near Ziph and as Saul settled at the Hill of Hachilah for his own camp (vv. 2-4).

---

3. I have no zeal to discuss in detail the critical problem of chapters 24 and 26. Biblical criticism commonly assumes these chapters to be "doublets" or duplicates or "divergent" accounts of the same incident. William McKane would speak for many when he says such a position is "more reasonable than the assumption that the Ziphites informed against David on two separate occasions" (*I & II Samuel*, Torch Bible Commentaries [London: SCM, 1963], 154). (Surely the Ziphites would *never* try to turn David in twice!) There is no doubt that the two chapters are very similar, even in structure. Note, for example

Saul and his three thousand	24:1-2	26:1-2
Peril of Saul and restraint of David	24:3-7	26:3-12
Speech of David (including "flea plea" and asking for Yahweh's judgment)	24:8-15	26:13-20 (two parts)
Saul's "repentance" and knowledge of David's success	24:16-22a	26:21-25a (with David's remarks)
Each to his place	24:22b	26:25b

However, real history shows that detailed similarity does not require identity. Marc Bloch, drawing upon Father Delehaye, cites an apt example: "Anyone reading that the church observes a holiday for two of its servants both of whom died in Italy on the very same day, that the conversion of each was brought about by the reading of the Lives of the Saints, that each founded a religious order dedicated to the same patron, and finally that both of these orders were suppressed by popes bearing the same name—anyone reading all this would be tempted to assert that a single individual, duplicated through error, had been entered in the martyrology under two different names. Nevertheless, it is quite true that, similarly converted to the religious life by the example of saintly biographies, St. John Colombini established the Order of Jesuates and Ignatius Loyola that of the Jesuits; that both of them died on July 31, the former near Siena in 1367, the latter at Rome in 1556; that the Jesuates were dissolved by Pope Clement IX and the Jesuits by Clement XIV. If the example is stimulating, it is certainly not unique" (*The Historian's Craft* [New York: Vintage, 1953], 123). Moreover, should we assume that there was only one Battle of Bull Run in the American Civil War (W. G. Blaikie, *The First Book of Samuel,* The Expositor's Bible [Cincinnati: Jennings and Graham, n.d.], 374)? Watch the assumptions. The differences between the episodes of chapters 24 and 26 the reader can easily isolate for himself or herself.

David, who must have been on higher ground near by, saw the precise place where Saul and Abner bivouacked—Saul was lying in the middle of the camp with the troops camping around him (v. 5). That's the way David and Abishai found them when they slithered into the camp at night (v. 7)—plus Saul's spear stuck into the ground near his head.

The emphasis falls on the conversation between Abishai and David (vv. 8-11). Abishai may have surmised they were on a commando raid, a blitzkrieg of terror to dispose of Saul and Abner in particular. In any case, the opportunity was too good to pass up and Abishai broke into his most theological whisper: "Today God has shut your enemy up in your power [lit., hand]—and now let me nail him with the spear into the ground just once; I won't need to try again" (v. 8).[4] David whispers back, also theologically: "Don't destroy him, for who can put forth his hand against Yahweh's anointed and remain innocent?" (v. 9). Then he explains:

> By the life of Yahweh, surely Yahweh himself will strike him down, or his day will come and he will die, or he may go down into battle and be swept away. Yahweh keep me from putting forth my hand against Yahweh's anointed! And now, get the spear that's at his head and the water jug, and let's go." [vv. 10-11][5]

Here is the same patience and restraint as in 24:6, 10, but it is a deeper patience, a more informed restraint. For one thing, David has learned something from his near-fiasco with Nabal (ch. 25). In that situation "Yahweh struck down [Hebrew, *nāgap*] Nabal so that he died" (25:38), and here (26:10) David considers that Yahweh may also "strike down" (*nāgap*) Saul. The use of the same verb may indicate that David has learned that Yahweh can be trusted to handle both fools and oppressors when such matters are left in his hands.[6] Yahweh

---

4. "The irony would then be superb—that Saul should be killed by David's man with Saul's own spear, the symbol of his authority, and in the manner in which he, for his part, had sought to kill David" (David M. Gunn, *The Fate of King Saul*, Journal for the Study of the Old Testament Supplement Series 14 [Sheffield: JSOT, 1980], 102.

5. Four times David refers to the evil of putting forth one's hand against Yahweh's anointed (vv. 9, 11, 16, 23); noted by Robert Polzin, *Samuel and the Deuteronomist* (San Francisco: Harper and Row, 1989), 212. Cf. 24:6, 10.

may be pleased to dispose of Saul as he did Nabal. Or then again he may not. Yahweh may work by some other method — he may permit Saul a "natural" death or he might see that Saul is swept away in battle. There are numerous possibilities. The important matter is that Yahweh will handle Saul's destiny. It is not in David's hands.

A couple of footnotes on David's restraint here, especially the faith that informs it. Note that faith sets imagination to work. David can conceive of various ways in which Yahweh will deliver him from Saul. He may work directly, as he did with Nabal, or he may bring Saul's end in a more "natural" way. The primary matter is that Yahweh will see to it, yet lively faith can envision numerous ways in which Yahweh will work. And there is nothing wrong with that so long as one realizes that Yahweh is not restricted to our range of possibilities and methods.

Many contemporary believers, in fact, would do well to let their imaginations run riot in regard to the adequacy and sufficiency of God. Regretfully, we probably associate imagination with falsehood or fancy. But "faith-full" imagination cannot be accused of that. In fact one might say that faith needs imagination to pull out all the stops if it is even to begin to grasp the grandeur, majesty, and ability of Yahweh. I am thinking, for example, of the stirring comparisons, questions, and pictures of Isaiah 40:12-31. In this sense imagination will not lead us beyond but will help us arrive at the truth of God. Such imagination does not falsify God but finds him. Our minds are so sluggish, uncreative, and proud (i.e., that we insist on only the facts, the dry facts) that we have desperate need of an imaginative faith. Surely God is praised when his people ask, "Who can guess how he will work here?" (see comments at 14:6). As long as we do not try to imprison God's freedom we should feel perfectly free to speculate on the measures he may use to deliver his people.

And now a counter point. Note that although David did not know how providence would work he knew what obedience required. He could imagine diverse ways in which

6. Cf. Robert P. Gordon, "David's Rise and Saul's Demise: Narrative Analogy in 1 Samuel 24-26," *Tyndale Bulletin* 31 (1980): 49.

Yahweh might take Saul out of the way (v. 10); he did not know how Yahweh would do it. But there was something he did know: Yahweh did not want David himself to dispose of the anointed king (vv. 9b, 11a). This situation is not limited to great figures of salvation history like David. Any believer will face predicaments in which he does not know how God will bring relief but does know what is or is not God's will for him. For example, a Christian cannot guess how Christ will bring resolution to a marital problem but does know that he (for instance) must not commit adultery against his wife. Sounds prosaic. God's ways will frequently baffle us but God's will is sufficiently clear to lead us in the meantime. God's ways may not be clear but our way is—at least enough of it to know what obedience requires. We may wait for God's providence but we already have God's law, and that is all we need for the moment.

Abishai may have been severely disappointed. We'll never know. It wouldn't take much imagination (pardon the reference) to hear him telling others: "Saul was snoozing right at my feet—and David wouldn't let me do it! Risked my life tonight for a canteen and a spear!"

The Encouragement Faith Receives (26:13-16)

A reader's mind simply refuses to be quiet when reading verses 6-11. How is it, we ask, that David and Abishai gain unhindered access to Saul's and Abner's location? How can they carry on such an animated debate (though we assume by gesture and whisper) without waking up the troops? How can they filch spear and water jug with no interference? Why are the anti-David forces so helpless? At the end of the section the narrator explains: no one saw, knew, or roused "because a deep sleep from Yahweh had fallen upon them" (v. 12b). We are watching not merely David's daring but Yahweh's hand at work.[7] Saul is helpless because Yahweh made him that way. Once it was by God's mighty Spirit (19:22-24); now it is by his deep sleep.

It must have been unnerving. David escapes to higher and safer ground and destroys the deep sleep with his piercing cry

---

7. Cf. Walter Brueggemann, *First and Second Samuel*, Interpretation (Louisville: Westminster/John Knox, 1990), 185.

into the night: "Aren't you going to answer, Abner?" (v. 14).
Abner staggers to collect his wits (v. 14b) while David continues
his gibe. David's satire is simple: For such a premier career man
Abner has proven a shoddy bodyguard; indeed, all of them
have (the "you" becomes plural after the first clause of v. 16).
The whole lot of them are "sons of death," that is, all Saul's men
should be court-martialed and executed for failure to protect
the life of the king. David isn't joking. The evidence is damning.
Look where the king's spear and water jug are (v. 16b)!

One needn't be too awake to figure this out. For all
his protection (Abner + three thousand troops) Saul is
defenseless. The omnipresent symbol of his power (18:10, 11;
19:9, 10; 20:33; 22:6) has been effortlessly pilfered. David has
"disarmed" Saul—a clear parable on future developments.[8]
With both truth and irony Saul could have said, "There is but
a step between me and death" (cf. 20:3). Even at night one
thing was clear: Saul's power is gone; nothing can keep David
from obtaining the kingdom. It was a sign for Saul but also
for David. David should receive it as encouragement, as an
assuring token from Yahweh.

Yahweh tends to be that kind of God, One who reaches
out to his tired and wearied servants and in the midst of their
discouragement grants them some plain token, some small
evidence, that he has not forgotten his word and promises to
them.[9]

Sometimes the Lord's encouragements can be quite dramatic,
at other times rather mundane. John Flavel wrote of a certain

8. Cf. Karl Gutbrod, *Das Buch vom König,* Die Botschaft des Alten Testaments,
4th ed. (Stuttgart: Calwer, 1975), 213, 215.

9. In applying this text I certainly do not assume that what God did for David he
must do for me. I hope I fully recognize the difference between David and myself. He
is Yahweh's chosen covenant king and occupies a place in the story of redemption
that I do not. I do not look at David primarily at all but at Yahweh as he deals with
David as David's God and Lord. Yahweh reveals himself as a God who acts in certain
ways with his servant. Hence I infer that if Yahweh gives tokens of encouragement to
David, that is likely typical of the way he deals with his servants generally—not only
major servants (e.g., David) of salvation-history stature but common servants who
have now entered the kingdom through the death and resurrection of One greater
than David. In this narrative I look for the revealed character of Yahweh, and when
I see *him* as the One eager to lift up and assure his servant, I assume that if he is
the same God he may be expected to deal similarly with his people today. David's
situation does not control our application of the text; it is the character of David's God
that does so.

Mrs. Honeywood, an earnest Christian who nevertheless felt God had cast her off and that she was without saving hope. One day a minister was meeting with her and marshaling reasons against "her desperate conclusions." It was then she took a Venice-glass from the table and said, "Sir, I am as sure to be damned as this glass is to be broken," and with that she threw it mightily to the ground. To the astonishment of both, the glass remained intact and unbroken. Obviously the minister did not fail to apply the assuring sign![10]

We needn't go around looking for royal spears or unbroken glass. It is enough to have a God who knows when we may need such and who in the midst of pressures likes to show us why we should go on believing.

The Distress Faith Feels (26:17-20)

Saul's stomach must have lurched when he recognized David's voice in the dark. It was no dream; he really was at the Hill of Hachilah listening to David's voice come across the "great gulf" David had been careful to fix between them. As he recovered his wits Saul gave David the "my son" treatment (v. 17a), but David fastened not on Saul's address but on his injustice: "Why does my lord keep pursuing his servant—for what have I done? And what harm is in my hand?" (v. 18). Then David presses on with his major concern and underscores its importance by expressly and formally requesting that Saul listen to "the words of his servant":

> If Yahweh has stirred you up against me, may he accept an offering; but if the sons of men have done so, may they be cursed before Yahweh, for they have driven me out today from joining myself to the inheritance of Yahweh, saying, "Go, serve other gods." And now may my blood not fall to the ground away from Yahweh's face; for the king of Israel has come out to seek a single flea like someone who pursues a partridge into the hills. [vv. 19-20]

Conceivably, Yahweh has instigated Saul's hounding of David as a judgment on David. In such a case David should offer a sacrifice to appease Yahweh. More likely, Saul is egged on

---

10. John Flavel, *The Mystery of Providence* (1678; reprint ed., Edinburgh: Banner of Truth, 1963), 71–72.

by vicious advisors or personal envy (a possibility David, kindly, does not suggest). His unrelenting hunt for David has pushed David to the point of leaving the land of Israel (the inheritance of Yahweh). Wherever he flees he will be in Paganland. It is as if people were saying to him, "Go, serve other gods." How does David mean this? Did David think Yahweh was imprisoned within Israel? That one could only praise him and pray to him on Israelite turf? That if David were in another land he would be coerced to worship its gods? Strictly speaking, I think the answers to these questions are no and no and no. Didn't David know what every "enlightened" Christian knows—that you can pray and commune with God anywhere? Apparently the writer of Psalms 63, 139, and 142 was well aware of that. But David was more enlightened than many enlightened Christians; he knew that to be cut off from "Yahweh's inheritance" (v. 19) was to be cut off from "Yahweh's face" (v. 20), that "when one had left Israel there was no possibility of public worship."[11]

This is not the place to sketch a biblical theology of worship. Suffice it to say that David would have made a poor space-age evangelical; he would never have been content with his study Bible, prayer list, and a quiet cave. Yahweh's face (or presence) was especially seen in the sanctuary (Ps. 63:2); yet David was being driven away and cut off from tabernacle and sacrifice, from priest and festival.[12] He was being shut out of the land and sanctuary where Yahweh met with his people. To be cut off from the ordinances of public worship is David's most severe grief. Would that cause me anguish? Christians have surpassed David in privileges but few have approached him in appetite.

The Hope Faith Holds (26:21-24)
Saul responds to David's speech with a confession, invitation, promise, and rationale all rolled into one:

---

11. H. L. Ellison, *Scripture Union Bible Study Books: Joshua–2 Samuel* (Grand Rapids: Eerdmans, 1966), 68.
12. For a helpful orientation to the relation of Yahweh's presence to the temple worship, see Willem A. VanGemeren, "Psalms," *The Expositor's Bible Commentary*, 12 vols. (Grand Rapids: Zondervan, 1991), 5:809–15.

I am in the wrong. Come back, my son David, for I will never harm you again, seeing how you have held my life precious this day. Yes, I have been a fool, and I have erred so very much. [v. 21 NJPS]

And David responds to Saul abruptly:

Here's the spear, O king! Let one of the young men come over and get it. [v. 22]

Saul can save his breath and his promises. Of course, some readers may question David's bluntness; after all, Saul really sounds sincere this time. But what has sincerity to do with it? Whether Saul expresses a momentary sincerity, a deranged sincerity, a deceptive sincerity, makes no difference. Because Saul has been a fool (v. 21) is no reason for David to be one. On that score Saul spoke the truth but David need not be duped by it.

Instead of returning to Saul David will remain with Yahweh. "But Yahweh will repay to each man his righteousness and fidelity, because Yahweh gave you into my hand today, yet I refused to put forth my hand against Yahweh's anointed" (v. 23). David then proceeds to cast himself and his future upon his only hope (v. 24): "Just as your [Saul's] life has been highly esteemed this day in my eyes, so may my life be highly esteemed in Yahweh's eyes, and may he deliver me from every distress." We might have expected David to say, "So may my life be highly esteemed in your [Saul's] eyes," but David is not looking to Saul, not hoping on Saul, not believing Saul. He places himself under Yahweh's eyes and in Yahweh's hands. "May he deliver me from every distress."

No contemporary believer can find better words with which to face life's way, littered as it is with both unusual and common troubles. We have no other help than David's, we can go forward with no other prayer on our lips. David himself saw the time when he could turn this prayer to praise, this trust to gratitude (see 2 Sam. 4:9, Ps. 54:7 [v. 9, Heb.]). In the meantime we go on praying his prayer.

The writer's closing sentence draws a line across the story: "So David went on his way, and Saul returned to his place"

(v. 25b). Very matter-of-fact, but David and Saul never saw each other again. One is tempted to say that they both go on alone from here. That is true in one case but not in the other. The other has a Lord who is determined to deliver him from every distress.[13]

STUDY QUESTIONS

1. Receiving assurance and feeling assured may be two different things. If this is true of you, which should you trust, the word of assurance or the feeling of insecurity?

2. 'Faith sets imagination to work.' This is true, but can you think of instances in your own life or those of other Christians you know when what the Lord did went even beyond what imagination could picture?

3. Use your imagination on the scene set out in Revelation 4 and 5. Here it will certainly find 'waters to swim in'. You will, of course, realise that there are some symbolical descriptions here.

4. Understanding sometimes has to wait but obedience cannot. Do you agree?

5. How great is your appetite for the worship of God amongst the people of God?

---

13. On the human level the stories of 1 Samuel 24-26 would function as a powerful apologetic for David in his quest for the throne. They clearly depict David as the one who refuses to seize the throne but who waits for the throne. He operates not by blood but by promise. There would be many in Israel who would need convincing, because they suspected foul play in events like those of 2 Samuel 3:22-30 and 4:1-12. For more detail, see my "A Proposed Life-Setting for the Book of Judges" (Ann Arbor: University Microfilms, 1978), 25–48.

25

What Can a God-less Text Teach Us?
(1 Samuel 27:1–28:2)

We should have known it. We heard what David said. He was already considering a "forced" exile (26:19-20). We shouldn't be too surprised to see him heading for Gath—again (cf. 21:10-15). Nor can we really blame him. Hunted, tracked, and attacked by Saul; treacherously exposed; making thrilling escapes (e.g., 23:24-29) and executing daring escapades (e.g., ch. 24, 26)—nine chapters full of high-blood-pressure narrative. It's the stuff that makes great movies but takes its toll on real people.

And now we arrive at our present text. Admittedly, 27:1-28:2 does not constitute a complete story. At the end of 28:2 the writer leaves his readers hanging. He deliberately chops the story off (more on this later). We have then a slice of a story, an incomplete story, yet one that, for the time being, stands by itself, and so we must consider it.

The story itself is rather straightforward. It breaks into four sections:

David's plan, 27:1-4
David's town, 27:5-7
David's practice, 27:8-12
David's dilemma, 28:1-2

This time David would be welcomed in Gath; he comes with six hundred men, whom Achish could use as a mercenary force. Under the guise of giving Achish elbow room and/ or of alleviating the drain on expenses for the royal court, David requested that he be transferred to one of the outlying towns—where he would not be so constantly under Achish's surveillance. So David took up quarters at Ziklag instead of Gath.[1]

At Ziklag David seemed to be both having and eating his cake. David and his men became desert raiders who raided desert raiders. He would attack bands of Geshurites, Girzites, and Amalekites (27:8),[2] carry off their livestock and goods, and bring to Achish the king's share of the spoil (27:9), alleging the plunder had come from attacks on Judah or clans associated with Judah (27:10). Achish was delighted with David's turncoat tactics; he really "believed in" David (27:12a), confident that all red-blooded Israelites must now despise this Philistine convert. There was, naturally, one hitch. David wiped out any human captives taken—he couldn't risk anyone blowing his cover, ratting on what he was really doing in Ziklag and beyond. Any human captives, therefore, were put to death (27:11). So far so good. David is helping Israel while both duping Achish and convincing Achish.

David, however, was so successful at making a fool of Achish that Achish unwittingly would make a traitor of David. He wanted his trusty David-contingent in the ranks of Gath in the massive Philistine assault on Israel (28:1). When in doubt use your mouth, so David answered: "Therefore you will know what your servant can do" (v. 2a)—ambiguous jargon but said with a turn of braggadocio that left Achish assured (28:2b). In the meantime David can ponder how to keep from being gored on the horns of a dilemma.

---

1. The locations of both Gath and Ziklag are problematical. Many identify Gath with Tell es-Safi, about twelve miles east of Ashdod (and about twice as far west of Bethlehem); Ziklag, if it is Tell esh-Sheri'ah, would be about twenty-three miles mostly south of Gath—if Gath is Tell es-Safi! See A. F. Rainey, "Gath," *ISBE*, rev. ed., 2:410–12, and "Ziklag," ISBE, 4:1196; see also Yohanan Aharoni, *The Land of the Bible*, rev. and enl. (Philadelphia: Westminster, 1979), 291, and the discussion in George A. Turner, *Historical Geography of the Holy Land* (Grand Rapids: Baker, 1973), 176–81.

2. We are familiar with the Amalekites (cf. 1 Sam. 15). The Geshur of 2 Samuel 3:3 and 13:37-38 is in the north, east of the Sea of Galilee; these Geshurites are operating in the south. Nor do we have any family data on the Girzites.

The story has enough tension to hold our interest, but what makes the story so fascinating and difficult is the fact that it is God-less; that is, the text does not mention God, does not say precisely or directly what Yahweh is doing in this episode, does not even inform us of Yahweh's point of view.[3] Nor is there any overt indication of the writer's position. He offers no moral commentary on the events. He simply does not say if he thinks David is in the right or the wrong. His silence in the matter does not necessarily mean he approves of David's course. One can report activity without endorsing it, as someone may testify about a robbery without approving theft. But how is David's activity here to be evaluated? One can only sift clues.

On balance, I would say that the text is sympathetic to David's difficulty and yet presents him as in the wrong. I suggest that the record of Yahweh's repeated protection (1 Sam. 18-26) should have convinced David that Yahweh was able to keep him even in Israel, especially when chapters 24 and 26 show Saul's protection gone and the king so exposed and helpless. Then there seems to be a negative cast behind the human slaughter of David's raids (27:11). I am not trying to foist an alien moral standard on an ancient episode. The writer himself tells us that the rationale for the human butchery was not a God-directed ban (as in 1 Sam. 15) but David's need to keep his front intact with Achish. Ordinarily raiders tried to avoid bloodshed.[4] Certainly, and happily, the Amalekites were more restrained than David (30:1-2) in that particular (though they had their reasons). Hence I think the text is both sympathetic to and critical of David. There is a sort of balance; the text understands David and yet is not willing to justify all his conduct.

Not all readers will agree with my assessment of the text—which only proves that God-less texts are tough to interpret. But at least readers will know the basis on which I build the exposition that follows. Even a God-less text teaches godly truths and gives godly directions to the Lord's people.

---

3. Richard L. Pratt, Jr., *He Gave Us Stories* (Brentwood, Tenn.: Wolgemuth and Hyatt, 1990), 131.

4 Claus Schedl, *History of the Old Testament,* 5 vols. (Staten Island, N.Y.: Alba House, 1972), 3:144–45.

Lean on Your True Security (27:1-3)

David is quite convinced that his only security rests west of the Shephelah in Philistia. He must think of more than six hundred men. Wives and households are involved. So they settled in Gath—perhaps to the first full night's sleep in months (27:2-3).

However, the thinking that led David to this move points to one of faith's fainting fits (as H. L. Ellison calls them):

> Then David said to his heart: "Now I am going to be swept away one day by the hand of Saul; I have no good (here), but I must escape to the land of the Philistines—Saul shall despair of me, of searching any more for me in all the territory of Israel; so I shall escape from his hand." [27:1]

David's verb, "be swept away," is significant. It is the verb *sāpāh*, which David uses in 26:10 when he tells Abishai that Yahweh would surely dispose of Saul in his time; for example, Saul might go down into battle "and be swept away." Now, however, David is convinced that he himself will be "swept away" by Saul if he does not exit Israel. It is a revealing reverse. Contrary to Yahweh's record of protection, contrary to Yahweh's promise via Jonathan and Abigail, David is certain he will now be swept away. I do not mean this in a detached way, as if I were saying, "Why didn't he read J. I. Packer's *Knowing God* and make the right decision?" No, I realize it is too easy to be a spectator of the biblical text, and, yes, David was under severe pressures here, yet at this point he looks to Philistia rather than to Yahweh as his security.

David has a special niche in salvation history but he shares common dilemmas with all the Lord's people. Covenant kingship is not at stake in our situations, but we still know the subtle danger of leaning on something else and less than the everlasting arms. Our concern is practical: Is there any way I might avoid deceiving myself with a substitute? How can I, how should I, go about leaning on Yahweh? Answer: By talking to yourself, by talking truth to yourself, especially by speaking to yourself the truth about your God.

I am only suggesting a reversal of David's procedure in verse 1. I had a reason for translating it literally: "Then David *said to his heart,* 'Now I am going to be swept away one day by the hand of Saul....'" David was talking to himself and what he kept saying to himself determined his action. What you say and keep saying to the center of you will direct your way. All of us propagandize our souls, that is, we constantly talk to ourselves. (Not many do this audibly, but we continually do it, and, if you don't believe it, you haven't been listening, and your self is probably angry with you for being so unreceptive!)[5] How crucial it is to feed our souls true propaganda, especially about the adequacy of our God.

Soul talk is quite a familiar idea in the Bible. Remember how Jesus depicted the farmer whose silos and bank account were full; the farmer says, "I will say to my soul, 'Soul [imagine!], you have ample goods laid up for many years...' " (Luke 12:19 RSV). There is a whole world and life view in that statement. The junk you tell yourself can make a difference. Actually, David himself knew how to talk to himself (Ps. 62:5 NIV).

Happily, sometimes others will rivet our minds on the right propaganda. It was 1854, Charles Spurgeon's first year of ministry in London. Cholera struck. One family after another called Spurgeon to the bedside of loved ones and almost daily he stood by a grave. At first Spurgeon threw himself into his visitation of the sick with all his youthful vigor. Soon, however, "weary in body, and sick at heart," he began to think he was about to succumb. He was on the Great Dover Road dragging himself home from a funeral when a large broadside posted in a shoemaker's window arrested his attention. It did not look like a trade announcement, nor was it. In the center of the large sheet, in good bold handwriting stood the words,

> Because thou hast made the Lord, which is my refuge, even the Most High, thy habitation; there shall no evil befall thee, neither shall any plague come nigh thy dwelling.

The words of Psalm 91:9-10 took immediate effect. Spurgeon reported: "Faith appropriated the passage as her own. I felt

---

5. On this talking to oneself, see Martyn Lloyd-Jones's application of Psalms 42–43 in his *Spiritual Depression* (Grand Rapids: Eerdmans, 1965), 20–21.

secure, refreshed. . . . I went on with my visitation of the dying, in a calm and peaceful spirit."[6] In any case, lean on your true security, be careful what you speak to your heart. That is the exhortation of this God-less text.

Learn the Craft of Wisdom

Secondly, this incomplete story, this God-less text, presses us to learn and use the skills of wisdom.

The words of Proverbs 14:12 might come to mind as we read of David's decision and its developments: "There is a way that seems right to a man." It is not that David didn't think—he surely did. In fact, if we think a bit about David's thinking we cannot help but understand how Philistia seemed to spell deliverance. Sheer tiredness must have dogged David. The malice and troops of Saul are enough, but the treachery and betrayal from local folks (23:19-20; 26:1) are too much. Moreover, David and his men have wives and households (27:3). Who knows how many of all these were with David and his six hundred men, but one can surmise that quite a number of David's men could not afford to allow wives and families to remain at home subject to the tender mercies of Saul's intelligence network. The sheer logistics of safety and provision for families probably weighed heavily. Such concerns took the thrill out of hair-raising escapes. And constant living in the shadow of death wears and unnerves a man. Murder mysteries are only for readers, not for the prey.[7]

Our narrative is fascinating. David's scheme, it says, is successful; David's decision is vindicated; David's thinking is accurate. He had thought that, if he made the move to Philistia, Saul would give up looking for him (27:1), and he

---

6. C. H. Spurgeon, *The Treasury of David*, 7 vols. (London: Passmore and Alabaster, 1876), 4:235.

7. See H. L. Ellison, *Scripture Union Bible Study Books: Joshua–2 Samuel* (Grand Rapids: Eerdmans, 1966), 69. Any disciple with some experience can sympathize with David's predicament and understand the difficulty of discernment. How often we ask as we ponder a decision, "If I do that, am I being prudent, or am I failing to trust?" What is the difference between prudence and unbelief? If I were in David's dilemma I might ask, "Do I lack nerve if I go to Philistia? Or do I lack sense if I stay in Israel? If I stay, am I believing God or tempting God?" I am not saying these were David's questions but only that many believers understand David's position, because they know how demanding proper discernment can be.

did (27:4). David is right on target. Perhaps David's men and their families enjoyed their first sound sleep in months. Gath may be Philistine, but it certainly beats a cave. So David's plan works—Saul does not pursue him any more. Mission accomplished. And David's request works, for when David asked Achish for a country town away from Gath, Achish granted him Ziklag (27:5-6). So David enjoys some freedom in addition to his security. And David's deception works, for from Ziklag David can attack Israel's enemies (thus helping Israel) while alleging he is attacking Israelite territory (thus convincing Achish; 27:8-12). The whole scheme has been a masterstroke. If it is not faith-full, it is nevertheless successful. There is a way that seems right to a man.

But David's evangelism had worked too well. Achish had become such a believer in David that he insisted on David and his men fighting with Gath's troops in the united Philistine offensive against Israel (28:1-2). It may well be that David had already considered this possible dilemma. David was certainly smart enough to have asked, "What if?" However, he may have considered his danger so desperate that he decided it worth the risk. Now . . . if he marches with the Philistines, he will lose credibility (to say the least) in Israel. His decision led him to a point where he is risking his kingship over Israel. David's rhetoric would never turn aside the charge that he had loved Philistia and stabbed Israel. If, however, he plays false at some point in some way with Achish and the Philistine brass (29:2-11), he may find them far more efficient than Saul in disposing of him. There is a way that seems right.

We must avoid cheap shots at David when he was in such straits; yet we must not ignore the import of the story, which we might summarize as: The will of God for us includes more than escaping from Saul. No one disputes the malice of Saul or pretends that escaping him was a merry lark. But the peril from Saul may not be so nasty or so damaging in the long run as being dubbed a traitor. It is, however, hard to see such difficulties when the immediate emergency looms so large. We fall into the "if only" fallacy. If only this insoluble problem that is right now wrenching my heart, monopolizing my thinking, and consuming my energy—if only I could get relief from it, I would get on well.

I know of no magical formula that can easily spit out the discernment we need. The Bible gives us perspectives and principles for facing these circumstances (e.g., Prov. 3:5-6; note: that text does not say, Don't *use* your understanding, but Don't *lean* on it; lean on the Lord and use your understanding; don't lean on your understanding and use the Lord). But there is no instant insight, no quick fix. We must *learn* the craft of wisdom. And it helps to remember that our Teacher is more merciful and patient than Saul or Achish.

Get a Grip on Grace

Finally, I propose that this God-less text is a gracious text, directing its readers to get a grip on Yahweh's grace.

I have argued earlier that the text seems to reflect a certain sympathy and understanding for David. Yet the writer does not hide how calculating and ruthless David was while a "Philistine." David the raider is one thing, David the butcher another. In 27:9, 11, David seems to be practicing overkill even in the customs of his time.

By now you may have become an angry reader. You may be angry at David because over the last number of chapters you have become pro-David. You have been moved by the sad lot of the afflicted, hunted servant of God, who runs from Saul because Saul in his frenzied envy insists on bathing his hands in David's blood. David, you might say, has won your heart. And now he has disappointed you (as most of God's servants will do at some time). You have been, as the current interpersonal jargon has it, betrayed. Conceivably you could be angry at the Bible as well, for telling you the unvarnished truth about this man David. Or you may even become angry at Yahweh, because he chose David and rejected Saul, and you can understand why he'd reject Saul, but how can he choose, support, sustain, and protect one who deceives and butchers like this?

Did you ever think that perhaps the writer is trying to correct *your* mistake? Yes, you, Bible reader that you are, may have fallen into the trap of hero worship, of looking on your pet Bible characters and exalting them too highly. Why should you be surprised, shocked, offended? Why should you talk about "betrayal"? The text is saying that this chosen, anointed servant is made of the same stuff as all the Lord's people. Must we throw out God's kingdom because not only its subjects but even its premier servants are sinners? Karl Gutbrod is right: the text will not allow us to view Saul with only contempt and save nothing but admiration for David; the text resists every attempt to make David the mirror of all virtue.[8]

Instead you must get a grip on grace. The Bible does not claim that God's servants are dipped in Clorox so they will be infallibly sin-free and attractive to you. The living God does not have clean material to work with. And don't get sentimental when you sing hymns about the Potter and the clay; remember it's only sinful (i.e., sin-full) clay the Potter works with. We should not criticize the Potter because of the clay but rather marvel that he stoops to work with such stuff. As long as we wallow (however subtly) in some idea of human worthiness we will never understand the Bible, never tremble before this God, and never delight in this God. We must get a grip on grace. Maybe a God-less text can do that for us.

STUDY QUESTIONS

1. 'Even a God-less text teaches godly truths.' Note that this is true of a whole Old Testament book and make time some time to study the lessons that can be learned from the Book of Esther.

2. 'Talking to yourself' – take a look at Psalms 42 and 43 (probably originally one psalm) for a good example of this, an example worth following in times of spiritual depression.

3. 'Faith appropriated the passage as her own' (CH Spurgeon). These words would make a fine description of devotional Bible study. Do you practice this?

4. 'What is the difference between prudence and unbelief ?' Do you think part of the answer may relate to the presence or absence of guidance from God as to a prudent course of action?

---

8. Karl Gutbrod, *Das Buch vom König*, Die Botschaft des Alten Testaments, 4th ed. (Stuttgart: Calwer, 1975), 224. Pratt (*He Gave Us Stories*, 292) suggests that this note stands at the center of the theme of 1 and 2 Samuel, namely, that Israel should hope in the Davidic line, despite the trouble caused by David's shortcomings.

5. We know that Jesus is 'great David's greater Son'. Think through some of the ways in which he is infinitely greater in character than David

26

And It Was Night
(1 Samuel 28:3-25)

The telephone rang down in the Führerbunker. It was for Hitler. Joseph Goebbels, Minister of Propaganda for the Third Reich, was on the line. He was ecstatic. The reason? The news: Franklin D. Roosevelt was dead. It was April 1945. Germany was caving in. The Allies were pressing from the west, the Russians from the east; soon Berlin itself would crumble. But none of that mattered to Goebbels, for, as he told Hitler: "It is written in the stars. The last half of April will be the turning point for us." He was referring to two previous astrological predictions that had forecast the hardest blows for Germany during the first months of 1945, especially in the first part of April, but an overwhelming victory in the second half of the month.[1] Unfortunately for Goebbels's horoscopes, Hitler committed suicide on April 30. Goebbels was not so unusual. Facing ruin, men will sometimes turn in their desperation to any resource that, they think, will give some hope, some direction. So it was with Saul.

Our writer begins with background information: Samuel's death (v. 3a), Saul's orthopraxy (v. 3b), Philistia's aggression (v. 4). The note about Samuel's death is a flashback (see 25:1), but for this story it is important for readers to remember that Samuel has died. Saul's ban on necromancers and soothsayers

---

1. Cornelius Ryan, *The Last Battle* (New York: Simon and Schuster, 1966), 318.

(v. 3b) was simply in accord with Deuteronomy 18:9-22. The Philistine assault, however, was something to worry about (v. 5). This would be no mere border skirmish. The Philistines bivouacked at Shunem, a site at the base of the Hill of Moreh at the east end of the Plain of Esdraelon (approximately seventeen "crow" miles southwest of the Sea of Galilee). They plan to fight on ground where chariots can maneuver to advantage, to control the trade route through the Plain of Esdraelon, and to cut off Saul from his northernmost tribes.[2] Primarily, they plan to mash Israel, camped several miles to the south on the slopes of the Gilboa range.

Such conditions could bring on ulcers for anyone, but all the more so for one in Saul's state (v. 5b). The first and proper step, of course, is to ask direction from Yahweh. But Yahweh did not answer him—not by dreams, Urim,[3] or prophets (v. 6).[4] Yahweh's silence did not silence Saul's terror; hence he wrongly turned to what he had rightly prohibited. He asked his men to locate a woman skilled in necromancy. Perhaps a word from the dead would help him face tomorrow.

Though necromancy and associated arts have been banned, Saul's men seem to know precisely where a practitioner may be found (v. 7). With Saul disguised in nonroyal attire the company pays its nocturnal call in Endor. Saul's request is straightforward ("Please practice divination for me by contacting the dead and bring up for me whomever I tell you," v. 8), and the woman's suspicion is immediate (v. 9). She knows about government "front" operations and apparently fears she is being set up as part of another "pagan bust." Saul obligingly swears an oath of immunity to reassure her (v. 10). The reader must not miss the irony—Saul swears the oath *by Yahweh*, by Yahweh's life, as he seeks help from a source

---

2. On the logistics, tactics, and terrain, see Claus Schedl, *History of the Old Testament*, 5 vols. (Staten Island, N.Y.: Alba House, 1972), 3:145–48, and John Bright, *A History of Israel*, 3d ed. (Philadelphia: Westminster, 1981), 194.

3. "A means of revelation used by the high priest in giving Yahweh's answer to inquiries." See C. Van Dam, "Urim and Thummim," *ISBE*, rev. ed., 4:957–59. We have more questions than answers about how the Urim and Thummim functioned. Remember that Saul had decimated the priestly ranks (1 Sam. 22).

4. There is no real conflict between verse 6 and 1 Chronicles 10:13-14; see H. G. M. Williamson, *1 and 2 Chronicles*, New Century Bible Commentary (Grand Rapids: Eerdmans, 1982), 95.

that Yahweh has condemned. For all his degeneration Saul is orthodox to the last. The woman consents, asking the name of the contact (v. 11); but when she sees Samuel she screams as she also sees through Saul's disguise (v. 12). Saul persists with more reassurance and, when satisfied that Samuel is "up," bows down and does homage (vv. 13-14).

Questions come thick and fast. Wasn't Israel forbidden to engage in such practices? Yes (Deut. 18:9-22; Isa. 8:19-20); but people, even ancient Israel or contemporary church, regularly do what Scripture prohibits.

Was this episode a piece of fakery? I don't think so; I don't think the text intends to suggest that. Some argue that since the woman screamed when she saw Samuel (v. 12a), she herself must have not expected his appearance; therefore, her usual practice must have been imposture and duplicity. One cannot be sure. The sight of Samuel (v. 12a) may not be the sole explanation for her scream. Verse 12b may help explain the scream, that is, the sight of Samuel brought the sudden insight that only Saul would have such a passion to consult Samuel. Hence her client was Saul—and she was doomed (v. 3b). The story carries the stamp of realism, from the central and sobering prophetic message of Samuel (vv. 16-19) to the obvious reticence to answer all our curious questions, along with its (intended?) failure to provide any how-to information for budding necromancers. In any case, we must remember that Scripture describes such practices not as futile but as pagan. Yahweh forbids Israel to use these means not because they do not work but because they are wicked.[5]

How then does one explain this piece of necromancy? I suppose by the power and permission of God. For his own reasons God must have permitted Samuel to "come up" in order to speak his word of truth and doom to Saul. Yahweh's word was spoken even if it came via an illegitimate method.

---

5. Yehezkel Kaufmann, *The Religion of Israel* (New York: Schocken, 1972), 88: "The laws ban divination on the ground that it is an abomination; they nowhere intimate that it is vain." On divination and magic in the context of Old Testament theology, see Willem A. VanGemeren, *Interpreting the Prophetic Word* (Grand Rapids: Zondervan, 1990), 20–27.

Doesn't this case of effective necromancy open the way for justifying the practice of consulting the dead? No, because Deuteronomy 18 has already stated the doctrinal position. Moreover, this case (1 Sam. 28) is simply the exception that proves the rule. That is, it is as if 1 Samuel 28 is saying, "Now can you see why this sort of hoky-poky is prohibited in Israel? Look at Saul—it only incapacitates and destroys."

So much for preliminaries. What is the teaching of this strange and sad narrative? I will try to summarize it in several propositions.

Hopeless Misery (28:15)

The first proposition is: *The most hopeless misery in all of life is to be abandoned by God.* What the narrative had already reported Saul himself miserably confirms in verse 15: "I am in terrible distress; the Philistines are fighting against me, and God has turned away from me and does not answer me any more, not by prophets or by dreams." Certainly as king, responsible for the leadership of Yahweh's people, Saul would normally have the privilege of Yahweh's direction for battle. Now, however, he can hear the shouts of Philistines but not the voice of Yahweh. He faces the crisis of his life and God has nothing to say to him. Some of the saddest words in all Scripture are printed in 1 Samuel 28:15.

Samuel explains that Yahweh is carrying out what Samuel had previously declared—tearing the kingdom from Saul and giving it to his neighbor (here David is openly identified as Saul's replacement; v. 17). Why is Yahweh mute? Samuel harks back to the episode of chapter 15: "As you did not listen to the voice of Yahweh and did not carry out his hot anger against Amalek—therefore, Yahweh has done this thing to you today" (v. 18).[6] Samuel picks up the key word from chapter 15, to "listen," to "hear" (Hebrew, *šāmaʿ*). There Saul confirmed the tragic tendency he had shown in chapter 13. In chapter 15 he tailored Yahweh's command to his own and the people's preferences. Saul would have called it accommodation; Samuel called it rebellion. Saul thought it prudence; Samuel

---

6. Please see my previous exposition of chapter 15 ("Rejecting the Chosen") for necessary background.

labeled it stubbornness. Perhaps Saul liked to think he had only reinterpreted Yahweh's word; Samuel charged that he had simply rejected Yahweh's word (see 15:22-23). "You did not listen." That is the explanation for Yahweh's absence.

The text is not gentle but it is clear: If you despise God's word he will take it from you. If you persistently refuse to obey God's speech you will endure God's silence. How crucial then are one's first responses to the gospel, to the initial call to enter the kingdom of God. Spurgeon tells of a man on his deathbed who sent for him. In his lifetime the man had jeered at Spurgeon, had often denounced him as a hypocrite. Now in desperation and death he called for him. Of this instance and of this man Spurgeon wrote:

> He had, when in health, wickedly refused Christ, yet in his death-agony, he had superstitiously sent for me. Too late, he sighed for the ministry of reconciliation, and sought to enter in at the closed door, but he was not able. There was no space left him then for repentance, for he had wasted the opportunities which God had long granted to him.[7]

What could be worse? To know you need to repent—and can't. It is horridly solemn. The most hopeless misery in all of life is to be abandoned by God.

Lighter Burdens

Looking at this passage in its larger setting leads us to a second proposition: *Burdens appear lighter when seen in their proper context.* Here we want to understand 28:3-25 in connection with 27:1–28:2 and 29:1-11. In order to do so it would probably be best to set out at this point the overall structure of chapters 27–31.

David's dilemma: with the enemies of God 27:1–28:2
Saul's dilemma: without the word of God 28:3-25
David's deliverance: saved by the Philistines 29-30
Saul's downfall: destroyed by the Philistines 31

---

7. C. H. Spurgeon, *Autobiography*, rev. ed., vol. 1, *The Early Years* (Edinburgh: Banner of Truth, 1962), 274.

You have not forgotten, I trust, the dirty trick the biblical writer has played on you—provided you had really thrown yourself into the flow of his story. He wound your mental rubber band as tightly as he could at the end of 28:2. At that point your question was, How will David ever get out of this mess? You knew it was 11:00 p.m. and that you needed to get to sleep, but you simply couldn't put your Bible down; you told yourself you must read on to see what happens to David. "Now Samuel had died and..." (28:3). You've been tricked. The writer does not tell you what happened to David. You are left hanging in his literary noose until chapter 29 (where he answers your anxiety over David). What's worse, the writer did this to you deliberately, for 29:1-11 happened chronologically before 28:3-25. Had he followed chronology his story would have taken this sequence:

27:1–28:2
29:1-11
28:3-25

But how do we know that the chronology has been inverted in these sections? In a word, geography. In 28:4 the Philistines and Saul are located at Shunem and Gilboa respectively, and the story takes place the night before the decisive battle. In 29:1 the Philistines (including Achish and David and men) were assembling their combined forces at Aphek in the Plain of Sharon roughly ten miles northeast of Joppa. A rough schematic may help:

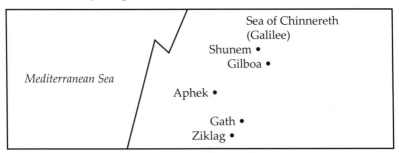

Clearly, the Philistines' movement goes from Philistia proper, including Gath and Ziklag (27:1–28:2) to Aphek (29:1-11), the assembly point for all Philistine forces, then through the Plain of Esdraelon and on to Shunem (28:3-25), near the chosen site of battle. By the geographical notes of 28:4 and 29:1 the writer cues us that he has reversed the chronological order.

Why would he want to do that? Why not finish a perfectly exciting story of David? Why not go right on from 28:2 to 29:1? Why interrupt this sequence with an account that took place some time later? Why interject 28:3-25 here?

Television programming suggests an answer. Suppose you are watching a Mississippi State-Texas football game on your set. Suddenly, six minutes into the second quarter you hear a voice as the game audio fades: "We interrupt our regular programming to bring you this special news bulletin: At approximately 3:30 Eastern time this afternoon the Canadian Air Force from bases in Saskatchewan launched a bombing attack against Bismarck, North Dakota, completely destroying the city...."[8] Why do that? Why interrupt a perfectly enjoyable football game on a lovely October afternoon? Because at that moment there is something far more urgent for you and others to know. Matters of greater importance have the right to preempt time.

I do not intend it in a hoky way, but this is essentially what the biblical writer does in 28:3-25. "I interrupt this tension-filled story of David's dilemma to tell you of something of far greater importance," even though it's out of proper chronological order. The reason he intrudes 28:3-25 is because he wants to place David's dilemma (27:1–28:2) and Saul's dilemma (28:3-25) side by side. By doing so he is saying to you, "Don't worry your head right now about David. You must see something far more critical. I interrupt this narrative to tell you that there is something far worse than being caught among the Philistines, namely, being cut off from all communion with God." Hence by selecting this sequence in his story the writer emphasizes our previous proposition: Nothing is so utterly miserable than finding in the hour of greatest need that you had long ago placed yourself beyond the sound of God's voice and that you are totally alone.

Does this not put David's trial in perspective? David's trouble is no light one; he is caught among the enemies of

---

8. Apologies to both Canadians and Dakotans. I wanted to give what I might reasonably assume would remain a hypothetical example.

God. But Saul's is far worse—he is without the word of God. Burdens appear lighter when seen in their proper context.

I must say that I do not write that lightly, nor do I mean it flippantly, as some do when they say (perhaps with a little whine in the voice), "Well, there's always some one worse off than you are." But I do mean: Believer, put your trials in context. You may be exhausted from work. In fact, your employer may be giving you a raw deal, dealing unjustly and underhandedly with you. You have lost your health, or family troubles are now cropping up. The text says there is something far worse.[9] Do you realize what a solace it is in the face of all your losses, all your pressures, all your disappointments, and all your failures to have access to the throne of grace and the smiling face of God in prayer? Do you realize that all that you have suffered is not nearly so tragic as someone moaning, "*God* has turned away from me"?[10] No, I am not saying you should be ashamed of yourself; I am not telling you not to weep in your troubles. Only keep the right perspective.

Misdirected Desperation

The map itself suggests how desperate Saul was. Endor was two or three miles northeast of Shunem (Shunem was on the southern slope of the Hill of Moreh, Endor on the northern). This means that Saul had to skirt the Philistine camp in order to arrive at Endor. He took a considerable risk. But what is the object of his desperation? According to verse 15c ("so I called for you to tell me what I should do"), Saul wants direction(s) for the day of battle—which lends cogency to H. L. Ellison's remark that "Saul, like not a few others, had to have guidance, not out of love for God but for fear of making mistakes."[11] So we are led to a third proposition: *Spiritual desperation can be misdirected.*

Samuel's response to Saul contained a broad hint that Saul was on the wrong track. "Why are you asking me when

9. Cf. John 5:14, where Jesus implies that there is "something worse" than thirty-eight years of helpless paralysis. Thirty-eight years is a long time, and helpless paralysis a horrid scourge.

10. The subject is emphatic in the Hebrew in verse 15.

11. H. L. Ellison, *Scripture Union Bible Study Books: Joshua–2 Samuel* (Grand Rapids: Eerdmans, 1966), 70.

Yahweh [emphatic] has turned from you and become your enemy?" (v. 16). If anything, Saul's quest should have been to face Yahweh, not to seek Samuel. His need was not for information but communion, not so much to prepare for battle but to recover God's presence. Saul, it seems, wanted the results of God's favor more than he wanted God's favor.

Here I think it is important to address a problem, to go on a tangent—but a related tangent. It is this. Some believers are convinced that they are in Saul's shoes—that they are cut off from God's presence, doomed to his silence, forever under his frown. For example, William Cowper, the hymnist, was at least at times convinced he was a reprobate. One can understand why believers in Jesus might draw such conclusions: God's presence does sometimes seem distant; sometimes he has seemed to cast them off. Sometimes God leaves us in our affliction so long that we are tempted to say he has forsaken us. And the Bible acknowledges that such conditions can prevail in the lives of God's flock. The Bible recognizes that someone can be—shall we say?—objectively forsaken by God (as was Saul) and that others can seem to be forsaken or fear that they have been.

Have we any clues to help us distinguish the one situation from the other? I would at least point to one. Look, for example, at Psalm 13:1:

How much longer, Yahweh, will you go on forgetting me? Forever?
How much longer will you keep hiding your face from me?

Notice what happens. What does the psalmist do since he thinks Yahweh has forgotten him, has hidden his face, or, could we say turned away from him? Does he turn to necromancers or check his horoscopes? No. After his "how much longers" he prays: "Pay attention, answer me, Yahweh my God..." (Ps. 13:3). Do you see what is happening? When believers are terrified at God's absence (Ps. 30:7), they instinctively turn to the God they think has forsaken them and complain *to him* about forsaking them (Ps. 13:1)—and then they go on having dealings with this God, crying to this God to answer (Ps. 13:3), because they have nowhere else to go and so keep clinging to him. Psalm 88 is almost as bleak as 1 Samuel 28, for that psalm does not have a positive ending with confidence in Yahweh's deliverance and favor. The faithful man's anguish is still unrelieved at the end of his prayer (Ps. 88:14-18) but he is still speaking *to Yahweh* about it. Cool rationalists will never understand it but warm believers do. Eventually they see that the clearest evidence that God has not turned away from them is that even in his "absence" they keep turning to the God who has turned from them (cf. John 6:67-68).[12]

Faced with God's "absence" the believer is concerned with *God's* absence rather than with a lack of insight for his or her current problem. Others, however, may be more concerned with guidance than with knowing the Guide.[13] Spiritual desperation can be misdirected.

Shining Light

I want to focus now on the concluding scene (vv. 21-25) of the narrative, heavy with all its hopelessness for Saul and Israel. And yet, if we allow the text to push us beyond itself, we can suggest a fourth proposition: *There is a light that shines in the darkness.*

At the words of Samuel, Saul was overcome. Fearful and foodless, he suffered total exhaustion (v. 20). The woman saw how utterly terrified Saul was and begged him to listen to her advice to eat what she wanted to prepare.[14] Saul initially refused but finally consented (v. 23).

It is a sad scene. The woman provides a meal truly fit for a king—butchering the calf in the stall and baking unleavened bread (vv. 24-25a; the "bit of food" she promised in v. 22 was typical eastern underkill; cf. Gen. 18:5-8). Yet all this only consists of making someone as comfortable as possible before he faces total disaster. What sheer hopelessness and despair ooze out of the last sentence: "Then they got up and went away that night" (v. 25b).

---

12. On this whole matter of apparent God-forsakenness in the believer's life I would urge a careful reading of an old (1649) Puritan work, William Bridge, *A Lifting Up for the Downcast* (Edinburgh: Banner of Truth, 1961).

13. Cf. Ellison, *Joshua–2 Samuel*, 6–7.

14. It is rather ironic, in light of chapter 15, to see the verb *listen/hear* (šāmaʿ) repeated four times in 28:21-23.

Does the scene not remind you of another last supper? Does it not bring to mind another religious and very talented individual? One who had preached Christ and had done miracles in his name? And you remember how you shudder every time you read those words about him in the Fourth Gospel: "So, after receiving the morsel, he immediately went out; and it was night" (John 13:30 RSV). You remember the scene—and Judas' exit. Surely we do not think John merely wanted to tell us the time. He wants to tell us it was *night*. Oh, yes, it was night; it was like entering the outer darkness itself.

But there was someone else who entered the darkness:

> And when the sixth hour had come, there was darkness over the whole land until the ninth hour. And at the ninth hour Jesus cried with a loud voice... "My God, my God, why hast thou forsaken me?" [Mark 15:33-34 RSV]

There is a mistake you can make if you're not careful—you can begin to think that you are quite detached from all this, that you are better than, not quite so stupid as, deserving of better than Saul or Judas. And, of course, you're wrong. But the glory of the gospel is that God's Son went through the darkness of God's absence for us, the darkness and agony of God-forsakenness. Is not Jesus' cry of Mark 15:34 very much like "God has turned away from me and answers me no more" (v. 15 RSV)? At the Battle of Golgotha Jesus has walked out into the outer darkness in order that you might walk in the light of life. Now the question presses upon you: Have you yet been seeking this One who has endured the darkness for you?

"They got up and went away that night"; but there is a light that shines in that darkness.

STUDY QUESTIONS

1. 'For all his degeneration Saul is orthodox to the last.' If you read the newspapers or watch TV you may be able to think of some examples of this in modern times. What is important though is that you cast yourself on God's grace lest you too go that way.

2. Do we sometimes excuse rebellion by calling it accommodation?

3. Do you agree that nothing could be more important than being more and more sensitive to God's Word, a sensitivity expressed in repentance, faith and obedience?

4. When you read the psalms it is worth noting that the psalmist always brings his problems to God, no matter what they are and even if they are problems with God. Read some of the psalms to get the force of this.

5. Luke and John each record three sayings of Jesus from the cross but Matthew and Mark one only, the same one (Matt. 27:46; Mark 15:33-34), leaving it starkly on the page to compel us to think; so think about the depth of suffering Christ endured for you – and then come to him in thankful worship.

27

Accepting the Philistines
as Your Personal Savior
(1 Samuel 29)

The biblical writer persists in his frustrating technique. At the end of chapter 28 we readers are eager to hear the report of the next day's battle, even though we know it is to spell disaster for Saul and Israel. It's not that we relish disaster but desire a certain literary cleanliness; tie up, clean up, and pull together this one story before going to another. But our writer doesn't share our compunctions about tidiness; he leaves Saul and his adjutants wandering in the night back to Gilboa, pulls us backward in time (perhaps several days' worth), drops us at Aphek in the Plain of Sharon, and shows us David and his men caught in their dilemma. They are part of the Philistine build-up against Israel. I suspect, however, the writer has his reasons for his vacillating pattern. He wants to maintain a continuing David-Saul contrast, and he may also prefer to put off telling about the debacle at Gilboa until the end.[1]

In any case, the biblical writer has given us in chapter 29 an interesting, humorous, yet orderly story. It breaks down easily:

Locations, 1
    Objection of Philistine commanders
    and explanation by Achish, 2-3
        Announcing decision:

---

1. Please refer to the previous chapter for the primary discussion of the literary technique and structure of 1 Samuel 27-31.

commanders suspect David, 4-5
Communicating decision:
Achish trusts David, 6-7
Objection of David and explanation by Achish, 8-10
Location, 11

Three times Achish defends David (vv. 3, 6-7, 9-10), a sort of emphatic irony. Achish takes up almost 50 percent of the chapter's ink. We will review the chapter and then summarize its import and teaching for the church.

Here are Philistine troops arriving at the Aphek Assembly Grounds as they prepare to launch Operation Shunem. All five Philistine lords have arrived with their various contingents. At last Achish and his Gath division pass in review, and the commanders observe David and his men among them. They are aghast: What are these Hebrews doing here? (v. 3a). Achish, don't you know who we're fighting? Achish is not slow on the draw: Haven't you ever heard of mercenaries? That's what David and his men are. He's been with me a long time and has been totally dependable (v. 3b).[2] But the military brass will have none of it. They argue from prudence (v. 4b) and from history (v. 5). How better, they contend, for David to get back into Saul's favor than by being a fifth column within Philistine ranks and rolling Philistine heads? And then the argument from history—or is it music? Every kid in Ekron Elementary School knows that Israeli song—"Saul has struck down his thousands, David his ten thousands" (v. 5; see 18:7; 21:11). The commanders are irate (v. 4a): how could Achish be so dense, so naive?

Achish comes back to David to deliver the bad news that is good news: "And now go back in peace..." (v. 7). There is more than a little humor in this scene (vv. 6-8). Achish stands there, apologetically emphasizing how he thinks David should go with him in this campaign and extolling David's faithfulness,

---

2. Achish might have had better success if he had not identified David as the (former) "servant of Saul, king of Israel." That was bound to set off red blinking lights in the commanders' heads. Cf. J. P. Fokkelman, *Narrative Art and Poetry in the Books of Samuel*, vol. 2, *The Crossing Fates (1 Sam. 13–31 & II Sam. 1)* (Assen/Maastricht: Van Gorcum, 1986), 571–72. Of course we can't miss the irony that Achish's emphatic confidence (vv. 3, 6-7, 9-10) rests on absolute deception (27:8-12). The Bible tends to depict Philistines as a bit slow; see, for example, my discussion of Judges 14–16 in *Such a Great Salvation* (Grand Rapids: Baker, 1990), 177–81.

which he has no reason to extol. On the other hand, David with disbelief on his face and exasperation in his voice protests the rejection he has no reason to protest. The deceived defends his deceiver, and the relieved disputes his relief![3] After David's tirade Achish so much as says, "Look, look, I know you're as solid as Gibraltar, but the commanders of the Philistines... well, they command. My hands are tied; majority rules. So, come morning, you must leave for Ziklag" (vv. 9-10).

Now what import does this chapter have for God's people? Certainly we begin with the assumption that 1 Samuel 29 is not the story of a lucky break but of a divine deliverance, a merciful deliverance. But what particular witness does it bear about our God that will lead us to know him better? We can summarize this witness in several observations.

God's Presence Is So Quiet

Perhaps the most obvious mark of this story about Yahweh's goodness is that it says nothing about Yahweh's goodness. Indeed, we have a text that almost refuses to mention Yahweh at all. I say "almost," because Achish does make a courtesy reference to Yahweh (v. 6) and alludes to God (v. 9). (As if only pagan Achish saves the text from secularism!) Yet we have met this sort of thing before. The Holy Spirit does not make everything so obvious in these narratives. Perhaps he intends us to think, to ask questions.

We hardly need, however, a concluding "Thus the Lord delivered David from the clutches...." We don't require a

---

3. Some think that David was not acting in verse 8 but was genuinely disappointed because he was counting on operating as a fifth column in the Philistine ranks. See William McKane, *1 & II Samuel,* Torch Bible Commentaries (London, SCM, 1963), 166; and P. Kyle McCarter, Jr., *I Samuel,* The Anchor Bible (Garden City: N.Y.: Doubleday, 1980), 427. However, I think the writer means to present this as David's crisis, not his opportunity. In these last chapters he intends to portray both of the anointed ones in their respective dilemmas. David may have considered operating as a wrecker among the Philistines if, as it appeared, there was no escape from his jam. But even his appearing among Philistine troops would have destroyed David's credibility with many Israelites. In fact, the story in chapters 27–29 may have circulated in Israel as an apologetic for David (trying to overcome northern Israelite objections to David's kingship), as if to say, "Yes, you're right—David did desert to the Philistines for some time; but you must realize he was almost forced into it by Saul; but don't think David ever joined them in fighting against his own people—he was marvelously spared that ordeal."

didactic punchline to see that Yahweh is here, delivering his servant—silently so. Walter Brueggemann is surely correct:

> There is no mention of God here, but we are dealing with a highly self-conscious theological literature that observes the undercurrent of divine governance without being explicit. Yahweh is with David everywhere (18:12, 28), surely with him among the Philistines as elsewhere, surely in chapter 29 as in those places where it is explicitly stated. The narrator is not so disbelieving as to perceive the outcome of the narrative as luck.[4]

Is it not then the task of the church and of the individual believer to go back over life and experience and try to itemize those moments when Yahweh was clearly but quietly present to save and support? I don't mean a kind of self-fixated, trivial existential overkill: "I was so afraid I'd be bored at the dentist's office, but the Lord showed me there on the table in the waiting room a copy of *Vogue* with an engrossing article." But as you ponder the ground you've traveled, the murky stuff the Lord has carried you through, the twists and turns of your life, can you not see glimpses of silent mercy, of quiet care? There was no noise or tempest. Yahweh was there, but not obviously.

We may wonder why Yahweh frequently works in such a subdued way. Perhaps because it is interesting and challenging. Perhaps it's something like a couple who begin to date in their college days. Each likes and cares for the other person. But they do not feel at ease to divulge their true feelings. One or both may fear they will "scare away" the other person if feelings are discussed too overtly. There is some uncertainty, exciting uncertainty. The fellow would like to hold hands with her but wonders if the girl might think that inappropriate; maybe she views him as merely a friend. She may not share the growing affection he has for her. But one evening as they are taking one of those reflective walks across the campus, it happens! Their hands happen to brush and quietly clasp. And that is precisely the beauty of it. An overt discussion about the proper calendar date on which they should hold hands would have wrecked it all. The reserve and the silence about

---

4. Walter Brueggemann, *First and Second Samuel*, Interpretation (Louisville: Westminster/John Knox, 1990), 199.

the matter make it so joyful and memorable. Might we not say the same of God's presence? What a relief that his work doesn't come blasting at you like a television commercial. He doesn't necessarily declare it but allows you to discover it, for if you have to think and struggle over the matter, there is more likelihood you will be led to truly *intelligent* worship.

God's Ways Are So Surprising

It may seem highly amusing to us but the Philistines were deadly serious. First, the commanders of the Philistines are exasperated and incredulous: "What are these Hebrews doing here?" (v. 3a); then they are angry at Achish for his soft-headedness (v. 4a) and proclaim the glad news of deliverance:

> Send the man back, and let him go back to his place where you have stationed him. He must not go down with us into the battle—that way he will not become an adversary to us in the battle. How could the fellow win back his master's favor— wouldn't it be with the heads of these men? [v. 4b]

Even Achish's hands are tied. He can only repeat this gospel to David: "Only the commanders of the Philistines have decided: 'He will not go up with us into the battle' " (v. 9).

We see it again. What instruments does Yahweh use to rescue his servant from his dilemma? The commanding officers of the Philistine army. It was not the first time Yahweh had turned enemies into saviors (see 23:19-28). Philistines make such unwitting but effective servants! Who has ever been his counselor?! (cf. Isa. 40:13-14). This text, of course, carries no guarantee for me. It does not promise me that if I get my life so tangled by my own cleverness and foolishness, off track by my own short-sighted decision, that Yahweh will infallibly rescue me from my mess. What he's done for David he may not do for me. What the text does teach is that even in our folly and fainting fits, we are still no match for our God, who has thousands of unguessable ways by which he rescues his people—even by the mouths of Philistines. He can make the enemy serve us as a friend. He not only prepares a table for us in the presence of our enemies but also has the knack of making the enemies prepare the table!

I remember reading a children's story in which a Christian woman, alone and out of food, was telling her plight to her heavenly Father and asking for her daily bread. Somehow a neighbor, an agnostic or an atheist, overheard the woman praying and decided it was time for a little divine fun. He went and purchased two loaves of bread and left them at her door. Upon discovering them, the woman burst into a devout and grateful prayer of praise. But her neighbor accosted her to demythologize the incident, informing her that he had happened to hear her praying, that he bought the bread, and he had placed it on her step. It was not, then, *God* who had answered her prayer. But the lady was "armed": "Oh, yes, it was the Lord who answered my prayer—even though he used the devil to do it."

"God's ways are so surprising" is not merely an observation. Whether in Scripture or in living, whether he uses Philistines or agnostics, whenever we catch a glimpse of this, we are meant to respond. The wonder and surprise of God's ways are meant to lead us to worship and praise. There ought to be those times when you throw up your hands and say out loud that God's decisions *are* unsearchable and his ways untraceable (Rom. 11:33).

God's Mercy Is So Tenacious

Perhaps all is over (for now) but the acting. At verse 7 one can imagine what massive relief flooded David's insides. But that must not show. Hence, no doubt, Achish sees the shadow of disappointment then the flash of anger cross David's face. "But what have I done? What have you discovered in your servant from the day I have been before you to this day that I may not go and fight the enemies of my lord the king?" (v. 8). A reader gets a trifle nervous at this point. Lest Achish should press for reconsideration one is almost tempted to holler at David: "Don't mess it up, David—just accept the Philistines as your personal savior and get out of there!" And he does. Morning comes. David is heading for Ziklag (v. 11).

A reader must connect chapter 29 with 27:1-28:2. I have already argued that David's original decision to go to Philistia was ill-advised, that it was understandable but not wise, explainable but not faith-full. Now, however, when one places chapter 29 alongside 27:1–28:2, the character of God shines brilliantly. Now one can see how Yahweh's mercy still pursues his servants even in their follies and fainting fits. How strong, tenacious, and un-let-go-able Yahweh's mercy is! Yahweh is not short-tempered with his people. His mercy and patience are not exhausted when we choose our foolish Philistias. Some of us have a tendency to construct and to believe in a god made in our own image, who, when once one of his children has botched a section of life, goes into a huff (as we would) and out of holy glee abandons him to fry in his own juice.

Is that the God and Savior of David, his servant? Do you see David here? Marching with the Philistines, caught in his own trap, overdosing perhaps on antacids, he and his men on their way to attack his own people at the side of these pagans. Does his God allow him to stew in his own gravy? Oh no, Yahweh's mercy can find David even in Philistia. The God who saved him from Saul again and again will surely save him from himself. Inexhaustible mercy does not dry up easily.

Christians should take heart from this text. As some believers look back on the time line of their lives they have no trouble picking out the occasion (or occasions) when they were depending on their own cleverness, sure of their own ability to assess and handle their situation, confident they already knew the right way. And it proved disastrous, nearly destroyed them. And they fear God's mercy has withered. After all, *their* mercy would have done so. Then there is some glad news for all Yahweh's servants in this fainting fit of his chosen king. God does not cast you off in your foolishness. Our bungling does not evaporate his mercy. It is yet full and warm—and stubborn, so stubborn it insisted on pursuing David into Philistia. He really did know something of goodness and mercy *pursuing* him all the days of his life ("follow" is too weak for the verb in Ps. 23:6a). However, David's jam and Yahweh's deliverance by his chosen pagan saviors shows that David's success is due not to David's savvy but only to Yahweh's mercy.

There is a striking contrast between the endings of chapters 28 and 29.[5] It is interesting if not significant, arresting

---

5. Pointed out by Fokkelman, *The Crossing Fates*, 578.

even if not intended. The reader well remembers how the last line of chapter 28 breathed despair as it told how Saul and companions trudged off into the darkness (28:25b). But it is not night at the end of chapter 29. David walks away in the morning (29:11a), saved by the Philistines who would destroy Saul. Not that David knew nothing of darkness. But David's night was not like Saul's night. He knew the tale of the mercy of God: "Weeping may endure for a night, but joy comes in the morning" (Ps. 30:5b NKJV).

Study Questions

1. Consider the quiet mercies of God. What dangers might we fall into if everything God did was exciting?

2. Does the analogy of a TV commercial suggest why God is sometimes reserved with us? Have you found that overkill with commercials is counter-productive as far as you are concerned, and you simply shut off?

3. Do you think it is true that God can be both surprising and consistent at the same time?

   Do we perhaps have to distinguish his methods and his character in thinking about this? Of course, it goes without saying that his methods are never out of line with his character.

4. Spend some time thinking about the fact that our God is not only merciful but patient and then praise him for the way the two are expressed in his dealings with you.

28

When the Bottom Drops Out
(1 Samuel 30)

Amos once used a graphic sermon illustration (Amos 5:19). He pictures a man fleeing from a lion only to meet a bear! He runs, so I assume Amos implies, from the bear, finally reaches and piles into his house, leans panting and heaving and relieved against the wall—and a snake bites him! He thought he had reached safety only to discover he had failed to see his enemy slithering along the top of the wall.[1] It must have seemed like that to David and his men in 1 Samuel 30. They had just escaped from the trap of having to fight with Philistia against Israel thanks to God's mercy and Philistine suspicion (ch. 29). How relieved they must have been to start out for Ziklag that morning. Even a multiday, sixty-mile journey (from Aphek to Ziklag) is bearable when such a burden has been lifted. But when they arrive home the snake bites. No town, no families. Still another blow in the tally of David's sufferings. It will seem as though the bottom has dropped out of the pit itself. Let us work through the chapter with a series of observations.

God's Servant Is Overwhelmed (30:1-6a)
Again, we are given the reader's edge. We know what happened (vv. 1-2) before David discovers it (v. 3): Amalekite raid, Ziklag

---

1. I can still recall Dr. Walter Kaiser illustrating Amos's illustration in Old Testament class.

hit and torched, all the women taken captive and carted off. Some may see a mercy in the fact that Amalek did not kill any of the captives (v. 2), especially in light of David's practice in 27:8-9. But normally it was a minor mercy. Everyone knew why captives were kept alive: they could be sold for profit to merchants or others and would eke out the rest of their lives in isolation, bondage, and misery. Soon enough David and men discover what we already know (v. 3): the shock of the smoldering rubble, the sorrow of wives and families taken. There was but one thing to do—wail. They did, until there was no strength to cry and scream (v. 4). What little strength was left was exercised in blaming David and lobbying one another to stone him.[2] Grief was transmuting into bitterness and rage.

The problem with the disaster at Ziklag is that it is not an isolated one. For David the pounding had been going on since 1 Samuel 18. Yet it seemed more unbearable given its immediate context. From the latest emergency (27:1–28:2) he had just received a marvelous deliverance (29:1-11). How they had looked forward to arriving in Ziklag; how long those sixty miles seemed; how fine it would be simply to enjoy the relief among loved ones. Then this. The yo-yo effect seems to make the battering more excruciating. A marvelous escape, a moment to breathe, a grand relief—only to be thrown into the pit again. Better never to have been lifted out of the slop than to be lifted out only to be dashed into it again. How could David be Yahweh's chosen king and be suffering like this? In 1 Chronicles 29:30 we are told that the written accounts of David's life and reign tell of the "circumstances [lit., times] that passed over him." Indeed they did, wave upon wave. David, the king-designate, was indeed a suffering servant.

Here is a sobering and disturbing picture for God's people. Are there not times when you think it cannot get any worse? And 1 Samuel 30 says, Yes, it can. There are times when you conclude that your present trouble is the last straw; you simply

---

2. Perhaps some argued David should have left a detachment of men to protect Ziklag. Surely the Amalekites knew the Philistines were campaigning against Israel; hence Philistine settlements were in greater danger. Some of David's men may have opposed the whole idea of the Philistine sojourn (27:1-2) and thought it was wrong-headed from the first.

cannot take any more. Then comes Ziklag, the last straw after the last straw. Sometimes you are tempted to add another line to Psalm 30:5: "Weeping may endure for a night, but joy comes in the morning" —and disaster strikes next afternoon.

A Christian woman once wrote to encourage J. B. Phillips, the New Testament translator. Phillips endured a great deal of depression and mental distress. In the course of her letter the woman described some of her own sufferings. She had had what many would call a terribly unhappy childhood. She had suffered several severe illnesses, but seven years ago had been stricken with polio, which left her (fortunately, she said) with a caliper and elbow sticks. But some sort of systemic gangrene set in and made life much slower and more cumbersome. Her husband, a political refugee, developed psychotic tendencies and took on a whole different personality. When he saw the effects of her polio, he could take no more, left her, and went to Canada. She was to raise three small children on no income (though, in answer to prayer, the Lord provided). In addition, her daughter's fiancé was killed by a car. That, of course, would have been plenty. But then she returned to Ziklag: two years after the fiancé's death the daughter herself was in a car accident, suffered a concussion but told no one about it. It was so baffling then when she tried to take her life with an overdose of pills. That was caught only to be followed by two more serious attempts. At last, Phillips's correspondent says, she had to commit her daughter to a mental institution. That was almost unbearable, for she knew her daughter was suffering and was not able to communicate or reach her in any way. Yet, she wrote, in all these times she never knew God to fail.[3]

We have a disturbing text. God's special servant, David, is overwhelmed with trouble. By implication we understand that this could be so for any of God's servants.[4] The text says

---

3. Vera Phillips and Edwin Robertson, *J. B. Phillips: The Wounded Healer* (Grand Rapids: Eerdmans, 1984), 93–95. The older daughter fully recovered after it was discovered what had brought on her condition.

4. However, Christians must avoid a perverted response at this point. We are not to take on a mass of false guilt if we are not crushed, if God spares us from such affliction. James 5:13b instructs us that praise, not guilt, is the proper response to God's goodness and happy circumstances.

that your distresses and troubles could intensify. Even this, however, does not leave us comfortless. For here is the realism of the Bible. Here is no hiding of truth or preaching of half-truths. Here is no false advertising. As the Lord's servant you may be overwhelmed with troubles. You may receive more than you think you can even handle. But God in his word tells you this. You can *trust* a God like that; you can depend on a Scripture that tells you this. When Jesus said, "In the world you have tribulation," he didn't reduce it to small print or hide it in a footnote.

God's Strength Is Sufficient (30:6b-9)

David was under severe pressure. In addition to his own sorrow he faced the rebellion of his men (v. 6a). Who knows how many votes there were to stone him? It is at this point we meet with an important statement: "Then David strengthened himself in Yahweh his God" (v. 6b). David is in the pit but this is the turning point down in the pit. We must ask then what it means to "strengthen oneself" in Yahweh.

We begin by specifying what it is not. In our day it is necessary to say that strengthening oneself in the Lord is not some kind of gospel magic. It is not a quick fix. It is not recognizing that the pressure is on and so deciding to seek help in religion. The Lord is not a genie you rub in trouble in order to make you feel better. Jesus is not your own personal pain reliever to get you on top of life's aches. Strengthening yourself in the Lord is nothing so superficial or superstitious as that.

Nor is it merely venting, that is, letting go emotionally. That was done in verse 4 when David and his men wailed to the point of exhaustion. There is a difference between pouring out sorrow and strengthening yourself in God. This should be obvious, but among contemporary psychologically sophisticated Christians it is necessary to say this. Some make much of the need for believers to be open, to talk about their distress, to get it all out and not hold it in. And normally there is nothing wrong with that. Some of us pastors keep urging God's people to do that, not to be afraid to pray like the psalmists. But one can cry tears and vent emotions and yet not be strengthening oneself in God. (Saul was in great distress [28:15, esp. the Hebrew] just as David is in verse 6a, and he could express it and grieve about it, yet he did not strengthen himself in the Lord.) No one is saying we must stifle our moans and cries; but is there anything more? Does our distress bring us before God? You may let it all out but not strengthen yourself in Yahweh your God.

One more negative qualification. Even if you freely and openly express anger and assign blame in your troubles, that is not the same as strengthening yourself in God. David's men did that (v. 6a), but they did not strengthen themselves in Yahweh as David did. I point this out only because in some Christian circles there is a sort of anger cult whose devotees have come to recognize that they have a "right" to be angry and express anger and to hold people responsible. And so "it's o.k." to be angry at what parents did or didn't do, at one's spouse or children, and so on. If the anger is accurate and within biblical confines there is no problem. But that is not the same as strengthening yourself in God. Verse 6 makes that clear.

Where does one begin in this matter? Precisely where David did—with a personal God. "Then David strengthened himself in Yahweh *his God*" (emphasis added). Alexander Maclaren has rightly underscored this point.[5] There was ever a danger in Israel of holding to the official covenant faith without having a vital personal faith. It could be all too easy to speak of the "Shepherd of Israel" (Ps. 80:1) but not be able to say "Yahweh is *my* shepherd" (Ps. 23:1), just as church folks might affirm Jesus is the Son of God but would not dream of calling him "the Son of God, who loved *me* and gave himself for *me*" (Gal. 2:20). As Maclaren has said, David could no longer say, "My house," "my city," or "my possessions," but he could say, "My God." That is where the strengthening must begin.

How then do you strengthen yourself in God? Does the text provide some clues? Perhaps. It implies that you strengthen yourself in Yahweh by remembering the promises and affirmations of his word; that is, the promises that pertain to

---

5. Alexander Maclaren, *Expositions of Holy Scripture: Deuteronomy, Joshua, Judges, Ruth, and First Book of Samuel* (reprint ed., Grand Rapids: Baker, n.d.), 385–87.

you and the affirmations about Yahweh's character. This text does not say as much, but we can scarcely read 30:6b without calling to mind the similar language of 23:16, where Jonathan, at considerable risk, went and found David in his haunt and "strengthened his hand in God." That obviously involved encouragement, but of what kind? The next verse explains: Jonathan assured David that "the hand of Saul my father will never find you, but *you* [emphatic] will reign over Israel" (23:17). That is, Jonathan only reaffirmed and emphasized the promise of the kingdom that Yahweh had already made to David. That is what strengthens. Hence I surmise something similar in 30:6. If David "strengthened *himself*" in Yahweh his God he must have recalled Yahweh's promise and how Yahweh had not yet allowed that word to fall to the ground.

God's people strengthen themselves legions of times in precisely this way. Andrew Bonar, Free Church of Scotland pastor, wrote in his diary for October 15, 1864, of his grievous "wound"; Isabella, his wife of seventeen years, died, apparently of complications following childbirth. He wrote that on the day of her death he had, according to his custom, been meditating on a Scripture text between dinner and tea. On that day it had been Nahum 1:7—"The Lord is good, a stronghold in the day of trouble; he knows those who take refuge in him" (RSV). Bonar adds, "Little did I think how I would need it half an hour after."[6] Bonar never forgot Isabella's death; again and again he mentions it in mid-October entries. I dare say he never forgot Nahum 1:7. But why did he mention it in his diary along with his wife's death? Because he was strengthening himself in Yahweh his God. It was that promise of God's word, that affirmation of God's character, that was keeping him on his feet.

A second way we can strengthen ourselves in God is by using our access to his presence. Note the apparent connection between verse 6b and verses 7-8:

> Then David strengthened himself in Yahweh his God. And David said to Abiathar the priest, the son of Ahimelech, "Bring me the ephod." So Abiathar brought the ephod to David. And David

---

6. Marjory Bonar, ed., *Andrew A. Bonar: Diary and Life* (Edinburgh: Banner of Truth, 1984), 226–27.

asked direction from Yahweh: "Should I pursue after this band?
Will I overtake them?" Then he said to him: "Pursue, for you will
certainly overtake and you will certainly deliver."

We have not heard David ask for the ephod since 23:9, and we
have not heard David speak of Yahweh since chapter 26.[7] Here
he recovers himself and seeks guidance through Abiathar
the priest and the use of the sacred lots connected with the
ephod.[8] He strengthens himself (v. 6b) by using his access to
Yahweh's presence (vv. 7-8).

The Christian does not have Abiathar nor the ephod. Yet
the same recourse is open to him. For he does have a priest, a
greater than Abiathar. "Since then we have a great high priest
who has passed through the heavens, Jesus, the Son of God,
let us hold fast our confession" (Heb. 4:14 RSV). Because we
have such a priest we are confidently to "draw near to the
throne of grace, that we may receive mercy and find grace to
help in time of need" (Heb. 4:16 RSV). We may not get precise
answers to our questions but we will find "grace to help,"
which we usually need more than answers. I don't often need
information but endurance; I don't need to know something—
I only need to stay on my feet. Use your Priest; use your access;
it's part of strengthening yourself in Yahweh your God.

God's Providence Is Essential (30:11-15)
A few years ago the city of Louisville, Kentucky, had giant ads
slapped on its buses, proclaiming that its bus transportation
system was "ubiquitous," that is, found everywhere. And it
seems that the doctrine of Yahweh's providence is ubiquitous
in 1 Samuel. We seem to meet it everywhere; and, of course,
we meet it everywhere because it is there.

David and his men are off and we catch up with them
by the Wadi Besor (v. 9), perhaps the Wadi Ghazzeh, some
twelve to fifteen miles south of Ziklag.[9] David presses on

---

7. Cf. H. L. Ellison, *Scripture Union Bible Study Books: Joshua–2 Samuel* (Grand
Rapids: Eerdmans, 1966), 72. It is likely a significant silence, though one must not put
too much weight on omissions in narrative literature.

8. See 14:41-42 and 23:9-12; see my references on the latter passage.

9. Cf. Joyce G. Baldwin, *1 & 2 Samuel*, Tyndale Old Testament Commentaries
(Leicester: InterVarsity, 1988), 167; also P. Kyle McCarter, Jr., *I Samuel*, The Anchor
Bible (Garden City, N.Y.: Doubleday, 1980), 435.

with 400 men; 200 remain at Besor, too exhausted to move on (v. 10). We might assume that David knows he is after the Amalekites. He may know that, but the text does not say he knows whom he is looking for. Tribes who made raids and burned towns didn't leave calling cards in the ashes of city hall, so it is conceivable, unless David had word from some survivor, that he was even unsure of who had carried off Ziklag's families.[10] But supposing David did know that the Amalekites were the culprits, how does he go about finding them? Nomadic raiders were hard to find. They floated. How could David find their whereabouts?

I raise these questions to put verses 11-15 in proper perspective. Here David's men find a used-up Egyptian slave in the open country (v. 11). Readers must appreciate that this discovery is not an optional luxury but an absolute necessity if David and Co. are even to locate the Amalekites. God's providence is essential; it is no neat extra.

We won't get any information out of this dehydrated Egyptian for two verses. Not until he eats bread, drinks water, consumes a slice of fig cake and two bunches of raisins (vv. 11-12). Now he can be interrogated. Now he can talk. "I am an Egyptian fellow, servant to an Amalekite man" (v. 13). His master, he tells us, trashed him because he became sick. They had raided various places, one of which was Ziklag, which they had also burned (v. 14). On promises of immunity from death and extradition the Egyptian leads David's men to the Amalekites and their captives (vv. 15-16a).

Happening onto this discarded Egyptian is the whole key for David's recovery operation. How important he becomes, making it possible for Yahweh to fulfill his assurances to David (v. 8). No theological bells go off at verse 11 in order to announce Yahweh's providence to you. You are expected to suspect it on your own and to hear its quiet work. It seems like such a little providence, finding this puny Egyptian. But little providences make big differences. Only Amalekites think that mustard-seed matters never matter. Little did that Amalekite

---

10. Cf. Hans Wilhelm Hertzberg, *I & II Samuel*, The Old Testament Library (Philadelphia: Westminster, 1964), 227: "David cannot, of course, know who the plunderers are and where they have gone."

master realize that the piece of human machinery he had discarded three days ago would prove his undoing! Maybe he never put it together. After all, there's not much time to reflect when a Ziklag sword slashes your wineskin and then recoils to finish off its drinker.[11] "And they found an Egyptian...." God's providence is essential.

God's Grace Is Decisive (30:21-25)

It wasn't hard to surprise the Amalekites. They were "eating and drinking and partying with all the massive plunder they had taken from the land of the Philistines and from the land of Judah" (v. 16); so the Judeans "struck them down from twilight up to evening-time of the following day—and not one of them escaped, except four hundred fellows who rode off on camels and fled" (v. 17).[12] The writer then describes David's success in the most emphatic terms; David recovered everything—both his wives, all the people, all the kids, all the plunder (vv. 18-19; more on this later). He returns to Wadi Besor to meet and greet the two hundred men he was forced to leave there for rest and recovery (v. 21).

We already knew that, by and large, David's men were hardly specimens of good breeding (22:2), but now we discover that some of the four hundred fighters are simply mean and nasty scoundrels. Using a guise of justice to hide their greed, they propose that the two hundred "laggers" may take their wives and family members but will not get their hands on any of the plunder the four hundred had liberated (v. 22). It was their version of "Whoever does not fight does not eat." Perhaps it was not so much greed that drove them after all; maybe it was only selfishness and malice.

David stifles their scheme with an astute blend of warmth ("You're not going to act that way, *my brothers*, v. 23a), argument ("... with what Yahweh has given us; now he has kept us and given this band that came against us into our hand," v. 23b), incredulity ("Who will listen to you about this

---

11. "The lack of watch by the Amalekites [v. 16] was because they knew the Philistines to be far away" (Ellison, *Joshua–2 Samuel,* 72).
12. For our purposes we needn't resolve the debate about whether *nešep* here refers to twilight or to early morning.

matter?," v. 24a), and authority ("For the share of the one who goes down to battle and the share of the one who stays by the equipment will be the same—they will share together," v. 24b). The last became standard military procedure in Israel (v. 25). Perhaps that combination of psychology, theology, and decisiveness explains how David could effectively command such a gang of unhomogenized characters.

Our primary concern must be with David's rationale, with his theological argument. "You're not going to act that way, my brothers, with what Yahweh has given us..." (v. 23). David's theology determines his viewpoint and stands behind his directive of verse 24. It is a theology of grace that keeps its eyes riveted on Yahweh's giftiness. The troublemakers function on a philosophy of works that is always impressed with its own contributions: "We will not give them any of the plunder we have liberated" (v. 22). The latter makes sense and sounds logical provided one never lifts his eyes to look to the hills to ask where his help has come from. But David knew better. This is not plunder *we* have recovered, he insisted, but what Yahweh has *given* us. The difference between grace and works is the difference between worship and idolatry. The man inebriated with the thought that all he has is Yahweh's gift finds himself repeatedly on his knees, adoring, thanking, praising. But if we do not grasp grace (v. 23) we plummet into idolatry, for that is the inevitable corollary of self-sufficiency. Then we walk around talking about the plunder we have recovered—and such other ridiculous notions.

It is urgent for Christians to see that for David here grace is not merely some theological concept but world-viewish stuff. It is not something that applies only to how one enters the kingdom of God but to every moment of that royal life. "What Yahweh has given us" dominates David's thinking and controls his decision and action. So grace must always be the decisive and dominating factor in the Christian's practical theology. He or she must constantly confess that this success, this employment, this loved one, this health, this meal is "what Yahweh has given us." "What do you have that you did not receive?" (1 Cor. 4:7). Every Christian then has no choice—you must be a good theologian who both speaks and lives a theology of grace. You will find it humbling, but it is the only thing that will keep you from worshiping yourself.

God's Victory is Encouraging (30:26-31)

David is Yahweh's servant. He is also wise as a serpent. Nothing wrong with that combination. Biblical faith never asks us to check our brains at the door. Hence David uses his. Back in Ziklag David sends some of the plunder seized from Amalek to the elders of Judah, some of whom were apparently his friends (v. 26a); at least they knew him, for David and his men had haunted their locales (v. 31). The writer includes a list of the recipients' addresses (vv. 27-31a), sites in the southern part of Judah mostly around or south of Hebron.[13] David's gifts were only just. Many of these communities had likely endured Amalekite raids; it was only right they should receive Amalekite loot.[14] But David's gifts were also shrewd—they would win him friends and support and grease both palm and path to David's kingship in Judah (2 Sam. 2:1-4). Nothing illegal about it (cf. Luke 16:9). One can be sharp without being sinful.

A reader, however, may underestimate David's victory. Because hordes of Amalekites are not on our list of most feared phenomena we are apt to consider David's victory a minor episode. The text, however, will not allow us to do this, for it stresses that David's victory is central and complete. Note how the general structure of 1 Samuel 30 places David's victory at the heart of the narrative:

> Ziklag—destruction, 1-6a
> 　Seeking Yahweh's guidance, 6b-8
> 　　Division of troops, 9-10
> 　　　Discovery, 11-15
> 　　　　Victory, 16-17
> 　　　Recovery, 18-20
> 　　Reunion of troops, 21
> 　Appreciating Yahweh's grace, 22-25
> Ziklag—distribution, 26-31

---

13. Some of the sites cannot be pinned down. Jattir (v. 27) was about twelve miles south/southwest of Hebron; Eshtemoa (v. 28) eight miles south of Hebron; Bor-ashan (v. 30) a little northwest of Beersheba. On locations and some emendations of place names, see McCarter, *I Samuel*, 436; also Robert P. Gordon, *I & II Samuel: A Commentary* (Grand Rapids: Zondervan, 1986), 201.

14. Baldwin, *1 & 2 Samuel*, 169.

If we discount this structure as too stylized and artificial, we must still deal with the way verses 18-20 emphatically insist on David's total recovery of all that had been lost: David delivered all Amalek had taken, including his two wives; nothing was missing, whether young or old, sons or daughters, plunder—whatever. In case we missed the point, the writer summarizes: "David recovered *all*" (v. 19b; emphasis in Hebrew; our colloquialism, "the whole shooting match," catches the idea). The writer pounds the point home in order to highlight the fidelity of Yahweh to his previous word, "You will certainly deliver" (v. 8). And he did—fully and totally (vv. 18-19; note how *nāṣal*, "to deliver," is used twice in v. 18, picking up its use in v. 8).[15]

Yet David himself catches the importance of the victory in a single line, his greeting to the various elders of Judah: "Here's a gift for you from the plunder of Yahweh's enemies" (v. 26). We are prone to regard the Amalekites as only Israel's enemies. And they are—always have been (see Exod. 17:8-16; Deut. 25:17-19; and our commentary on 1 Sam. 15). But because they are Israel's enemies they are Yahweh's enemies; and because they have mangled his flock they must deal with its Shepherd. We do not merely have an ancient altercation here between Israel and Amalek. Rather this conflict is symptomatic of the greater war. There are Yahweh's people and Yahweh's enemies; there are two kingdoms, the kingdom of Yahweh and the kingdom of this world; there are two humanities, the seed of the woman and the seed of the serpent. And here in 1 Samuel 30 Yahweh's enemies have been trounced! This victory then is not an episode but a promise, a scale-model scenario of how it will be when Yahweh makes the Davidic Messiah's enemies his footstool (Ps. 110:1). God's victory here is encouraging, for it is both preview and pledge of final victory. It is because of assurance like this that Andrew Melville dared scorn the Earl of Morton's threat to hang or banish the Scottish reforming ministers. "Tush, sir," said Melville, "threaten your

---

15. David recovered all—and more. Verse 20 indicates that David gathered plunder from the Amalekites that was designated his personal plunder. This is clear in spite of the difficult text. From this store David sent the gifts to the various elders of Judah.

courtiers after that manner. It is the same to me whether I rot in the air or in the ground. The earth is the Lord's.... Let God be glorified; it will not be in your power to hang or exile His truth."[16] Knowing that Yahweh's enemies will perish (Ps. 92:9) breeds a holy defiance in God's people against all the threats of the enemy. Yahweh will rule, this I know, for the Amalekites tell me so. If not, why get out of bed tomorrow?

First Samuel 30 is a long chapter and covers a lot of turf. It begins in tragedy and ends in triumph. Yahweh has a way of doing that.

STUDY QUESTIONS

1. Make time to read through the Book of Psalms, Book 1 (Psalms 1 to 41), noting references to David in the headings, to confirm the fact that being God's king did not exempt David from suffering and from problems. Remember too that this drove David to God not from him.

2. Sometimes preachers give the impression that all the hearers' troubles will be over if they become Christians. Do you ever give people this wrong impression in your personal witness?

3. The Word of God and prayer – two great means of strengthening ourselves in God. Consider then the importance of making recourse to them a life-habit.

4. 'Little providences make big differences.' Think this through in the light of your own experiences with God.

5. 'From the fulness of his grace we have all received one blessing after another' (John 1:16 NIV). Do you tend to think of grace mostly as connected with the beginning of your life in Christ and not the whole course of it? Is that wrong?

---

16. J. D. Douglas, *Light in the North: The Story of the Scottish Covenanters* (Grand Rapids: Eerdmans, 1964), 18.

29

The End?

(1 Samuel 31)

"We now join the Battle of Gilboa in progress." The biblical writer actually begins like a television announcer introducing scheduled programming that has been delayed for some reason. The initial verbal form (v. 1) is a participle indicating continuing action. It is not to be translated as a past tense (as RSV, NIV, and NKJV do) but rather: "Now the Philistines were fighting against Israel." We readers have arrived a bit late and must catch up on things. I have a hunch, however, that the narrator has deliberately made us late. I sense he was in no hurry to arrive at Gilboa. He could have nicely and chronologically related the Battle of Gilboa immediately after chapter 28. Instead the writer switched us back to David and to something that had happened earlier. He makes us spend two chapters with David and his men (ch. 29–30) before he gets us back to Gilboa—late. It is such a sad, tragic, and dark story that the writer loathes to tell it. He drags his literary feet as long as he can. But it cannot be postponed forever—even this must be told.[1]

Actually, there is not much to tell. It can all be said in one line: "The men of Israel fled from the Philistines and fell slain

---

1. It is interesting to note the primary locations and associations in chapters 27–31: David at Gath—desperation, 27; Saul at Endor—desperation, 28; David at Aphek—deliverance, 29; David at Ziklag—despair, 30; Saul at Gilboa—death, 31. Cf. my comments about structure in the exposition of chapter 28.

on Mount Gilboa" (v. 1b). Hebrew narrative frequently gives
such a terse summary at the beginning of a story and then
fleshes it out with details. The details will follow. Like a bad
dream we must reach the end of it. Readers are under no
illusions, however; the writer has given a blunt and bloody
synopsis at the start. David had enjoyed double deliverance
at Aphek (ch. 29) and at Ziklag (ch. 30), but there is no
deliverance here. At Gilboa the enemies of Yahweh (cf. 30:26)
win the day.

The witness of chapter 31 centers on tragedy, truth, shame,
and gratitude. I will summarize the teaching of the text by
expanding on these themes.

Tragedy: The Steadfastness of Yahweh's Servant (31:2)

This chapter is frequently dubbed a tragic narrative, "tragic"
alluding to Saul and his end. I propose the tragedy, if one
wants to call it that, is in verse 2:

> Now the Philistines dogged the tracks of Saul and his sons; and
> the Philistines struck down Jonathan, Abinadab, and Malchishua,
> the sons of Saul.

Actually, Jonathan is the first reported casualty on Mount
Gilboa. I will not linger long on this bare notice about Jonathan's death. David will do that later (2 Sam. 1). But when
Jonathan has played such a central role in previous narratives
(cf. chs. 14, 18–20, and 23) his death notice certainly deserves
that—notice.

I will not repeat what I have already outlined (see "The
Air of Tragedy" in the exposition of 1 Sam. 14). Here then is
Jonathan's obituary. He remained a true friend to David and
a faithful son of Saul. He surrendered his kingship to David
(18:1-4); he sacrificed his life for Saul. In this hopeless fiasco
Jonathan was nowhere else but in the place Yahweh had
assigned to him—at the side of his father. As I noted before,
maybe that is not tragic at all. What is tragic about remaining
faithfully in the calling God has assigned us? Was it tragic
when Jonathan laid aside a kingdom he could not have to
enter a kingdom he could not lose?

Truth: The Fulfillment of Yahweh's Threat (31:3-7)

The verbs tell a tale of brutal disaster: to flee (three times; vv. 1, 7), fall/fallen (four times; vv. 1, 4, 5, 8), strike down (v. 2), writhe or wounded (v. 3), pierce through (twice, v. 4), die (four times; vv. 5, 6, 7), strip (twice; vv. 8, 9), cut off (v. 9), nail (v. 10). In the thick of it all Saul pleads with his armor-bearer to finish him off (v. 4a). Saul wills to die the way Abimelech, Israel's unanointed king, died (Judg. 9:54), by the sword of an obliging armor-bearer. But Saul's armor-bearer will not comply (v. 4b) precisely, no doubt, because Saul is Yahweh's anointed.[2] Hence Saul plunges himself upon his own sword (v. 4c).

Four times the verb *mût*, "to die," is used (vv. 5-7). Saul has died, his sons died, his armor-bearer died, his bodyguard died.[3] Israel is licked. All this matters, not only because it is sad but because it constitutes the fulfillment of Yahweh's word spoken through the "disturbed" Samuel (28:19; cf. 15:28).[4] As the word of God announced the end of Hophni and Phinehas (2:34) and as that word "found" them (4:11), so the word of Yahweh has done with Saul and his men. Israel may fall on Gilboa, Saul may fall on his sword, but the word of Yahweh will not fall. It will and has surely come to pass.

This is hardly a happy fulfillment of Yahweh's word, and yet it is not without its comfort. It is a dark time for the kingdom of God, but God's word (15:28; 28:17-19) shows that even this darkness is not outside God's purpose. It falls within the boundaries of what he has already announced. By the same token, it is far easier to stomach Pharaoh's big mouth when you know his hard heart already stands under the decree of God's word (e.g., Exod. 4:21b). In any case, if Yahweh's word of judgment on Saul is true, we can be equally assured of his word of promise to David. In darkness or light what matters is having a God who speaks a true and faithful word.[5]

---

2. For some of the parallels between Saul and both Abimelech and Samson, see Sam Dragga, "In the Shadow of the Judges: The Failure of Saul," *Journal for the Study of the Old Testament* 38 (1987): 43.

3. The last is what is meant by "all his men" in verse 6, that is, not the whole army but the king's contingent of crack troops. Cf. C. F. Keil, *Biblical Commentary on the Books of Samuel* (1875; reprint ed., Grand Rapids: Eerdmans, 1950), 279.

4. Ralph W. Klein, *1 Samuel*, Word Biblical Commentary (Waco: Word, 1983), 288.

5. Note that Mount Gilboa also exposed the folly of Israel's idolatry (8:7-8). Israel had craved a king, salivated for royalty. In chapter 8 Israel claimed they needed

Shame: The Problem of Yahweh's Honor (31:8-10)

Next day the Philistines swarm over Mount Gilboa collecting prizes from Israelite corpses. They discover their premier trophies (v. 8b) and mangle them to their liking—at least they do Saul's body (v. 9a). They chop off his head and strip off his armor. Then we have fits with grammar and geography (in the Hebrew text). Do the Philistines send Saul's head and armor all over their home territory or do they keep head and/or armor in the north and send word (i.e., through messengers) to preach the good news in their idol-temples (v. 9b)? And is the "house of Ashtaroth [Astarte]" (v. 10) in Beth-shan or back down in Philistia? One cannot be sure. I take verses 9-10 to mean that the Philistines sent messengers back to proclaim the gospel of victory in their temples and to their people, and that the house of the goddess Astarte, where they placed (at least initially) Saul's armor, was in nearby Beth-shan. Saul's head may have ended up in Philistia (cf. 1 Chron. 10:10). But the corpses of Saul and his sons were spiked to the walls of Beth-shan (v. 10b; cf. v. 12).

In spite of its uncertainties the text is all too clear. The idols (v. 9b) have won! Astarte has carried the day! The gory head belongs to Yahweh's anointed; therefore Yahweh has been defeated. Saul's armor is in the adversary's temple; Yahweh could not protect his king. No question about how the media would construe it. If Yahweh's king and people were trounced, so was their God. Never mind that the Philistine idols couldn't even salivate when the spoils of war were placed before them. As if Ebenezer (4:1–5:2) were not enough. Now, again, pagan evangelists were running all over Philistia chanting, "Yahweh is a loser!"

The sadness of our text is due not merely to the fact that Israel is crushed. That is sad. But there is a deeper sadness in that Yahweh is mocked. Every true Israelite mourns over that. Worse than Israel's defeat is Yahweh's disgrace.

This concern for God's reputation ought to strike God's people individually as well as corporately. There is a striking

---

a new system, that the issue was defense, and that the solution must be political. They called it progress; Yahweh named it idolatry. Chapter 31 shows where trust in the political process (as such) brings a people. Some idols, like Dagon, lie shattered before the ark of Yahweh (5:1-5); others lie slain on Mount Gilboa.

example of this passion for God's honor in the life of Esther Edwards Burr. Esther, daughter of Jonathan Edwards, had been bereaved of her husband Aaron (father of the infamous Vice President). He was a bright and shining lamp of the Spirit, president of Princeton College, and cut off at age forty-one. Esther's sorrow was mixed with anxiety, with a holy worry, as she wrote to her parents:

> O, I am afraid I shall conduct myself so as to bring dishonour on my God and the religion I profess! No, rather let me die this moment, than be left to bring dishonour on God's holy name— I am overcome—I must conclude, with once more begging, that, as my dear parents remember themselves, they would not forget their greatly afflicted daughter, (now a lonely widow), nor her fatherless children.[6]

That is what matters, whether it involves the church as a body or an individual believer; whether it is at Mount Gilboa or in New Jersey; whether those around are Philistines or Presbyterians. The honor of Yahweh himself must be at the top of our agenda.

Gratitude: The Kindness of Yahweh's People (31:11-13)

When Saul's ranks were cut to shreds at Gilboa Israel evacuated the area. Those "on the other side of the valley" (v. 7a), that is, people to the north of Mount Gilboa and across the intervening Valley of Jezreel, and those on the other side of the Jordan (v. 7a; I take this as meaning east of the Jordan River) abandoned their towns to Philistine occupation. It is difficult to know how extensive Philistine dominance was at this point; it seems they had at least cut off the Galilee tribes from those south of the Plain of Esdraelon. They controlled the fortress town of Beth-shan, located several miles to the east of the battle scene and dominating the area west of the Jordan River.[7] Four mutilated Israelite bodies now hang on the town walls.

---

6. Iain H. Murray, *Jonathan Edwards: A New Biography* (Edinburgh: Banner of Truth, 1987), 434.

7. On the strategic location and archaeological history of Beth-shan, see Keith N. Schoville, *Biblical Archaeology in Focus* (Grand Rapids: Baker, 1978), 329ff.

Verses 11-13 come as close as one can get to a tender note in this raw chapter. Residents of Jabesh-gilead heard how the Philistines had abused Saul's corpse. Some of their strong and daring men took an all-night trek to Beth-shan, removed the rotting bodies from the walls, and vamoosed back to Jabesh-gilead.[8] They had stamina, for Jabesh-gilead was to the east of the Jordan River and about ten miles southeast of Beth-shan, hence a round trip of twenty to twenty-two miles. They had courage, for there was a great deal of risk in such a bold stroke. They also had memories, which explains it all.

Jabesh-gilead had never forgotten. Nahash the Ammonite was as skilled a mutilator as any Philistine (11:2), but when he threatened Jabesh-gilead, Saul in the power of the Spirit (11:6) had marched to their rescue—and a night march at that (11:11). Saul's reign began with his deliverance of Jabesh (ch. 11) and ends with Jabesh's "deliverance" of Saul (ch. 31). The Spirit may have departed from Saul and Yahweh may not answer him, but time was when Saul was their savior and they remain grateful. Proper burial and fasting are in order (v. 13b).[9]

It was a debt of gratitude. Paying it couldn't reverse Gilboa. Yet one has the sense after reading verses 11-13 that at least something was right in this whole mess. Gratitude carries its own "ought," whether it changes anything or not. The women who kept watch at Jesus' crucifixion (Mark 15:40-41) couldn't do anything, but they were there. When they watched him being placed in the tomb (Mark 15:47), they couldn't do anything, but they saw. When they took spices to anoint his body (Mark 16:1-3), they had no idea how they could do it, but

---

8. Burning the bodies was not normal Hebrew practice, but it may have been judged necessary. "The bodies will have been considerably damaged by the process of decomposition, which sets in quickly during the heat of the day, and by the ravages of carrion birds; and it was important to remedy the disfigurement of the bodies and rescue the bones for burial" (Hans Wilhelm Hertzberg, *I & II Samuel*, The Old Testament Library [Philadelphia: Westminster, 1964], 233). See also A. F. Rainey ("Beth-shean," *ISBE*, rev. ed., 1:477), who notes that such burial rites were carried out in honor of heroes among the Homeric Greeks (e.g., *Iliad* 23).

9. Cf. J. P. Fokkelman (*Narrative Art and Poetry in the Books of Samuel*, vol. 2, *The Crossing Fates [1 Sam. 13–31 & II Sam. 1]* [Assen/Maastricht: Van Gorcum, 1986], 628) and Karl Gutbrod (*Das Buch vom König*, Die Botschaft des Alten Testaments, 4th ed. [Stuttgart: Calwer, 1975], 254) for some parallels and contrasts between chapters 11 and 31.

they went. Love offers the kindness it can—it doesn't forget the King even in death.

First Samuel is not a biblical "book" in itself; 1 and 2 Samuel constitute the whole document. Nevertheless there is something appropriate about the imposed division of the "books" after 1 Samuel 31.

It will not do to smile the tragedy away. Modern faddists notwithstanding, Israel needs far more than a shot of self-esteem. The picture is hardly sunny: leadership annihilated, territory evacuated. Some fled; others couldn't—their bodies litter the slopes of Gilboa. It is a sad sight: Israel scattered like sheep without a shepherd (Num. 27:15-17). In fact, 1 Samuel is simply a sad book of one disappointment after another: the judgment on ungodly leadership (Hophni and Phinehas, ch. 1–4), the rejection of prophetic leadership (Samuel, ch. 8, 12), and the disintegration of royal leadership (Saul, ch. 13–31). Here is the kingdom of God enduring one failure after another. Yet Yahweh, who looks on the heart, has chosen a shepherd for these scattered sheep (Ps. 8:70-71). Presently nothing looks quite so dismal as Gilboa, but then it's not what man sees... (16:7).

Study Questions

1 Jonathan's death can be looked on either as a tragedy or as his entry into God's better future. Does that put some apparent tragedies in the lives of Christians into a different perspective?

2. Many in our society care little for truth even in small things. 'I'm sorry, the boss is out,' may simply mean, 'He does not want to see you.' Reflect on the fact that truth is a primary virtue and that God's commitment to it is total.

3. How high on your agenda is the honour of God?

4. Itemise the chief lessons you have learned from 1 Samuel. Keep your record of this near you and use it in your devotions for some time, 'for I forget so soon.'

Persons Index

Index of Bible Characters

Subject Index